WEAVERS OF LIGHT
A Channelled Book of Knowledge
For our Changing Times

By The Council of Elders
Channelled through Krow Fischer
Received by Wendy Murdoch

Copyright © 2006 Here On Earth

Fischer, Krow
Murdoch, Wendy
The Council of Elders

ISBN 0-9782344-0-5

Front cover photography by Sally Ann Schweikhard
Poetry by Krow Fischer

For information or to order more books please contact us at
www.hereonearth.ca

Acknowledgements

We first would like to thank the Mother and Father of Creation for... well, everything!

We thank the Council of Elders, for entrusting us with this project. The honour is deeply felt by us.

We thank Cindy Fougere for all her editing help and encouragement.

We thank the forests of Oakendell for holding space for us, granting us serenity throughout all the seasons we worked under your protective canopy.

We thank our families for all their support, and for managing without us, as we placed our focus on the bringing through of this work.

We thank our friends for their incredible support, enthusiasm and faith.

"Are we there yet?"
"Yes!"

Dedicated to our brothers and sisters,
And All Our Relations,
Children of the Mother and Father of Creation,
In honour of our path of lovingness manifest,
Here on Earth, as it is elsewhere in the Universe.

Table of Contents

We find each other.
In the oddest places
Eyes
Look the same
Memories
Those faces
Close our eyes
And breathe
Share an atom or two.
Touched by accident or design
Electric comet
Moves on through
Our universe
And we smile.
No confusion in this moment
That's saved for tomorrow
Distance
Doesn't matter
Nor time.
Nor pain,
Nor sorrow.
Thoughts run the same……..

Chapter I
In the Beginning...

At the very beginning of Creation there was a plan, and this plan evolved according to the natures of the Creators. The creative essence that you call God is the source of energy from which all manifestation springs forth. This energy is both receptive and creative; it both gives and receives. In the consciousness held now, this can be interpreted as the parents of creation. In the place that these energies combine, you have manifestation, and for this to happen, you must have a merging of the two. In the merging is a build-up of creative energy which explodes outwards causing a pushing apart.

During the times of merging, you have excitement, hope, expression, creation, energy, vision, and light. This culminates into creation, and the power of that creation causes the pushing apart. During the times of the pushing apart these two forces are separate. In the separation comes reflection, solitude, introspection, and sometimes doubts. These doubts come in during the violent pushing apart, thus, were in the beginnings of creation.

This universe was birthed in this way; merging the creative forces of union and the receptive forces of separation. Some see it as the inhalation and exhalation or as the ebb and the flow of creation. This is the basis of all that you know. Every thought, every idea, that was brought into this union became manifest as a physical reality. Where you, as a soul, put your conscious intention, is where you manifest yourself. You are all made of the same stuff as this universe. The reality manifesting on this little particle of the universe that you call Earth is an absolute manifestation of all that is.

The thoughts and ideas of the Creators manifest the physical reality of Earth. The essences of the Creators manifest the souls and it is this essence that made you! Just as their thoughts and ideas create the manifested reality, so your thoughts and ideas create your manifested reality. In this mini-universe that you call Earth, here on this planet, you learn your birthright in manifested creation. So your hopes spring forward into joyous creation and your fears and doubts tear apart that creation. The very fact that there is life here at all shows that the hope far exceeds the fear.

Planet Earth is a collection of atoms spinning in configurations with each other causing molecular structure, giving form to the ideas of God. The Earth is a soul and an essence of creation that has given itself form. It was, is, and will be, all at once. The atoms that were first manifested are the same atoms that are the building blocks of all things on Earth today. The soul of the Earth bursts forward her ideas of creation and the atoms make these ideas manifest. The essence and energy of the soul of this Earth are such that she is in a constant and continual dance of creation. The life force of this planet is continually manifesting life.

Some people think of the Earth as experimenting, but the Creators do not need to experiment; better to say that the Earth is creating with different ideas. The arrangement and rearrangement of atomic matter creates the realities upon which souls bring themselves into manifestation. There are as many layers of reality on this one planet as there are planets circling the stars in your skies. This can seem very overwhelming from the state of consciousness in which you find yourselves now, yet it only requires a little bit of investigation for you to see the truth in this.

As a simple example, look around you at any object, perhaps a table. You see before you a table that you may have purchased from a shop in response to your desire of having a surface to put things on. Simple, but somebody built that table, somebody you do not know. They were paid to build that table. Some other people purchased it, brought it across the ocean, maybe in a plane, but probably a boat. Then somebody else bought that table, other people advertised it, shareholders bought stock in it, and it arrived at the shop where you purchased it.

In another reality there was a creature getting ready for the rainy season, collecting and gathering food. It dropped some of its food because a predator startled it. A big creature, like an elephant, came by, stepped on that food, pushing it deep into the ground. Then the rains came and that seed burst out of its nut, and another tree fell over, protecting that little sprout. That little sprout reached out trying to get to the sunlight, and it kept reaching up and the rains kept coming down and no elephant stepped on it, so it grew each year in height and girth.

One day a family decided to stake claim to this land and grow their food there, so they wanted to push back the forest. They cut down this tree and they sold it. The man who bought this tree took it on a cart with other trees into the village, and there he sold it. All of the trees that had been brought to this village were loaded onto a big truck and taken to a mill, where straight pieces of this tree were cut. These pieces were sold to a buyer from a factory, where they were piled up high, and the mice ran through them, and you could smell the fresh wood. They were then all chopped up into uniform pieces. A man, who had five children to support, then took these pieces of wood and quickly put them together, so he could get to his lunch, because he was hungry. These are some of the many realities of your table, and there are more.

The molecules of this table were once the forest floor, an elephant's dung, and the body of a snake. Before that, they were part of the bottom of an ocean, a piece of coral, salt and gases; all that has ever been is in your table! The atoms have agreed to make up the molecular structure that is expected of them, and thus, your table is what you expect it to be. But it is also all of these other realties as well.

The wood is still growing, and if you put it out in the sun and let the water penetrate into it, it will continue to grow. Since its life force still exists within it, it will want to continue changing. Given the correct circumstances, it will swell, grow mould, and continue its journey to become part of the forest floor, giving its life force and atomic matter to become another form of creation. That is another reality of your table. So you see, your reality is far more complex then you first observed. When we look at the complex realities that involve personal experience, we can add a billion more dimensions.

Let us start with your conception. You have, again, a merging of two essences causing a build-up of life force resulting in conception. This ignition and igniting of life, creates the energy force that an individual soul can utilize to begin their dance in the physical reality. The patterns of your life force must match in close enough proximity, to the patterns that the ideas of your individual soul are projecting. The ideas of your soul then manifest the DNA strands according to the patterns these ideas stimulate.

These ideas call forward the DNA from the sperm of the masculine, and eventually imbed themselves in the receptive DNA of the ovum of the feminine. During the time of incubation, your soul proceeds to manifest your physical being from the heart outwards. Your soul pulses its longing for life, your ideas of manifestation, and your hopes for your future manifestations. In response, the molecular structures form the DNA blueprint that then manifests the physical body, based upon and loosely adhering to the original pattern of the universe. In essence, your soul manifests into human experience by creating a body based upon the image of God or Goddess.

Within this manifestation is room for many variations, depending upon the ideas and beliefs of the individual soul attempting manifestation. This involves having faith and knowledge concerning the mother that you have chosen as the incubator of your expression. Once you make the conscious intention to leap into manifested reality, you must trust the mother you have chosen to serve and provide the proper environment for your growth. You must overcome any obstacles that her environment or her choices create. You must work within the framework of the physical reality that she provides. You will be washed with her hormones, her chemical responses will be felt by you, and during this time of incubation you will be strongly imprinted by all that she experiences. She will in fact represent to you in a tangible way, your ideas about the Mother of Creation or the feminine aspect of God.

The masculine or father, now that his spark has ignited for you the possibility of life, will begin to play out his supportive role towards your birth mother. How he chooses to support your growth and development will match your ideas of the nature of God as Father. During this incubation experience you always have the free will to change your mind and leave. If you decide to stay, you will create within the very structure of the atoms of your body, all the ideas and beliefs about yourself and your relationship with the Mother and the Father of Creation.

The experience of your actual birth, the time, the day, the place, and the people involved, reflect your ideas of coming into manifestation. You can, by observing on as many levels of reality that you can see, discern the entire story that your soul came in with. This is the blueprint, the hopes and the fears, the ideas and expectations that you are bringing into this lifetime. From here you have your life force, which you can increase or decrease according to the choices you make.

You have your basic intelligence, which you can increase or decrease, and you have your health, which you can increase or decrease. For the first few years of your life you have allowed yourself to be dependent upon the basic choices that you made in the parental souls. They may keep you, kill you, or pass you onto somebody else. By now you have some idea of what they are going to choose and have obviously decided to trust your luck.

You will again have to work with the raw materials provided for you, which will manifest according to your ideas of what the universe will provide. You will eat or starve, be fed nourishing food or synthetic chemicals, according to your beliefs or ideas of the universe.

Even with the choices available to you, your body will have its reactions of sickness or health, assimilation or rejection, again according to your beliefs or ideas.

In the same way that you have the basic blueprint of God or Goddess to follow for your physical body, the manifestation of form, so you have the blueprint of the unfolding of the universe to follow as the blueprint for the unfolding of your psyche.

In all of the places where you, as a soul, believed and judged there to be disharmony, injustice, pain, terror, or any harmful characteristics present during your experience of the unfolding of the universe, so you will re-experience these same patterns in your growing up and in the unfolding of your individual psyche.

In the places that you have resolved these trauma points in your experience of the unfolding of the universe, so they will be easily handled in your current experience of growing up and developing in this current lifetime.

All points of trauma and psychic scarring in your current lifetime will correspond to the unresolved and unhealed points experienced in the unfolding of the universe.

She moves through me, she moves through all
If you allow her in .
Ripples of earth, waves washing through
Damp green moments between.
The rising and falling and hold....
Intensity growing..
First face is presenting it's light
Beacon steady glowing.
The final ripping bursting forth
As sacred water flows
The final cut, the first breath drawn
And always that she knows.
The dance of stars holding their time
The light they enter in
Form the dreams and hopes of this life
The challenge will begin.
Lines of blood and lines of life
Here gathered into skeins
Weave with the colours of the stars
Tapestry code in genes
This life is yours, what you have spun
From all you have described
For every breath you drew on earth
And all thoughts you inscribed
Will weave your destiny and choice
Of what you will make here
Your statement of self made in form
She grants you your free will.

Chapter II

The Unfolding of the Human Experience

From the first expression of human life on this planet, to the point of existence in the now, there has been an evolution of consciousness that corresponds to the birthing of consciousness in this universe.

Collectively, on your planet, you can witness various states of group conscious evolution developing and presenting in different places. Your brain has different points of development, just as your psyche has different states of consciousness. Your psyche and your personality have within them varying stages of maturity, development, and consciousness through which you act. All of you have experienced yourselves acting and reacting from these different places within your personality and psyche. You all find yourselves acting from as many child points at times as you do points of your current age experience. Some children, nay, all children, have points where they are acting from their adult selves.

On your planet you can witness group consciousness at the same state of development. Some areas on your planet seem to be collectively acting from the state of consciousness of a disgruntled five-year-old. Most group consciousness appears to be behaving from the awareness of an eleven or twelve-year-old.

Within your own psyche, as you agree to be consciously aware of your own thoughts, actions and reactions, and agree to be parental to yourself, you begin to bring your consciousness into the point of now.

As you each, individually, dedicate yourselves to becoming whole in the now, so the consciousness of your whole planet can bring itself up to the speed of the universe. As you witness a deeper level of conscious maturity within yourself, you will change the resonance of those with whom you have contact, and thus the consciousness of the human souls expressed on this planet matures.

As the human experience deepens its resonance, animals and plants can be seen to respond. When people began to be afraid of their disconnection to the planet, they began to lose their conscious ability to influence the natural reality expressed by the Earth.

You can witness the response of animals to people who love them, just as you can witness their response to people who are afraid of them. There is a different interaction in each of these cases.

A farmer, who loves their land, will have a different response than a commercial agricultural industrialist, who is trying to squeeze the highest yield from their acreage.

These are different states of consciousness interacting with the consciousness of the planet, and will generate different outcomes. In this way, collectively, you are influencing and thus co-creating the reality expressed by this planet.

The ideas that were being presented to help people understand their relationship with the planet were brought forward during times when it was noticed that there was a loss of consciousness happening on Earth. This was translated and twisted into the concept that man must have dominion over nature. This is the basis of many religions and has become the basis of western civilization.

As the consciousness of the individual evolves and matures, so this attitude shall also evolve.

Just as the eleven-year-old child wishes to test their power by sometimes behaving in ways that are not pleasing, so we witness the collective consciousness operating at this stage of maturity.

The key point to remember here is that each individual has within their psyche, all places of consciousness, and the free will to choose which place of consciousness to express from. We cannot emphasize enough the importance of the individual taking responsibility for their personal states of consciousness. Bringing this planet back into a healthy ecosystem involves creating a healthy ecosystem within your own consciousness.

Again remembering that within your brain are billions of points of reference, or rather referring points, so it is within all of the varied cultural expressions. You have within yourself points of reference that witness the beauty, the colour, the movement, and the joy that is expressed by all life.

Hopelessness is experienced from the point of perspective that is trapped in belief patterns. For example, when you are looking at a rose bush in bloom with its first flower, you are intoxicated with its scent, enchanted with the beauty, and are at one with the bliss of creation. Then you worry about paying your bills. What if you lose your house and nobody cares for this rose plant, or a neighbouring tribe may just come and burn everything down? Or, a spiteful neighbour may damage your plant, or those pesky rodents may eat at the roots, or a hundred different thoughts that tell you this bliss can be taken from you once again.

The pattern of belief that says moments of bliss can be stolen, or that beauty can be indiscriminately destroyed, is what causes the hopelessness. It is never the living object that causes the hopelessness; it is the belief in the pattern.

So how can you change your states of consciousness if you insist upon holding yourself in the belief in the patterns, rather than holding yourself in the experience of the living?

It has been said by many people that our fears mostly come from worrying about the future, which hasn't even happened yet. This is just another way to tell you this. Next time you are feeling hopeless and you are caught in the perspective of noticing the patterns that you are afraid of, spend some time with a living rose bush instead!

As you reconnect yourself with the joyous and loving beings of this planet, you will give less of your attention and energy to the feeding of the patterns that you do not like.

As these patterns are not actualized and empowered by your conscious attention, they will transform. For every pattern that you are afraid of, the Earth has a pattern that you will like better. She has been constantly and consistently presenting different patterns in living colour for you to choose from.

You, as an individual growing in wisdom and in consciousness, have the choice and the ability to create within your own psyche the healthy patterns that you choose to bring into existence through your personal experience. You must be conscious and aware enough to witness your own patterns.

One of the ways you can witness what is going on within your own psyche is to look at your awareness of the world's psyche.

How do you feel about the interplay between the different countries, cultures, religions and races? Can you see the places of conflict within your own psyche as it is played out in the group consciousness expressed in the world? What beliefs of darkness versus light, black versus white, do you hold within your consciousness? What beliefs do you hold about white light or coloured light? What beliefs do you hold about levels of consciousness being lighter or darker, denser or lighter? How do these beliefs that are so ingrained express in the realities of racial discrimination? What are your beliefs about ownership? What are your beliefs about personal rights?

There are, as I have said, a billion, billion realities to choose from. It will be interesting for you to observe and be aware of the realities being expressed in this world that come to your attention.

Some souls choose to take limited responsibility and may only be aware of what is being expressed in their neighbourhood. What comes into play within this one locality may have within itself many elements of the world at large, but the recognition of these elements will tend to be limited to what that person will accept conscious responsibility for within themselves.

Another person may choose to be globally aware of certain elements in the world, which will reflect the aspects of their own psyche that they are healing at this point in their experience. This soul may be very aware of the plight of the dolphins, the whales and the monkeys who are being experimented upon, and the suffering of all their fellow creatures.

You will find that this soul is healing their relationship with the creatures of the Earth. What goes on in their neighbourhood, their personal life, and with human societies, will be secondary to the problems faced by the pelicans in an oil slick.

A different soul may be fully aware of the rising and falling of the numbers in the stock markets of every country in the world, but be completely unaware of the child who has just been indentured to the factory, producing the goods represented by those numbers.

By witnessing where your attention is drawn and what you make yourself aware of, you can get a fairly accurate overview of your own personal states of consciousness.

Your head is round like the planet, your eyes are round like the planet, and you can see how your consciousness correlates, and therefore, co-creates the realities that are in expression in this world.

In the places where you accept the exploitation of your young and vulnerable emotional expressions, so you will condone the harm done to the child living in an impoverished reality.

In the places where you condemn and disempower yourself, there will be whole populations condemned and disempowered. In the places of your psyche that you demand respect, abundance, joy and bliss, so this percentage of happiness will be expressed in the world at large.

As you take parental responsibility for all of the varying stages of your own development, it will reflect in what you discover happening in the world itself.

Someone just becoming aware of their own personal pain may suddenly find out about atrocities being committed in another place on the planet. As they feel helpless and hopeless, they will want to know more and will want to uncover more, believing that these stories have been hidden with intent. As they seek help to heal themselves, they will discover that there are agencies such as Amnesty International, who are in these places doing their best to help that situation heal.

Information about the happenings of the world comes to your conscious awareness as you become consciously aware of yourself.

So as this hypothetical person makes a choice to put their energy toward healing painful places within themselves, you may find them volunteering their time or giving their money to organizations, that are doing the same work as it is expressed in the world.

In order to heal the patterns of the psyche within, you must heal how these are expressed outwardly in the world. In order to heal the patterns that are expressed in the world, you must heal the patterns within yourself.

Lucky for you, you live on a planet that expresses so many different patterns for you to choose from. A walk by the river can teach you more about the continuity of time than all of the clocks or Einstein's theories, and the passage of the seasons can teach you a different pattern on the same theme. Studying the operation of one anthill would be a lifetime's work that could help to organize the transportation system of any major city. Watching the growth and development of a sunflower can teach you all about prayer.

The Earth has the answer to every question; in fact, she has a thousand answers to most questions.

Notice

In between the stars is the place
In which all creation awaits...
So pay attention to this space
In it's receiving, lie your fates.
The night sky has been pulsing through
In varied frequencies of thought
All information just as new
As when the stars first brought
Their light of conscious intention
To guide the souls of Now
Wisdom written in suspension
Of time and space and Tao.

Chapter III

Starlight, Starbright...

When you look up at the night sky you see configurations of stars, and the light of those stars are coming to your eyes from varying points of time. Each star has sent this vision to you from a place that you would call the past, and each star has a different frequency of light. Your scientists have classified the different starlight into groupings according to colour, size of light, and intensity. From these classifications they expect to understand the nature of that specific starlight. Then you have the configurations! You observe the relationships of the stars as clusters from the viewing point of where you are located, usually on this planet.

Imagine yourself standing on a point on Earth and looking up into the sky. You have a circle around you now, and in that circle you have dots of light streaming down to your eyes. Your eyes take in this light and you imprint it on your brain. These star imprints have been in the same patterns that have been received by your genetic ancestors and your soul history experience.

For instance, you may have witnessed these same patterns in your Mohawk, your Cree, or your French, Indian, or Métis lifetime that you experienced from this reference point on Earth. The difference is that the light you are now receiving from these stars are different streams of light from different time points in the universe.

So you are now receiving light from one star, for example, that may be three billion, three hundred years ago instead of just three billion.

As you all know, a lot can happen in three hundred years. The energy information that you are now receiving on Earth is different energy information than what you received yesterday. Each day or night you will receive brand new configurations of light patterns. They will all look pretty much the same to the point that you can map out the pattern, and can trust that the maps from twenty years ago will suffice for your general observation today. But your astronomers, who have access to deeper vision, will tell you that there have been many changes.

With these understandings, you can see that the person standing on that point on Earth is receiving the billions of impulses of light from the billions of time realities in the heavens. These light impulses form patterns that your psyche relates to, according to the point of time that you first brought your consciousness to life in this incarnation.

These patterns will be the base patterns that you were born with. The change and flow of the starlight over the course of your lifetime will influence the patterns that you will be dealing with.

As you can see by looking up into the sky, you have a billion, billion answers to each question. As above so below! Here you stand, a soul anchored in place and time, surrounded by the unlimited possibilities of atomic configurations, continually impulsed by the swirling energies of molecular vibrations, while at the same time, you are impulsed by the streams of light pouring in from the heavens.

This is the warp and weft of the energy and light, out of which you weave your physical reality. It may be comforting for some of you to realize that you are weaving with ancient patterns of light, and that many of these patterns have long since evolved to different frequencies. Wherever you hold a point of reference in the universe, you are receiving the light impulses from forever.

To imagine how you could possibly figure out what light to work with, which patterns to choose from, and how to become conscious of your creation of life, can seem quite overwhelming. Yet, if I told you that you needed to become aware and responsible for how many oxygen molecules each one of the cells in your liver needed at this moment, you would think that was impossible too. Nonetheless, you do provide each cell of your body with what it needs in a very precise and orderly fashion. When you are honouring and trusting your body consciousness to care for and provide for your body, you do just fine. Can you trust and honour your spirit consciousness to be able to sort through and organize the energy configurations which are needed for your living experience?

In order to keep yourself from feeling so overwhelmed, you do not allow yourself to be aware of what is manifesting around you. In fact, you allow yourself a very limited awareness of reality. The increase in consciousness is the expanding of awareness; that is, to be aware of what you are conscious of.

Most of you are not aware that you are breathing, except that you imagine you would be dead if you weren't. If I ask you to bring your awareness to your breath, you may find yourself being drawn out of this book long enough to shift the position of your body.

Some of you may have forgotten that you have a body, so engrossed are you in trying to make sense of what we are telling you. Yet your body, has all this time, kept breathing and functioning, whether you were aware of it or not.

In the same way, your spirit is weaving your reality constantly out of the patterns of light and energy that you have chosen to receive. The more conscious of your body you become, the more knowledgeable of your body you become, the more consciously you choose what to put into your body and how to treat it. The more conscious and knowledgeable you become of your spirit, the more conscious you will be of what you choose to believe.

This is the dance that creates your individual reality, and thus your group reality on this planet. What you can work with and consciously understand is what your spirit will bring to your awareness at any given time. What you create before you and around you in your pathway, will be woven by the patterns that your spirit believes.

To understand belief, we can return once again to the stars. At this moment, pulses of energy from the universe from any given time or place are inundating you, and you get to choose what you focus your awareness on! As you hold these awareness patterns they become belief, and you create your reality according to that pattern.

As different impulses reach the Earth that changes these beliefs, you see the collective belief systems on Earth change. The impulses from five thousand years ago that reached the Earth may have created a belief system that included the concept of one person owning another person's life. These impulses became the belief of the majority of people expressing on Earth—it became a way of life in every culture. As different impulses reached your eyes, these old patterns were challenged and new patterns of light became reality.

Now you have some pockets of people focusing on old star knowledge, but most have accepted new knowledge and new patterns. Therefore, the majority of people on Earth are repulsed by the idea of owning another person's life.

Nevertheless, you can see this same old pattern underlying corporate belief systems, country belief systems, relationship belief systems, and parent/child relationships. It takes a long time for the light to change.

You are not yet aware of the light that has not reached your state of being on Earth. This gives cause for hope, for we can tell you that the evolution of God light into manifestation has continued into creation.

You have yet to receive the light of God in its state of bliss that it has evolved to. We cannot tell you what you are going to choose, or how you are going to weave from the multitude of realities yet to arrive to influence Earth, but we know the patterns of light that are coming because they have already happened at the source of their respective stars.

If you think that the energies of these stars have little bearing upon you, I would like you to realize that all life and all existence that you know on Earth is directly created by the star that you call your sun. The stars are the creative source of all energy that creates all existence.

We can see what is coming, what is heading towards your planet in light and in form, and therefore, we can prophesize the influences coming and the probable expression of those influences.

It is those of you who are here, physically incarnate on Earth at this time, who will choose which impulses of light you will weave reality with.

I am the river flowing ever
Filled and renewed
Sunk deep into the beds
Lapping the shores

I am the waterfall tumbling dizzy heights
Crashing against the rocks
To pool into sacred oasis
At the end of the fall..

I am the waves crashing
The beach wanting ever more
Pounding the shores
Who rise to catch the waves

I am pulsing through the veins
Pumping through the heart
And out into creation
Exploding into bliss

Chapter IV

Weaving of Realities

This Earth, therefore, is built with the impulses coming from a variety of places and times. It will reflect the weaving of all of the realities that have ever been.

If you think of each star impulsing its light from its corner of the universe as a different aspect of creation and aspect of reality, you will be able to see how Earth weaves its realities, and how people choose the various threads of light to weave with. These are all choices, ideas, and understandings; realities expressed, that come together to create the possibilities that you each bring into your lifetime expression on Earth.

In the same way that your physical body chooses from the DNA of your ancestors, in each lifetime that you express you bring through all of the choices that you have experienced in your previous existences. Each physical manifestation on Earth is a product of each thought, feeling, what is and has been, impulsed from the heavens.

With these understandings you can consciously create the reality of your choice by being fully aware of what light you are weaving with. One star is not better than another star, but the impulses from each star have different frequencies from which you may choose to weave your realities. What we would like to assist you with, in the information we are bringing forward at this time, is the conscious ability to weave the realities of your liking.

You can choose to follow your own DNA lines through the ancestry, or the blood that flows through your veins, as a way to reflect this to yourself. By following back each person's ancestral lines, you will find the basis of many of your beliefs, habits, accomplishments, and setbacks that you express in your current lifetime.

You can see the patterns of terror, injustice, joy, industriousness, art, music, and all of the accomplishments and disadvantages that your ancestors have expressed, fulfilled in your life. Just as you choose the DNA that you express in your physical being, so you choose the ancestral patterns that you wish to express in your lifetime.

If you think of your DNA as the choice of weavings from each star, you will see the point we are making of the realities woven on Earth. Just as you can travel back through your ancestral lines and find patterns of history that still affect you now, so you can travel back through the lines of light from the stars and see how universal history is affecting Earth life now. The microcosm is the macrocosm, and vice versa.

As you can see, whether you choose to keep your viewing point in your own one lifetime and learn of your reality through that, or you choose to hold a more global or universal viewing point, makes no difference.

One soul choosing to be born in a physically disabled body may be so tuned into their body that they notice every nuance, every pulse, the growth of every cell, and the release of every hormone. This soul is witnessing within their own body, the same effects from the impulses of the brain as a globally thinking person can be aware of the effects of the impulses from the stars.

To judge one being as more conscious than the other does a great disservice. The same patterns are witnessed in everything, no matter how tiny or big - it is all one.

Each lifetime that you live, you are expressing and noticing different patterns that make up your being.

Another way to think of this is to view the light from each star as being a roadway that you can travel on. Taking up the craft of your ancestors or witnessing the patterns that show up in your blood would be the same thing. The ability to bring full consciousness and awareness to what you are working with within this lifetime enables you to take power and control over your own life.

To witness yourself as a being created through lines of light, to stand in that experience in full power, is to be creator of your own reality. When you are aware of what you are made of and what choices you are making, you are then able to see the threads that you have available to you. It is time for those of you who are ready to hold this level of responsibility to begin to see how you are the weavers of the reality being currently held.

Most people on Earth at this time follow the lines of light like roadways. They expect these lines of light to be their roadmap, and they express their reality as if somebody has written this map for them. The belief system that these lines of light are your destiny, the belief system that "the sins of the ancestors are visited upon the descendents" is erroneous.

Closer to the truth is that you have the choice of all of the roadways available to chart your own course. It is easier for most people to follow a pathway that seems laid out; this way people do not feel the burden of responsibility and the burden of consciousness.

Those of you willing to take responsibility for the pathways you are creating actually weave pathways that others may follow - and they will! That is what many of you are doing this lifetime; weaving pathways for future generations to take.

Those of you listening to these words are listening to them because you are ready for this step. It does not make you any more enlightened or wiser or more advanced than anyone else, it is simply a choice in how you're going to express. It is working with different pulses of light from different stars. It is working with different strands of DNA from different ancestors. Not better, not greater, nor lesser; just choice.

Choosing to be weavers of the new reality can be fun, exciting, courageous, exhilarating, frightening and many other varied emotions, but it is the ability to respond to different frequencies than you have responded to before. We are bringing these frequencies through with this work.

To be able to witness the realities that you are creating here at this time will help you understand what lines of light you have chosen to work with. To take responsibility for those choices brings you to the moment of here and now. From this place you are able to choose what realities to weave next.

When you have most of yourself caught in other places, whether you call it past or future or alternate, you do not have the presence of awareness to create from the now. Everything that is, is spun out of what you are now. To be aware of all of the lines you are choosing to work with immediately makes you aware of all the lines you are not choosing to work with. Seeing this enables you to have different choices; much like an artist who can broaden their colour palette by using more than three colours. There is much more you can paint when you have access to the millions of colours that the universe truly has!

Even your eyes are geared to seeing only some colours. Those of you who have witnessed spirit light in the form of aura or light spirits understand that there are entire other spectrums of colours to weave with. It is the same story over and over and over again. What we are showing you is that you have a billion choices and a billion realities to choose from. Those of you who wish to weave a different reality can take that responsibility and do just that, on behalf of yourselves and anyone else who chooses to follow the patterns you are laying out.

Many cultures and societies have tried different weavings, creating different ideas that have played out throughout Earth history. Most of the societies have come to the same place at one point in history or another.

This is the place where another idea or culture became dominant over theirs. This is the place where they relinquished power and responsibility and allowed themselves to feel victimized by another reality. It has been popular to think of the dominant reality as being somehow evil, Luciferian, wrong, or any other blaming viewpoint.

We offer a different choice here. We ask that you see how each one of you lost faith in yourselves, in your truth, in the realities you were choosing to hold. We ask you to witness all the places that you put aside your own weavings, your own light, your own faith in self, and allowed others to dictate to you their light, their understandings, and the star systems that they were bringing through.

We ask you to witness where in your life right now you are allowing another reality to dominate over yours. Every time you think, "I may be wrong, this other reality might be right. This is what I have to do. This is the way things are. It's always been this way. I don't have a choice..." all of these thoughts, all of these beliefs hand your power over to another.

Each time you think and act in this way, you are in effect choosing lines of light to weave your reality with. It is far easier to blame the conquerors than it is to understand how their reality got allowed into yours in the first place!

One of the ways we see to shift the current world reality, that none of you seem to like very much, is to ask you to hold tight to the ones you want.

We ask you to recognize that you have a universe full of starlight to choose from, to recognize that you have millions of ancestors to choose the DNA from, to recognize that you have millions of realities that you, as a soul, have expressed and are expressing to choose from. There are a million thoughts in your mind at once and you choose which thoughts to fixate upon, thus creating the realities of your choice. When you choose a reality dictated by someone else, you choose to abdicate your responsibility. The state that your world is in right now is the product of this universal law.

So here are the ancient weavers of the fates. Each one of you an ancient weaver, reaching to the skies, pulling lines of light from what has come to pass in different times and different places in God's reality, taking the chosen lines of light from the night sky and weaving your dreams.

In the morning you bring yourselves into the consciousness of the one star that guides the daylight hours during the awake reality of your planet. The patterns that you replicate under this one sun are patterns you chose from your dreams in the night sky.

Each one of you are weaving the realities of your choice, creating between all of you, the tapestries that become the dominant culture on Earth. As the weavers become accomplished in their work and take pride in their creativity, so the realities expressed become more interesting and creative.

Collectively, you begin to create a variety of patterns, colours and possibilities. These weavings become clothing that you wear in each lifetime to express who you are. You change weavings as you change your clothes.

Each life has a slightly different weave. When you agree to weave together as a collective reality, you weave the fabric of your consciousness. Each culture has its own patterns that you can actually witness in the pottery, the clothing, designs of the buildings, and the structures of the societies. These same patterns will be dominant in different time periods in different cultures across the planet.

About the time of the so-called Industrial Revolution, one group of souls who understood this very well decided they would try their hand at creating reality. They began the industrialization of weaving, and these were the very first factories created. There was one pattern and all workers were expected to become the cogs, to become the wheels, to become the weavers, to churn out this one pattern. It was uniform and precise, without much creativity, but functional.

Since this time, the consciousnesses of the souls incarnate on Earth have become less creative and less varied. They began to weave according to the patterns dictated to them. Terror was used to keep weavers working on the big looms in the factories. Some were chained to the looms and others were held hostage by the withholding of food and water. Whatever means of fear and intimidation used, the workers found themselves weaving the patterns according to the dictates of this small group of souls who were trying their hand at weaving reality.

Most of you agreed to allow them to try their hand at being the creators of Earth reality for a period of time.

We believe that time has come to an end. We believe that most of you have decided that you like the creativity and innovation of your own weavings.

We believe that the time has come for the diversity of the weavers to create the new reality on your planet. We are interested in awakening you all to witness what you have been allowing to manifest here.

We do not say that these souls were wrong, bad, or evil, as many will claim. We say these souls realized and saw how easy it is to weave reality on this planet and decided to try their hand in the full weaving.

We ask that rather than projecting blame and creating a revolution, or going about beheading these souls, you instead learn from what they have done.

We ask that you see how easy it is to weave realities on Earth and try your hand at such weavings. We ask that each of you look, see, and discover what lines of beliefs and realities you are choosing to weave with.

We ask that you look, witness, and observe what other lines of light are available to you and make your choices with a broader range of colour.

If you do not like the weaving of the realities you are currently living in, you need to understand the pattern to enable yourself to change it. This is your individual responsibility.

As you take your individual responsibility, you will find yourself in the company of fellow weavers also taking responsibility. You will find that you can weave together by weaving your own reality.

We believe you have seen that large, collective looms create standardization of thought, leaving little choice in expression.

We believe you have become more interested in what a multitude of looms can weave.

We believe that new designs and colours excite you.

We believe that you are ready for far more choices in your current reality.

We cannot show you realities that you have not experienced. We cannot bring you new patterns. It is up to each one of you to examine your beliefs, examine your realities, examine your creations, and make the choices of what you wish to weave.

Each one of you is a beam of light woven from your personal encounters and experiences. Each one of you, by weaving the fibres of your own soul, is a part of the greater reality.

We would like to spend our time together here looking at the different weavings that have gone into the creation of today. We would like to help you understand what you have been weaving with, and to possibly offer some other choices of reality to bring in.

This love
stretches through bliss
and meanders
through time,
tumbling over centuries,
cascading over limitations
to pool gently
in your arms.

Chapter V

Threads of Time and Place

The patterns that are inherent from the beginning of creation of this universe have vibrated through all the lines of light that lead to Earth. From the perspective of standing on Earth, you are in the center of the universe.

You are a bowl in the center of the universe, which has lines of light coming from places far and wide in every direction, pointed directly to Earth. Your eyes are the receivers of this light; your mind is the receiver of this consciousness.

Your viewing point is a place upon this Earth, and this affects how you receive everything that comes in. The proximity of each star's light to your planet, the movement of your planet through the universe, and your placement on this earth, all are relevant to what you are receiving. In essence, in this moment, your expression is a result of where you are standing, what you are receiving, and what you choose to work with. If you were expressing from a different place in the universe, (and you are, I can assure you), then that would be the center of your universe.

For now, we are working with the context of Earth as the center of reality because that's whom we are addressing with this information.

All that has ever happened in this universe, every thought that the Mother and Father of Creation have ever held, every feeling that has ever been expressed, has an effect on the makings of reality.

Of the billions and billions and billions of light sources in this universe, only some of this light ever reaches Earth. Out of the few points of light that ever reach Earth, many do not reach Earth until millions of years after their initial expression. Earth only has available to it a limited number of lights. It is limited to the billions, but

33

there are billions more possibilities of light that have not reached Earth. You have enough to weave with here to create whatever you choose in Earth reality, but Earth reality is limited to the lines of light you have here to create with.

There are billions of other realities in this universe, which are constructed out of different lines of light, and you, as a soul, may find yourself in all of these different realities. Just as your life is a microcosm of all of the lives of your soul, so Earth reality is also a microcosm of all of the realities expressed in this universe. You are working on Earth with some aspects of universal light, just as in your one physical lifetime you're working with some aspects of your other lives. Just as you are a physical being expressing some of the DNA of your ancestors available, just as you as a personality, are expressing some aspects of the ancestry, so Earth is expressing some aspects of the universe.

As your entire solar system moves through the universe very slowly it seems, you are picking up different beams of light. This changes the realities available to you on Earth and creates what appears to be an evolution to you. Your concepts of time are based upon the rotations of your planet, in comparison to the rotations of the other universal beings around you. Your idea of place relates to where you are on your planet and where your planet is in proximity to other beings of the universe.

We understand that you need these concepts to grasp Earth reality, but it is only one aspect of the realities available to you. You may choose to view time according to the single rotations of your planet, as in day, following day, following day, appearing as if it is a continuous time line, directing you towards some destined place.

Witnessed from where we sit, we watch your Earth spin around and around, and as it is spinning around itself, it is slowly moving around your star, and as it is slowly moving around your star, your star is spinning itself.

You don't notice this from where you stand on your planet, nor do you notice that you are simply spinning in circles.

The part of your soul who sits where we are, knows this, sees this, and is aware of the spinning. The part of you who is standing on the Earth, sees consecutive days and nights, and experiences reality according to that pattern. You, on Earth, witness day followed by night followed by day in a consecutive order.

Your bodies are born at one point of the turn of your planet, your lifetime is a series of days and nights, and then your body dies and you leave your planet. This is the reality as most of you see it. The other part of you sitting where we are sitting witnesses yourself jumping down into that reality at one point and jumping back off that reality at another point. You witness yourself as light jumping down into realities of Earth and back into realities of spirit.

This has most of you weaving realities with the belief that you started out at one point in time, and have been evolving to this point in time, as if it is a straight line of accomplishments.

Some of you believe you are graduating from levels of reality through the experience of consecutive lifetimes. Some of you believe that you are evolving from some lowly experience to some great-heightened experience throughout the course of what you think of as linear time.

Most of you create your realities according to this belief of consecutive linear time. For you to be able to shift the realities you are creating, we ask that you sit in our viewing point for a moment and witness the simple spinning of your planet. There are no lines involved here. There are no levels involved here. There is simply a turning of the circle.

There have been many prophets who have tried to describe this wheel, within a wheel, within a wheel. There have been many who have seen and understood this concept, and therefore, have been able to be the weavers of their reality.

The atoms that make up physical reality also spin. The electrons and the neutrons and protons all spin in the same way, around and around and around; each spinning with different frequencies, different patterns, different numbers, all creating the weavings of physical reality as you know it. As you witness yourselves as part of this great dance of creation, we ask that you step forward, grasp the threads of light and the threads of consciousness that bring you joy, that excite you, that appeal to you, and begin weaving your dance.

Throughout history, as you know it, you will find these same stories among all people in every culture. There are the Beltane celebrations of the British Isles, where the young men and women each hold their ribbons of light and dance to weave the maypole, as an expression of the weaving of reality for their people and their village.

There are the Plains people with their trailing feathers and ribbon shirts, men and women weaving their dances to the drumbeats.

In the deep jungles of the African villages, the men and women with their coloured masks and their grass skirts, again, dance the weaving of the masculine and feminine.

To the creation of towns and villages, to the weaving of cloth, each village with its own blanket design. In the Scottish highlands and lowlands, each family and clan has their own weaves and patterns.

The coats of arms of the European families have their own distinctive patterns, and in the making of the outer coats, each has its distinctive stitch work.

Every culture knows this, and in the very core of their being, every soul knows this. It is up to you to bring it into consciousness and to actively, consciously, weave the realities of your choice.

We cannot emphasize enough how important it is for you to be aware of the patterns you are choosing, and to be aware of the patterns you are not choosing.

Bringing this awareness into your personal creations that you call your life, we ask that you witness the patterns and the colours that you express your life through. What are the styles of clothing you choose? What fabrics, colours, and patterns do you choose to express in?

This may seem trivial to some people, but it is a reflection of what you are choosing. Some of you choose patterns that have been made for you by others; so-called 'buying off the rack'. Some of you will prefer to clothe yourselves in creations made by your own hands, or the hands of those who love you, and they may look out of place in the reality you live in. The choices of colour and design, in how you clothe yourselves, reveal the beliefs systems you are currently holding.

I would like to point out that in the culture that most of you are living in, you clothe yourselves in fabrics made by those giant factory looms, with patterns chosen by a small number of individuals. The colours are chosen by whoever is dictating this season's fashion, and those same individuals also create the designs. Most of you will be wearing similar styles and colours. Some of you will be choose something that stamps you as a little different, yet, you will select the same styles and colours as others who are also trying to be different.

Some of you choose to dress in the styles from different time periods, and even different realities that appeal to that soul. You will see simply by looking at the patterns of the weavings of the cloth that people choose to dress themselves in, the patterns of beliefs they are choosing to express.

When you move into realities that most of you readers are not expressing in, for instance, a village in central Africa, you will see different patterns emerging.

Here you may see people clothing themselves in the cast-offs from the dominant cultural realities. They will be choosing from discarded patterns, fabrics, colours, and realities of the wealthier places on Earth. You will notice very few places on this planet where cultures are wearing the clothing of their own creation. What you will see is one basic pattern in a small variety of choices being worn by most of the people on this planet.

Most are wearing the fabrics woven by the giant machines, which have enslaved your reality on Earth. Most have agreed to be the workers churning out the one dominant reality, which was dreamed up by a few individual souls willing to try out their hand at being creators.

To see how this is being played out is not meant to have you feel helpless in the face of it; on the contrary, it is asking you to see how easy it is to do that.

How easy was it for a few individuals to stand firm and say, "This is the way it is going to be. This is the reality and there is nothing you can do about it."?

They stood firm and whether anybody liked it or not, they began pulling the levers and pumping the bellows to create that reality. You all fell into line and did what you were told to create this reality.

Why then, would it be so hard for a few of you to stand up and say, "This is reality," and have fun? Why should one group stand so strong that the whole planet aligns to it and another group allows it, but hates it?

This Earth is meant to reflect a multitude of realities. She has the ever-changing sands of the desert, the bright blue skies, the flowering cacti, the bright creatures that live in this reality.

She has the waterfalls and the jungles of emerald green, and brilliant flowers and birds and creatures darting about so full of life that it is an entire orchestra of colour, vibration and sound.

She has the mossy banks of the gentle flowing river.

She has the plains waving their grasses as far as the eye can see.

She has the ocean waves of blue that can turn so quickly to rolling, roaring, waves of grey.

She has a multitude of realities from the glistening white of the glacial snows of the far North to the tropical heat and beaches of the Caribbean.

Of all the possibilities she offers, why have you all agreed upon one? Why do you not allow the diversity that this planet offers to express? Why do you not look at the options and choices truly available in your lives? Why do you accept such a narrow reality as the basis of your experiences?

You have full choice here and it is up to each one of you to exercise that choice, to be creative and try out different realities.

There's no where to run to, no land that is free,
From the tyranny and oppression of, what they say must be.
If we threaten their lifestyle or question what they say,
Oppose their progress, or suggest a new way,
They're on us like sharks in a frenzy of rage.
Bomb us, drug us, lock us in a prison cage.
Tell us we're crazy and that we don't exist,
Except just to serve them and in this we persist.
They still hold the factories of slavery and pain,
And we buy the products believing this sane.
We agree to their rules, and by this we abide
There's no where to run to, and nowhere to hide.

Chapter VI

Pyramid Reality

Those who have been the weavers of the reality that you currently believe in have put a lot of work and effort into creating this. They began by understanding fear and how fear works in the psyche of the soul.

When you are expressing in physical reality, you are constantly creating and re-creating yourself on an atomic and subatomic level. You are meant to exchange and interact with the rest of the planet on this atomic level. You eat, you drink, you breathe, and this allows the life-giving dance, the exchange of atomic energy, between you, as a soul, and the planet that gives you life.

Some cultures consider this soul light as masculine and the Earth atoms as feminine, and the dance created between the two as what you witness as life. This dance requires an interaction with the physical. To end the dance, you must stop that interaction by stopping the taking in of breath, of food, and of water, so that the dance can no longer continue and that physical life ceases to exist.

Knowing this and understanding how to use this, these folks decided to create a reality using fear, and it worked. Fear of not having this interaction with breath, fear of not having this interaction with food or water caused most souls to give over their power.

The first thing the new weavers did was to take the food and control of the food; thus, the fear of starvation led many to come to work in the weaving factories.

Those who knew that the Earth could provide and who chose to live a different reality went further and further into the wilderness, relying on the forests and jungles to feed them.

Knowing that the tactic of food didn't work fully, they spread their net a little further and claimed the forests and jungles as their own, cutting down the sources of food and nurturance, and thus, creating the foreign dependency on food.

This caused the fear which brought the people out of the forests and into the factories. For those who still resisted, the net went further; to the sharp sword, the guns, the hunting of fellow man for sport. Therefore, the fear of losing the ability to breathe brought the rest of them into the factories.

It has gone even further now, and at this point in history it has come to be that to live on Earth, to have access to food, to have access to water, and to have access to breath, you must conform to the reality that these ones have created. Here, the denial of food, water, and breath, has caused most souls to hand their power over before they begin to even consciously live their life.

You raise your children in this way! You give them rules and expectations and punish them by taking away their food. You will find many children expressing this whole system of belief; when they don't have what they want, they will hold their breath. This is their way of saying, "You won't have power over me with breath, I will".

You find diseases in your culture with the eating of too much food or not being able to take in food as the same statement, "You will not control me through food".

You see people actively poisoning the waters, for there is no other excuse, as a way of stating, "You will not control me through water".

This is the backlash; the destruction and pollution of the physical reality is the backlash of the people against such control. Most of you blame the few in control for this. *They* are polluting the waters, *they* are poisoning the lands, and *they* are cutting down the trees! I ask you to look.

Although *they* are giving the orders, it is the bulk of the people on this planet who are actually creating the destruction. The few that are giving the orders are fully aware of what they're doing, and those who are following the orders would do well to become as aware of what they are doing themselves.

So this reality has been created on the fear of losing food, water, and air. This reality is created on the fundamental belief that someone else owns the food, the water, and the air. This reality was created and can be uncreated, too! Many of you believe, "This is the way it is. This is the way it has always been." You hold this belief because you were told this belief is the only possible reality.

This belief system does not go back too many generations in most ancestries. The belief systems held in the North American continent, going back only four or five generations, were different than what is held now as truth. Most cultures and peoples throughout the history of this planet have lived with the belief that the Earth is a provider. They believed that your personal interaction and your communal interaction with the planet resulted in the reality that you lived.

The belief was that if you gave to, honoured, and respected the planet, the planet would feed you and keep you alive. The belief was that this Earth cared for, fed, clothed, housed, gave water to, and gave breath to the people and the animals that lived here. The belief was that as long as you kept in balance and in honour with this planet, you were provided for.

The belief was you could stay here as long as you chose, and at the end of your journey you gave your body back to the planet with gratitude; you gave her back the atoms she lent you. The belief was that the heavens, the sun, God, spirit, whatever it is that you call it, gave you the life force to have this beautiful experience of interaction

43

with this planet. The belief was that each lifetime was yours to express your most courageous, most beautiful, most talented, and the most wonderful aspect of your soul that you possibly could.

This belief system led to a diversity of cultures. On this continent alone there were thousands of variations of tribal life. All patterns were based upon the circle; the spinning of realities.

On the African continent were thousands of diverse cultures. On the Asian and the European, as well as the Australian, and all the continents that no longer show above the water, this was the way. Each culture looked different, expressed different sizes and shapes of physical bodies, different colourings, different dances, different songs, but all flowing in the pattern of a circle. The European races had thousands of cultures, each with their own distinct patterns, beliefs, and ceremonies, all based upon the circle. The villages were created in circles, the stones were set in circles, and the altars were placed in circles. In the yellow race there were thousands of different cultures, peoples, and villages. In each of the four directions were thousands of different possibilities of reality, expressed as different cultural identities.

When one is standing and looking at these four directions, you are aware of the diversity in your own area, but the other areas tend to look the same. Within each one of these directions were a thousand possibilities of expression, and the soul was free to choose incarnation in any one of these places, and was free to express themselves in any of these aspects. Some of them were fierce, some were gentle, some were possibly more creative and colourful than others, some simpler, but every possible reality could be expressed.

As souls began more and more to try their hand at being creators, different realities began to be manufactured out of what was here on this planet; different realities were tried out. As those souls began to test their power, to test their strengths, they began to try to impose different weavings than what this planet naturally expressed. This began the concept of dominion over the Earth. This began the concept of harnessing energy and using that energy to create something different, according to the individual will. Thus, began a changing of molecular structure; the changing of reality.

The changing of molecular structure led to the makings of metals, which began wars on a scale that the Earth had not seen. The changing of molecular structure into different metals created the realities of the armies, which came forward to conquer and takeover the existing cultures. Your conscious mind can generally go back to the early years of childhood, and your collective mind can generally go back to Atlantean times, which was when these realities, that did not fit with the planet itself, were brought here. A different form was brought forward. The form of the pyramid was imposed on a place that expressed with the form of the circle.

The form of the pyramid relied upon a large base supporting a small pinnacle. The idea was to gather a base force and condense it in an upward movement to create a fine point of energy that could then be utilized by one or two individuals to create what they willed.

To build such societies required a great base. It required an attitude of evolving upward. It required an attitude of a small number on the top that one aspired to be. It required an attitude of climbing from the bottom to the top. To those cultures, and the wise among them that lived on the basis of the circle, this appeared quite ridiculous.

It was obvious that those on the bottom must never be allowed to climb to the top, or it would topple over. It was obvious that those on the bottom, creating a base, truly were the strength and the power, and those on the top were actually quite precarious and at the mercy of those on the bottom.

The wise of the circle villages didn't want anything to do with such a structure. But those that wished to try their hand at creation knew that to make it work, one had to have a large percentage believing in that reality.

If you wished to bring the pyramid reality to Earth, you had to get rid of the circle reality. To do this you had to convince the majority of the souls to believe in the pyramid reality over the circle reality. Quite a lot of effort has gone into this very creation. There have been various means of convincing you to walk away from the circle and to believe in the pyramid.

Each generation has believed more and more in this pyramid, until the reality you have culturally manifested on your planet mostly reflects this pyramid. This is the creation and belief system most of you accept as truth.

Standing in the place of the wise elder from the circle community, you would laugh at the folly of the people who are racing to be the base of the pyramid. You would chuckle to see the hordes of people scrambling over each other to get to the very top, believing they have now made it; they are now at the pinnacle. They never looked down to see how precarious it is where they stand, and no one wonders why someone would want to create this in the first place.

We would like to draw your attention back to the circle. The circle expands outward; its energy and its power encompass all, and all may partake as the circle expands. It creates space for many and encompasses many.

The shape of the pyramid puts its energy upward into a point, focused through, into one being. That is a lot of energy focused into one being. The circle, on the other hand, opens for all and it is collective power, collective energy, and all must equally partake within that. The pyramid is focused for one. One point to take one line of energy, generated from all that create this pyramid, and used by one entity. It can be directed to create reality as one entity sees fit. It is actually quite brilliant, but it only works if everyone agrees to be part of it.

When energy is directed from a point, this energy is deprived of the colours of its light; it is changed in form and structure, in essence, to a point. This goes against what you see in nature, doesn't it? A star is round, a star is round in every direction, and the light that emanates from a star comes from all points upon that star. When your sun, which is round, shines its light on Earth, it shines its light to encompass everything that wishes to be encompassed. It shines to give its energy and light to include all who wish to put themselves in that presence. When light is focused into one single beam it does not encompass, and that one beam has to be directed. I would ask that you look at what you are creating again here and decide if you want to focus all your light into one beam, and if you want to hand that over to the one person or one group of people who are choosing where to focus that one beam of light.

You can see this pattern in so many things that you do. You can see it in the way that you use your eyes, how you focus on one point. How in your schools your children are taught to focus their eyesight on one word, one letter, one point. You can see it in how your children are made to sit in boxes, in rows, with all their eyes pointed at one person in the front. This way of teaching creates, right there, the basis that continues to be the foundation of the pyramid that you use in your culture. These children are put in rows according to behaviour or according to intelligence. All of this dictated by what that one person in the front decides, and all eyes are supposed to be focused in a sharp point at the front. Any disobedience from that sharp focus will be severely reprimanded. You are not allowed to focus on anything else, but to put all your attention on one point in the front.

You send your children to these places where they are trained to behave in this way. They are trained to hold their energy, to hold their consciousness, contain it all within one spot, seated in one position, eyes focused forward on one point. This is not conducive to learning. Therefore, one would have to look and see why it has been set up this way. What would be the point of this system? This is not the best way for minds to learn and grow. It is not the best way to receive information. So, what good does it do? Its purpose is to train the base of the pyramid, isn't it? If you look at the systems set up in your education you are already creating the pyramid. You are already creating that in your classrooms; all points forward into one.

You also create through your marking system the idea of moving upward on the pyramid. Small numbers of students get good marks; it goes out and out and out to the average and the mediocre, and those who do not get those meridian line grades are pushed out to the exterior. Those ones are meant to clean up after the rest, isn't that so?

The ones in the middle are going to be expected to hold the pyramid. They are going to work in the factories or in offices, each with their own cubicle, in their own little box, again, to live in for their lifetime.

The next line up, those who achieve the middle grades, will learn to behave in a particular manner, or they might be able to bring in some new ideas, or some might be able to be overseers, but they will all try to go forward to the little points on the top again.

The ones who are expected to take the place towards the top points of the pyramid, you will not generally find in these public school systems. They generally will be in other school systems; expensive ones, too! That is where you will find them. They are being trained in a different way; they are being trained how to use the energy, they are being trained how control the masses; they are being trained how to work with all of this, and they are being indoctrinated in their own way as well. But you will find in a lot of those systems, they won't have the point on the top; they will have these kids thinking they are the point! So you grow up in your culture in this way.

In other cultures and other times, education was conducted with the students in a circle with their teachers, and generally there would be a few teachers in that circle, not just one. In this system of learning the interaction goes back and forth within the circle, like a weaving of ideas. These kids will be brought to places to learn things. And so, if the lesson is about growth, that circle will pick itself up and walk through the forest, or that circle will pick itself up and go over to the rivers, but it will maintain an entirely different focus; the focus of give and take.

In the circle story teachings we have the teachers talking about their experiences and knowledge, and we have the kids asking questions and bringing their experiences forward. In these ways, the teachers learn just as much as the kids. The kids tell their stories and ask the questions that cause the teachers to look further and deeper into themselves, and therefore, education becomes collective.

Oftentimes, you will find people doing their work on the outskirts. You may find a woman grinding grain while she listens to the stories and lessons that the children are hearing. One day you may find the kids are going to be learning perhaps how to make a rope. Well, they will be out with the folks making the rope. All is inclusive, all is one. You may find some of the kids asking questions that cause the rope-makers to say, "I don't know, let's try that way," and so the whole community learns through the kids learning. It seems a lot better way to educate; seems like it would fit better with the whole community.

In your present educational system, based on the pyramid, you can see how when the kids are taught to look and focus on the one person at the point, they miss everything else going on around them. Your brain is not allowed to notice what is going on outside the window, or that the kid beside you is squirming, or the kid over there is crying; you're not allowed to notice these things. You are not allowed to notice your own body or how you are feeling. You are not allowed to notice that the position you are sitting in is cramping your legs and your feet, or that your head hurts, or that you are thirsty. You are not allowed to acknowledge any of these things in the pyramid system. So, the kids are expected to sit in this discomfort, not noticing their bodies, not noticing what is going on outside the window, not noticing what their peers are going through. They are meant to block the whole community out and focus only on that one point.

Most of you observe the world in this way. You walk in this way, head up, eyes to the front of you. You think of your life in this way. You plan for yourself to go from this point here to that point there; you draw yourself a straight line and you think that is your life going from one point to another.

You train yourself not to notice what you are walking past. You want to get from your home to your place of employment, and you don't want to notice the person who is driving on the road beside you, and you don't want to notice the person who is lying on the streets as you walk by.

You focus only on your point, your objective, with all of your energy, and you believe this is going to get you where you need to go. You keep going and going, running and running and running, trying to get to the top of that pyramid. You set your timepieces to tell you, "I must be here precisely at this time. I am allowed to urinate at this time. I must pour this liquid into myself to stimulate myself enough to wake up at this time," and you set yourself to this pace of reality and you tell yourself that this is life— this is the way it needs to be!

So, at the end of the week you are given a piece of paper telling you how many points you have earned and where you are on this pyramid; where you are and what income bracket you are in. If you took the population base of everyone living here and divided him or her into income brackets and graphed it out, you would have a pyramid! It is exactly what you would have! Your paycheque at the end of the week tells you what level you have reached on this pyramid.

You all have been taught to believe that if you follow these exact precise rhythms and focus only on this straight line, you will be able to rise in this pyramid. Rising in this pyramid tells you how many swimming pools you are going have or how many cars you are going to drive.

In other places, lower down in the pyramid, it is reflected in whether you're going to eat or not. That's where it starts at the base; to eat or not to eat. The higher up in the pyramid you get, decides whether you're going to drive a car; higher up still, what kind of car you're going to own, how many cars you are going to have, and then possibly acquire an airplane. It is kind of a sad reality, for that is what has been created here, and it is what everyone has agreed to. I want you to begin to look at how ingrained this structure has become.

You can see it in your healthcare system. Who gets health care and who deserves to live? You can see it in how much pain you are expected to tolerate and what level of wellness you are allowed to have. In areas where the people are higher up on the pyramid they have better healthcare available to them and they have better doctors. For the ones lower down, if you have any health care practitioners in the area where you live, that's considered pretty good.

In this country, where we are sitting as we channel through this book, you can see this pyramid. You can see the base of it in the south, where the border between you and Rome lies, and you can see the wealth all along that borderline, and it gets less and less the further north you go, ending in a point. You have an inverted pyramid happening. So it's kind of funny to see how these systems are at play! The way your society has brought this reality in over the last ten thousand or twenty thousand years or so, can be seen in every aspect.

We have looked at education. We can see here how it begins right from the start, by sending your young ones into these boxes, as early as a few weeks old, to learn to focus their intent into the pyramid. You can see how, as the education goes higher and higher up, that there are less and less people. You start out at six years old, as the broad base, until those who make it to the seventh or eighth year in school are fewer. Even less who make it to their twelfth year of school, and all the way up to the highest point of education, the numbers become less and less until there are very few people. Your educational system is in the shape of a pyramid. It was never meant to be like that; it was meant to be all in circles.

You have a pyramid in the healthcare system. One's place on the pyramid determines whose lives are important and whose lives are not, and what levels of extreme measures will be used to save their lives. It also decides to which areas of the healthcare system the money will be allocated.

If you look in your system, the amount of money that is spent on studying heart attacks, which are the killers of those in the middle to upper levels of the pyramid, and compare the money spent on mothers who bear the children, which is where health really begins, you will see a gross imbalance.

If you graphed the kind of diseases found throughout the pyramid and graphed where the money is actually spent, you wouldn't see much money put in the basis of good health, such as nutrition or good food. That is not where the money is directed. Most of the funds go to the killers of the smaller group near the top of the pyramid. That's where the funding goes, where the attention and the focus is. Your hospitals are built for that. They are not built for health; they are built to save the lives of the upper ones on the pyramid.

If they were truly built for health, what you would have is nutritional counselling for pregnant women. What you would have is nutritional counselling and health for the children so that they would grow up to be healthy adults. That is not what you have in your society. You have the saving of the lives of the top ones of the pyramid. You have healthcare as being shown as a benefit of rising higher and higher on the pyramid.

In the same way, you have this in your financial world. At the base of the pyramid, the people there are only just getting enough to pay the bills and eat, maybe. As you go higher and higher up, at the top are the standard banks that own and hold all the money. As well, sucking from the bottom, are the moneylenders; so the moneylenders taking from the bottom and the top are really one and the same. That is how it is disbursed through to the top of the pyramid. You can use that money to make more money, to buy stocks, or to have more power. If you are at the bottom of the pyramid, you get to borrow all that money so that you can be further in debt, to make sure you never get out from under the bottom.

You can also see this in the spiritual ideologies that many of you hold; even many of yourselves who think you are new age thinkers—whatever that means, for I don't see much new age happening here. Your belief, that you are all evolving to a higher and higher consciousness, the belief that there are great masses of sleeping people, and very few elite awakened ones at the top. Some of you, who believe yourselves to be great spiritual people, think of yourselves as the top of the pyramid, don't you? You think of yourselves as better than the masses unconscious at the bottom. In the circle reality you realize that every soul is a spirit. It doesn't matter who they are, it doesn't matter what they look like; they are all children of the Creators and they are all equal in the Creators' eyes.

When you look at the spiritual, so-called spiritual, through the eyes of the circle, you see a group of people that the Earth has offered her atoms to, for each one of you equally. The Earth never said, "We don't like your ideologies so you don't get these atoms." The Earth never says, "We're going to take your body back because we don't like you." The Earth offered each person free use of her atoms to create life with. She didn't decide whose ideologies she was going to support and who she isn't. She says, "Go ahead and try it and see." She won't judge. The Creators don't judge which person is going to have light or not; the Creators just bring light and say, "Help yourself."

In the circle reality all are equal no matter what their spiritual ideologies are. In the circle reality you are able to dialogue back-and-forth; you are able to learn from each other. It is not that one is better than the other, not that one knows more than the other; it is a choice.

In the pyramid reality you are all led to believe that you are evolving in consciousness, that there are initiations and levels of consciousness you are to go through and at some point you're going to be up on that top point and you are going to be one with God. That is the belief system that has been held.

You have been taught that you must go through lifetimes of struggle, lifetimes of lessons, and those who did not learn their lessons are sent back down to the bottom of the pile. Down you go, and you have to live lives in misery, down at the bottom of the pile, until you learn your lessons and start climbing back up the pyramid.

This belief system has led to a lot of suffering and a lot of pain. It has left many people with the feeling that they're constantly climbing and climbing and climbing, and at the end of each lifetime, they lose their grip and fall back down. It has created a sad illusion for many people, and many have just given up believing that they are ever going to be accepted or reclaimed by God. This is, again, a choice of perspective.

The truth? The true truth is that you are! You are all of those things! You have choice of where your focus and energy is put. Those who think they are standing on the pinnacle of awareness don't realize they have aspects of their soul who are lying on the streets, discarded. Those who justify their reality of being in the middle of the pyramid say, "Well, you know, I am a good person in a good place. The ones above me are rich and bad. The ones below me are poor and bad. I am in the middle in the best place." They don't know that they have part of their soul in both places, above and below them in the pyramid structure. They don't take responsibility for all of themselves.

In the circle reality, you are taught that where you stand in the circle, when you look across at all the other points, that those points are all reflections of yourself, and may very well be a piece of your own soul incarnate over there. In the circle reality you learn you must stand on every point of that circle. You must be all of those things to be whole. These are very different teachings than the pyramid reality.

Using the models of this reality, I would like that you look in your places of business, in your religions, in your gatherings, in your families, all of the places that you interact in your life, and notice how this system has been imposed. Recognize for yourselves, that you have a choice of how and where you are putting the focus of your intent. Notice the ways in which you allow yourselves to conform to the shape of this triangle and recognize that this is your choice. Next, I would like to speak a little bit about the circle and the intent and the teachings of the circle.

55

She sits by the shore and she spins
The rhythm of the waves
Mark time with her treadle pulse
The summers fleece she saves
Through wandering hills and valleys low
From winter's growth she pulls
The sun and rain and green grass grown
One years turn she mulls
Through wisdom gained and time well spent
The healer, the midwife
She spins the harvest of the year
And thinks about all life

The spinner women ancestors all
Knew how to meditate
As well as a Zen master can
Took time to contemplate

They knew that rush and hurry can
Lead you to your own defeat.
While time and care and good thoughts make
A balanced skein complete

Chapter VII

Ways and the Weavings of the Circle

In your universe you have a giant dance. Every body of light, which are called stars, are formed in a ball of radiating light. The light radiates in every direction from these balls of light. Around these balls of light are balls of energy that receive light that you call planets.

These receivers of light move themselves in a circle so that they may receive the light from their stars from every angle. They revolve around their stars so that they may accept from as many aspects of light that that star is willing to give. They move in a circular pattern around their star. The systems of planets that move in the circular pattern around the stars move together like a spiral dance. These seemingly individual dances of the stars and planets also move in the greater dance with other stars and planets. The configurations of each one of these dances in the universe move together in a giant spiral dance that is forever flowing and creating. This is the basis of the pattern of reality.

The point in the universe where each star system is situated is precise. The proximity of one star to another is set in perfect balance so that the movement of each galaxy creates the coordinates of the heavens. The exact friction between each heavenly body is precise creating the exact balance needed for this universe to function perfectly.

Within the individual systems of stars and planets that have their own dance, you can find an approximate replica in each star system. One star, that may have twelve or thirteen bodies revolving around it, will be part of a whole network of twelve or thirteen systems that revolve together. These are the basic movements of the universe, the basic patterns of the universe, but within this are some random patterns.

There are heavenly beings that have different movements that go flying through these galaxies at seemingly random and irregular times. These asteroids, these comets that go hurling by, have their own patterns, their own momentum, and their own weavings, that bring a different spark of colour through that creates change as needed. That is their purpose and their place within the universe; to bring change. Because of the precision of each circling, because of the exact proximity of star to star, you have a pattern that can move forever; always giving and always receiving, creating a perfect balance of life that can generate power forever into eternity.

I want to talk about these heavenly bodies that seem to randomly fly through the universe. They have their own pattern within this pattern. They have their own cycle, their own pathways that encompass many different star systems, and as they travel through the different star systems, they are linking the energies of these systems together in a circle.

Wherever they travel through the universe, they create a circle of their own. Some of them take one million Earth years to complete their circle; some of them will come every hundred years, every twenty years, every ten thousand years, depending upon the size and momentum of their individual circles. As they come through each universe, traveling very, very fast, they gather their momentum by gathering energies. They bring their own stories every time they come! They affect each system precisely how they are meant to affect each system. They are not random; they are a big plan within a big plan!

On your planet, you have the same configurations of molecular structure as every other planet. The patterns of the light of the stars are the exact same patterns of the different molecular structures you find on Earth. The patterns of that structure coincide directly with the patterns the stars are in.

If you look at your atomic reality, you will see your atoms laid out purposefully within each structure in a precise and intricate pattern. You will see the protons and neutrons turning and spinning within your atomic world, exactly in the same patterns that your universe does.

Your scientists have not been watching long enough to see the comets that come through that cause the shifts in your atomic realities. Your scientists have spent a lot of time, a lot of innovation and energy to try to create systems and tools that they can use to look at atomic reality so they can map it. All they needed to do was talk to the astronomers and they would have received the same information!

This they will discover; the microcosm is the macrocosm. It is all one. The stars are representative of the atoms of the Creators. Your physical reality is based upon universal reality, point for point. You look at the structures and systems of the stars, see a configuration, and you call that configuration the Great Bear, the Little Dipper, or you call it Pisces or Orion's Belt. Whatever names you give these systems, the point is that you recognize the importance of the configurations of certain groups of stars.

Collectively, you recognize the importance of these configurations upon your Earth. You are, in essence, throughout history, recognizing where your impulses are coming from. With which system, which pattern of stars you are choosing to identify with, that you are choosing to align with, you are in effect choosing which patterns you are going to weave with.

This is not new knowledge. If you look on your Earth and you decided, perhaps, to take a map of your planet, and if you decided to put a dot every place a pyramid was built on your planet, you would have a map of one star system. It was not random where these places were put; it was with purpose. These places were mapped and built in areas where you did not have a pinnacle to work with. You will only find the pyramids built where there were no mountains because they needed to create a pinnacle to be able to focus the light to match the star systems whose patterns they were trying to re-create on Earth.

If two thousand years ago you were able to map every place a stone circle had been built, whether it was built of stones or of stone houses, you would also be mapping a star system, but it would be a very different star system than the one that would appear where the pyramids were built. All across this planet, everywhere, people have built stone circles in configurations to represent and to map out different star systems. This showed the choice of the weaving of realities that those people were wishing to bring to Earth.

Where you have the pyramids, the people were trying to build a focused reality because they were afraid that they were going to lose their power. They believed they had to gather and hold as much power and resource as they could. It is possible that they were mapping out a dying star system. It is possible they were afraid of losing this light. It is possible they were afraid they were losing God's light. There are many reasons why this came into being, but the point I wish you all to look at is, this was a choice; a choice made out of fear.

In the places that you had the circles, they were open to the sky, not closed. They were open for people to come into, not closed. They were not hidden, with underground tunnels or burrows and walled-in places; they were open to include. You will find these circles of stones in Africa, in Asia, in Europe, in North and South America, in Australia, and even beneath the snows of the Antarctic. You will find them in every village in every land.

You will find some pyramid systems in North Africa, Egypt, of course, and in the South America, and you will find some of them began to be built in other places where they could not be sustained.

Wherever you find them, you will find the pinnacles of power that spread out to take over all the other places in the world. We have seen how the system of the pyramid has become the ways of your religions, your societies, your education, your health, and your money. Most of your culture is built upon this system.

We have seen how it could be different using the circle as the model. In education, you could have children sitting in circles, learning as part of a circle, learning from each other's gifts, as well as from the teachers' gifts.

We have seen what a monetary circle system may look like. As an example; if people were sitting in a circle, each one generating their own wealth, whether the wealth be in food or clothing or materials, you can't help but notice who and what else is in that circle. It becomes pretty obvious that if one person has four bags of rice and another over there only has one and someone over there doesn't have any, you see immediately how you would want to put that extra bag of rice where it will be needed. One may say, "I have four pairs of moccasins here. My friend over there has all that rice, but their moccasins look pretty worn." It is easier to see what is needed when sitting in a circle.

Most of you are so afraid of being on the lower levels of the pyramid that you do not even look down to see what is going on. If you are only looking up, all you notice is those ones have more than you, and you will always be looking up noticing who's got more.

Some people will be looking down and they are going to say, "I should be content where I am because I have more than them," but you don't look across and see each other as equals, so it's hard to share.

When you're sitting in a circle you become aware of everybody around you; you become aware that that circle is only as strong as everybody in it is. It makes you want to help all those people to be as strong as you are. It makes you realize that what you have is important to share with

61

others. It makes you realize who you are in relationship to that circle.

When you begin to include in the circle, the plant people, the stone people, the flyers, and the swimmers, the crawlers, and walkers, then you realize that that circle extends out and out and out, and that you are part of all that. It changes your whole way of being.

When using that circle structure in the health system, a circle healer works very differently than a pyramid healer. The circle healer can sit in that circle and realize that a person over there experiences ill health as a result of the circle and how that circle affects that one person. They become aware of where illness comes into the circle itself and how it affects the individuals involved and how it is important to heal all of that.

You cannot heal the individual without healing their family and their community, as well. You begin to see how the health of that one individual is a result of the circle they are standing in, and the strength and the weakness of that circle.

The circle healer goes about things in a very different way than a pyramid healer, and the system of health is entirely different.

The pyramid healer and the hierarchy of health has to do with the expense of health; the more expensive the treatment the higher up on the scale it is.

In the circle of healing all things are inclusive; the tree beings, the plant beings, and the stone beings are all part of that healing, and all may be brought forward to assist in that work. It is more inclusive, more holistic, and it generates the health of the whole circle rather than the sharp focus being on the one individual. It is a different mentality.

In the pyramid system, and wherever you find the tribes that created the pyramids, you will find slavery. Slavery is the basis of these systems.

The tribes that came into South America and Central America came from the fallen cities of Atlantis, and they brought slavery with them and began imprinting the other cultures, the circle cultures that were there, creating slavery and making it a way of life.

Within that system you must, out of necessity, have ill health. You must, out of necessity, have the threat of death and the threat of ill health; either from not enough food or water, sleep, or air. You must have people that you can force to work in the poisoned mines, you must have people that you can force to do the damaging physical work; you must have slavery or it will not survive.

In the circle communities you cannot have slavery or it will not survive. When you encompass slavery within the circle you immediately weaken it. When you encompass poverty in the circle, you weaken the circle. If some people in the circle are hungry, the whole circle weakens, and you know this!

In the pyramid you have such a big base it doesn't matter if half of them are starving, because you don't concern yourself with such things. If your base is starving you don't realize that from the peak, but if your base is well fed, they are not going to work. The basis of the pyramid means keeping that base right at sustenance level, so that food can be kept as a threat and incentive. You are not going to be willing to do harsh work unless you have to eat. You are not going to go and clean out the toilets of the ones at the top unless you have children's mouths to feed. You are not going to be willing to knock twenty years off your life to work in a coal mine unless that makes a difference between your family surviving or not. You are not going to chop down trees in a forest that you love; you are not going to do all the dirty work unless your very survival is threatened.

In a circle society most of these jobs are not important, as they are not needed to sustain that reality.

They don't exist in the circle reality. If there are unpleasant things to do, everybody can see that they need to be done, and everybody can agree to help out doing them.

In a pyramid society you can't see that, and you push the lower ones to do it so that you don't have to notice. The people that are pushed out of the bottom of the pyramid are the ones who will look after the top ones. They are the ones who handle the garbage and they are the ones who will be sent to certain communities when they are finally pushed all the way out of the pyramid. They are the ones that are going to have to handle all of the things that others do not want to notice.

In the circle community you have to take responsibility for these ones. You also have to take responsibility for yourself. You come to understand that you are part of this great dance, that you are a star or planet, and that you are one aspect of this whole revolving consciousness of light, and that your place in that dance is important. If you weren't there, there would be a little gap in that circle. While you are there, you can hold your place.

In the pyramid you are dispensable, and no matter where you are on the pyramid, if you get knocked out, there will be somebody trying to scramble upward, really happy to fill that hole. And since it is based on a precise line, just about anyone could fill that spot. In a circle, nobody can fill your place except you.

I want to take this into relationships, too, because you can see your family systems based upon the pyramid, as well. You have the father as the head of the family, the mother underneath that, holding everything, and from eldest to the youngest child. Where grandparents get put in here is generally at the bottom of the pile because they are not of use to the pyramid anymore. You can see the family systems have been set out like this, with one person at the top point. It is very different in circle families where the whole tribe is part of it, where the whole extended family is a circle onto itself, and what's important for the children, what's important for the elders, what's important for the mothers and fathers, all of this matters, all of it is of equal value.

In the circle community everybody knows that they are important. In a circle community the children are generally gathered in the middle with the elders circle around them.

The elders, who are getting ready to leave this world, recognize that these children are their future and are going to make the possibilities for them to come back into the world someday. So they create the next layer around the children, because the relationship between the child and the elder is the relationship between past and future; it is the relationship between life and death.

The elders are going to put their energy towards these children because these children are going to produce the future generations that these elders can incarnate back into. These elders, they want to make sure that their experience and their wisdom is going to be part of the future, so they want to give to these children the basis of all their experience and all their knowledge. This way everything they have gathered in their lifetime, everything they have expressed, has a chance to be woven into the future realities. In a circle community the elders' focus is on these children. They want to tell them their stories and give them their knowledge.

These children, they know they are going to be the weavers of the future. They want to turn to these elders, they want to say, "Give us your tools, give us your knowledge, and give us your ideas and possibilities, that we may build the best realities for ourselves." They turn to the elders because they know; they know that's where it's going to come from! In the circle community the link between the children and the elders is strong.

In a pyramid community you do not want the children to have these choices. You want them to follow only one pattern and you want to break that tie between the children and the elders and separate them. You want to sever it and you have done that in your culture.

The next layer around in the circle community comes from the mothers, the women. The feelings and the attitudes that the women in the circle community carry are to be the givers and the receivers of light. The movement of the women in their dance around the circle is to create life, to create sustenance, to create home. They are the builders of reality. They are gatherers of all the materials needed and the creators of the basis of that reality. The elders are too tired to be building too much. The women are full of life and energy, and they build, and they build, and they look after the elders, and they build for them. They look after the children who are too young to do this. They create the basis of life. They create the food, they create shelter.

The men are the helpers of the women; that is their role in the circle community. They stand on the outer circle, look and see what the women need, and they bring them the food and they bring them materials. They go out from the circle and they get what is needed by noticing what the women are doing, and they bring in what is needed to the women.

The women create the future and the past that coexist in the center. The men, they hold the boundaries for the reality of the circle, moving in and out between the outer world and the inner world, bringing back-and-forth, weaving. The women take these threads and create with them.

You can see this in the very biology of the male and female and how they experience each other. You can see this in the very biology of the fast, rapid growth of the child, and the sinking back in, of the elder. You can see it in the physical makeup that each expresses in this world.

The pyramid people have still never been able to get it to fit. No matter how many types of drugs they have manufactured, they have not been able to stop the inner-moving physical process of age. They haven't been able to control the outward-moving physical expression of youth.

They try to stunt the youth by allowing your culture to use suppressive drugs on your children to stop their outward-moving conscious expression so they can be contained in their little boxes. They begin at very young ages by binding their feet up tight, by binding their bodies up tight, confining them to little cages with bars as soon as they're born. They swaddle them tight and put them in contraptions so they cannot move, right from the very start, trying to confine this growth, this movement outward. They build boxes to put the children in, and after they have confined them, they try to control the outward-moving growth.

As soon as people get to the age where the body starts going back in, they start injecting themselves full of chemicals. They dye their hair, cut off body parts and replace different ones, all in an effort to stop the inward momentum. But they haven't been able to do it, have they?

They try to force women to move from nurturing, creative beings and push them outwards to become slaves. As I look at the damage this pyramid culture has done to the bodies of women, I see breasts being cut off and uteruses being cut out; yes, the very creative life-giving body parts of the women are being destroyed.

I look at what they've done to the men by not allowing them to hold their place but forcing them into alignment with the pyramids. I see the hearts of your men broken, destroyed, and I see the balls of your men are damaged. That's where they get the men; in their hearts and in their balls. Those kinds of diseases, you do not see in the circle communities.

67

You could look at this as two opposing star systems, or as two very different realities, emanating from different places in the universe, that people on Earth have chosen as the basis of their realities.

One system seems to correspond with the reality naturally created on Earth and one system seems to oppose it. One system supports life, and one system tries to be controlling of life.

It is time for those of you who are here creating reality on Earth to decide which system you wish to embody, which system you wish to activate.

If what we say is true, that your very atoms, your molecular structure, is based upon the blueprint of the universe, that you have within yourself a choice of which very atoms to activate, which patterns to activate within the core of your being, then you have a choice of what arrangements of patterns you are going to identify with. When you identify with a pattern, you activate that within yourself, and in so doing, it becomes the blueprint of the reality you project outside of yourself.

When you think, understand, and perceive of yourself as part of the circle of life, you begin to behave as if all things that you interact with matter. When you behave as if all things matter, you can no longer live as part of the pyramid. The very reality of your physical being is dependent upon this. The atoms of the Earth interact with your spirit according to the pattern of your focus and your intent. The focus of your soul on the Earth at this time is creating the idea that allows yourself to have physical life. The belief in yourself, the belief in your soul gives you the life force that you have to create your life with.

How you focus your belief and your intent, what you focus on and how you perceive yourself, begins the reality you are living. If you make a choice to focus on the patterns within you that reflect the patterns of this planet

68

and of the universe, you are immediately moving yourself into a different dance.

Think of each star as sending a tone to the Earth that creates music, and whichever tones come together create the song you are listening to, and each gathering of impulses creates a different song. What you tune yourself to is what your body is dancing to. The patterns that you dance upon the Earth are the patterns that are being woven for the future. The song you are listening to creates the response in your body, which creates the reality on Earth.

As you begin to perceive a different rhythm than what you have been focused on, you dance a slightly different dance. It is as if you have two radio stations coming in. Somebody is playing a CD in another room and out on the front porch somebody else is playing a fiddle, and you have a choice of tuning into the different types of music. You also have a choice of silencing some of them if you wish. It doesn't mean they go away, it just means you're not listening to those ones right now. You also have a choice of which one to dance to.

In circle cultures they understood the importance of these dances, the importance of allowing your physical body to respond to the rhythms of the stars. They understood the importance of putting these rhythms into physical movement, and you will notice that many of the dances of the circle people will be in circles. They will dance the rhythms of the planets and the stars, thereby imprinting those rhythms on their very being. It is a wordless, thoughtless, experience. It is a physical manifesting of these impulses, and through this, the patterns become established as part of your physical being.

Your heartbeat is your drumbeat and this pulsing rhythm is the magnetic rhythm. When the light energy moves towards a receptive planet, it causes a pulsing in the planet itself. This back-and-forth pulsing is felt between every planet and every star, it is between every star system, it is a heartbeat pulse; the rhythm of drums.

This rhythm is found in every Earth culture. The movement of this rhythm in the circle cultures corresponds with the pulse of the Earth, and the pulse of the heartbeat;.

It is very different than the drumming that is used in pyramid cultures which are more rapid, like a heart in anxiety, like adrenaline running through, meant to create an adrenaline like movement. You hear, in this rhythm, the singing in every pyramid culture, what most of you would identify as a military type march. It has a completely different formation than the circle cultures have. You have a choice of what songs you dance to.

When you begin to recognize this, you start to tune your ear to the circle dancing and you start to tune your ear to the rhythm of the circle; you begin to be aware of yourself as part of everything around you. You realize that every person you have contact with is part of you. You share the same atomic realities, you share the same breath, you breathe each other's air, and you expel and inhale and breathe in what has just been in each other's bodies. You share the same water and the water becomes your blood. You die, and the blood returns to the Earth. Someone else drinks that water next lifetime, and they are you.

You recognize and begin to perceive of yourself as part of one great pulsing cycle of life. When this is the way you are dancing, you cannot help but be whole; you cannot help but change the way you relate when you recognize the greatness and the immensity of the universe. You recognize that all of this light is part of you, part of your rhythms. When you recognize that you are part of everything, you cannot help but begin to dance to the songs of the Creators, and reality changes.

All through known, remembered history you see the battles between different realities; fighting and killing each other and spilling blood, all trying to prove their right to be on the top of the pyramid. You see the constant scrambling up and down, climbing, climbing and falling and climbing and falling. Rising and declining is the reality that has been created.

You can see this because these are the only histories that get recorded. These are the only ones your children are taught and these are the only ones you recognize as valid realities. You don't have the pictures of the circle realities because you do not have the language to talk about them. You don't have the academia that rules your world with the understandings of the circle realities, so whatever they are talking about or writing about, is from the viewing point of the pyramid. If it does not fit in that viewing point, they just don't talk about it.

In your culture you have been taught the histories of Rome, and that's about it. You have all learned about the Romans, the lands and peoples they conquered, but you seldom hear of the cultures that were there before they went in. You are not taught those parts of history. You know very little of the Picts, the Celts, the Franks, and the thousands and thousands of other little cultures that were in Europe before the Romans came. You do not even know much about the Greek cultures before the Romans invaded, and you seldom hear about the Italian cultures that were there before the Romans took over.

So, where did the Romans come from? Where did the Egyptians come from? Where did they all come from? How did they gain hold of the consciousness of Earth so that only their histories are taught or are considered important?

It is not because they are the only ones who recorded their histories; it's because it's the only one you hear about.

It is the same choice as to what songs are you going to listen to, what radio station you are going to tune into, what stories you are going to teach your children.

I am asking here, those of you who are hearing these words, to tune into a different frequency. Find out what else is available; follow your own ancestral lines back. What were your ancestors doing? What aspects of creation did they revere? How did they build their homes? What shapes did their villages have? What did they eat? How did they dress? What were the patterns and weavings of their fabrics? Follow back as far as you can.

If you can follow your ancestry back to before the Roman Empire came in, before that way of being was brought forward, you are probably going to find your original circle dance. If you followed the threads back in history to before the Roman influence came into being, you would find Atlantis, of course.

Atlantis wanted that line of thinking, that way of being, to be the dominant culture on Earth, and there was a pushing and forcing forward that created the construction of that reality. There are remnants of that reality that came forward and gathered strength in the surviving parts of the world after the destruction of Atlantis, which created what you call the Roman culture, and it has been that force that has moved forward and dominated the rest of your world. These are the patterns that created the reality that most of you have now.

But, just as during the times of Atlantis, that pattern of the pyramid called forward the enslavement and manipulation of all beings to create a base. Just as then, the base began to topple and the whole thing fell over. It looks like that's what you have going on now, doesn't it?

There is another way to shift realities. It does not have to follow that old pattern of toppling the pyramid; it could follow a different pattern. You could choose new light and new configurations from the stars. What you listen to, what you understand, and what you believe, creates reality.

As you shift your perspective from the belief of the pyramid to the reality of your planet, you begin to perceive a spinning circle, with every body as a spinning circle of atoms, and your life as a circle, evolving and cycling through. As you recognize that everything moves in this way, you turn your focus to be in alignment with the Creators' reality. As your focus is there, your dance changes; the rhythms become part of this. As you move yourself to dance to the different music of the stars, you find yourself dancing as part of the circle with everything around you dancing too. You can witness all the little atoms leaving the pyramid, and coming out until a whole different reality is created.

You do this by shifting your focus, shifting your intent, and by being so consciously aware of the cultural set-up that you make a conscious choice to move yourself into a different rhythm; in essence, you are creating an alternate reality.

For a while these alternate realities will have to coexist, as you strengthen your reality, as you pulse your drum beat stronger. As you pulse that drum beat stronger, it draws the attention of others, who begin to perceive differently. As their attention is drawn, they are gathered into the rhythm and the momentum of a different reality. Then there are fewer people's intent and focus holding up the pyramid reality, and it simply dissolves; ceases to be.

Deep

    Drums

        Dance..

            I watch them.

Hop

    Turn

        Tremble

            Jump

          Stamp.

I get up to move..

            Responding to their rhythms.

Chapter VIII

Drumming In a New Reality

Some of you have experienced the sounds and the rhythms of the drums, and have probably noticed that when the drumbeats begin, they call, and many respond, bringing their drumbeats and their rhythms.

The feet cannot help but begin to drum upon the ground in response. Sometimes it takes one drummer to begin and hold their rhythms, hold their beat, and others come and are so absorbed in the drumming themselves, that they look up, and hundreds have begun to gather around, and dancing erupts. It is so easily done.

I understand that in many of your cities, you have regular gatherings of drummers in your parks and in your church basements. The people gather together simply for the very act of being at one with each other in the rhythm. I know that most of the original cultures still left from these lands have regular gatherings of drumming. I know that most of the original cultures from Africa have regular gatherings of drumming. The Celtic folk and the Australian aboriginals are beginning to do this, as well. All through the Orient the drummers are gathering. This is a recent phenomenon in the last forty years or so.

The drummers are gathering. They are holding the rhythm of the heartbeat, the rhythm of the Earth. By the very nature of this reality, you end up drumming and dancing in a circle formation. These drummers are calling to bring you all back.

You see the office workers in their cubicles; where the pyramid rules dictate that the higher up in their building they are, the higher their pay is and the higher their prestige is!

Can you see the vision of this worker in their cubicle on the twenty-seventh floor looking down in the park, watching a circle of drummers drumming? What happens to this worker who sees this? Do they turn away and say, "This has nothing to do with me; I must get to my board meeting?"

But what happens when they take that elevator down to the ground and they have to walk through that park? Do they not stop? Do they not get drawn the same as everyone else to the drum? If the drummers can open up their circle to include this worker, then this worker has a profound experience.

So, in the future when they are up in their cubicle and look down into the park and see those drummers, it completely changes their perspective. It's that simple! Shift your prospective. Choose your reality.

That one drummer sitting in the park awakened that lonely soul, so tightly strung high up in their cubicle. It changes their whole life. It changes the very core and fabric of their whole being by simply shifting the configurations of consciousness. It is powerful. It is powerful because it is based upon the rhythms of the stars; it is it is based upon the responding pulse of the Earth itself.

The structure of that high-rise and of the cubicle created within it does not correspond with realities of the universe, does not correspond to the rhythms of life. It is an aberration of life.

It won't take much to move the souls of the people to the rhythm of the drums, the rhythm of the heartbeat, the rhythm of the universe. It won't take much to awaken this within you. Each one of you feel and sense this call.

When the butterfly lands upon your hand, you feel that it is hope, it is creation. When you see a flower growing, you feel that it is hope, it is creation. A bird flying overhead, the sun shining on the dew; these are all calls of creation. If you can stop for one moment and answer with your soul, you have immediately made a connection between yourself and another part of the circle. The fear-based reality that has been so imprinted doesn't stand a chance in the focus of that bliss of creation. It doesn't stand a chance against the beating of the drums. It doesn't take much to shift it.

What happens with some; the butterfly lands on their hand, and we have seen this, and great pain wells up inside of the soul and they begin to think about what they have lost. And they get angry, and they think about getting on top of that pyramid and paying back and having vengeance upon everything that is the cause of this great hurt, this great loss that they have. Their response to that butterfly is to take their other hand and squish it. So afraid are they to feel it, to recognize the loss of their birthright. So this is what they do.

So some, when they look down on that drummer and the gathering of the drummers, call the police and say, "Stop this," or "Don't let them do this. They are disturbing the peace. Take them away. They have no right to be here." They will send in the police to keep these drummers away, they will send in the RCMP to break up the powwow, they will send in the soldiers to stop the dances in the Congo.

So afraid are they of feeling the loss of their birthright, so entrenched and ingrained are they that they must, and will, stay late at the office and get their work done so they can rise on the pyramid. These drummers are disturbing their peace, so they will destroy the drummers.

Have pity upon these souls for they are mourning the loss of their birthright. Have compassion for these souls; the souls that kill the butterflies, the souls that stamp out light, life, and creativity, for they are so afraid. Recognize where they are in the circle, recognize that they are that part of you that is really afraid to open and embrace, and recognize that they are following the impulses that are coming from the light of the dying stars.

Many of you are feeling as if you have been the drummer in that park, so many times, and every time you were just getting into the rhythm of your drumming, the soldiers on horseback came.

They take away your drums and trample them into the ground, they beat your body, and they put you to work in the factories where you can be of some good to the world. Your saddest songs and your saddest stories, your sad movies and your sad books tell the same tale over and over. The poet tries to breathe the rhythm into the words, the musician tries, the artist tries, the writer tries, and the beating and beating of reality tries to reach you – while the other reality seeks to impose itself upon you. That reality seeks to claim your soul as its own.

How many of you feel the futility of this constant, constant battle, or feel that you have set yourself against that reality and its great sadness and great pain? Life after life, being imprisoned and enslaved, life after life, tiny glimpses and pieces of this bliss; never allowed to sustain itself long enough, never allowed to go further. You feel the pain of every circle village on this planet, raped, pillaged and murdered. You smell the blood that soaks the lands everywhere. That is the way of the pyramid that enslaves the circle people. It is a great pain, a great sadness, when looked at from that perspective.

Standing in the circle, one realizes that every aspect of creation that is being manifested on this planet is still part of the circle. One realizes that every fear and doubt that you have in the circle of your own consciousness is manifested. Just as you are the drummer on the ground in the park, so you are also the worker in the cubicle, and you are the policeman that was called to come in and stop the drumming. You can recognize that you have parts of your consciousness and your belief in all those places, and the healing is simply making the choice of where you are going to hold your consciousness.

In one reality the cubicle person calls the police and the police beat the drummer. Let's look at everyone's reaction here. The cubicle person is afraid. His whole life is pressure, he has debts, he has fears, his boss is yelling at him, he has a presentation to do and he has a deadline to meet the next day. He believes that his whole life depends on whether he gets this promotion to a higher floor or not, and that is going to depend on what he has to put together for tomorrow. So when he looks down and sees that drummer, it makes him angry and he thinks, "How dare you have freedom to do this when I am so responsible and working so hard? You are frivolous, you do nothing, and you make me angry." These are all his beliefs.

The receiver of his beliefs down on the ground is probably used to this. The receiver has things going on too, as he is sitting there drumming in the park.

Maybe he just came from his home where his father has said to him, "You had better change. You cannot continue like this. You are useless. You do nothing," and the drummer is drumming his frustration of this out. He is too afraid to get a job, he is too frightened to look after himself; he does not know what to do. He is angry at the world the way it is and he has not found his place in it yet. He has not accepted himself as the drummer, and therefore, he is drumming in retaliation and in reaction. He is not centered in himself.

Do you see the polarization between the one in the tower and the one on the ground? The representations they make to each other calls in the police. This reality between the two of them that has been created, this dichotomy, this tension between these two poles, calls in the police. Who is the policeman? He is a person also, and maybe he is worried about his job. He may have just come from a lecture where he has been told, "Why are you letting the streets get wild?", or he may have come from a citizens' meeting talking about crime and vandalism and all the lay-abouts who do nothing, and how they should be thrown from the city. So he comes in response to the person in the tower, and he says, "Well, I'll prove how good I am. I'll get rid of them alright." And now you have this dichotomy everybody has created.

Can you see the circle? It is the circle, and this is what got created here. Let's change the dichotomy a little bit and see how it takes form.

The person in the tower has a deadline. They haven't spoken to their children for two days because they've been working late at night. They're beginning to wonder, "Is it worth all this? I am tired. I haven't eaten properly. My wife isn't talking to me."

So down the elevator they go to clear their head. The first person that they see is a soul who has just fallen in love. Perhaps they are a student of philosophy and they are learning their role in the world as a healer or an artist, and they have taken their drum to the park because they wish to express this joy they are feeling within themselves. They are making these rhythms and sounds and they are interacting with the squirrels running and birds flying. It is late in the day and they are enjoying the last of the warmth of the sun, and they wish to express this joyousness onto everyone. They feel good about what they are doing and they love the response of the people who are joining and moving with this rhythm.

This office worker walks through the park and stops to listen and says, "Boy, this is nice." The sun is shining. His body starts moving to the rhythms and his mood becomes lighter, and he thinks, "Maybe I'll just leave that presentation the way it is and go home and see my kids."

The policeman is walking through, too, and the policeman is thinking, "A crowd is gathering. I better go over and see how it feels."

The office-worker says to the policeman, "Hi. Nice day, isn't it? Boy, that's a good drummer over there," and walks on.

The policeman stops beside the drummer, arms folded, and watches the crowd bobbing their heads back-and-forth to the rhythm, and thinks, "This is nice. This is what the park is for. People are happy," and continues on his way.

Those are two circles, two realities. That drummer had a choice of what to call to himself. That office-worker had a choice of what to create, and that policeman had a choice of how to react. Each one's response was dependent on the attitude of the other. What happened? What transpired?

The beliefs systems held in the state of consciousness in that moment of every participant could be changed by any bystander. An unhappy drummer may have a bystander who starts to enjoy the rhythms and smiles until the drummer smiles back. The office-worker comes down grumpy and the bystander offers him some hot chestnuts and says, "You look pretty stressed-out. Relax a minute; it will help." It would take only one master in that circle to turn everything around. One member of the circle bringing through what they resonate with and what they hold has an impact on the whole circle.

No matter how many pyramids you try to build on the Earth, she still turns in a circle around the sun. No matter how you try to constrict your children into boxes, their atoms spin and their blood flows in a circle through their bodies. No matter what rhythms you try to dominate your airwaves with, your hearts beat the same rhythm.

There is a true pattern that is expressed in this universe, no matter what types of patterns you try to impose upon it.

You each have within you, true beautiful souls, which are beautiful aspects of creation. No matter how many experiences you imprint yourselves with, the original beauty of your soul, the original rhythms of your very being, are still there. They are underneath it all. They have

81

never been lost, they have never been damaged, and they are still there. These patterns that have been put upon them are no more than illusions.

You have a choice of what rhythms you dance to in this life, not for an outcome, not for a purpose, but to be in that moment dancing to your truth. This is freedom, this is bliss, and this is your birthright, all of you.

The circle of life on this planet has its arms open to each one of you. The circle of life of this universe has its light open to each one of you, for you are a part of it by the very nature of your being. You are a piece of this great dance; and how you dance and what you dance is important in the weaving of the whole, in the creation of the illusion of the reality that you all live in.

In truth, this moment in time, with the tall pyramid buildings that make up the cities, the damming of all the rivers, the capture of all the waters, the conquering and cementing of all the land, the imprisonment of all the creatures into their little nature reserves, the imprisonment of all the native peoples in every land onto reservations, the imprisoning of all the ideas, philosophies, music and art; all of this is a temporary moment that is transient and can change.

It is all part of a flow, and tomorrow it will be different, and the next day will be different again, according to the music you are listening to and how you are choosing to dance in response to that music.

All of you are your birthright; you don't have to earn it; you just have to uncover it.

Ancient history flows through our veins
Ancestors crowding in to see what they have made
Unfolding our destinies, like linen napkins
Waiting for the crumbs to fall.
But You, You come to this table presuming you'll be served!
Raising up a wine glass,
You propose a toast to all of creation!
And You,
Are received.
And fed.
From the bounty of the universe.
Just as You expected to be.

Chapter IX

Opportunity Knocks

So, here we are gathered again the weavers of light, at another point in creation with a decision to be made of what reality we are going to weave. What realities are we going to create for the future generations?

Throughout the history of the planet there have been pivotal points when you know everything is going to turn and change. These pivotal points often can be seen as times when there are choices to be made by the people on Earth. The choices they make are going to open up a pathway to a future reality. Which pathway gets opened up is dependent upon what the weavers of those times hold to be true.

It is interesting to note that each of these times has been heralded by changes in the heavens. They are heralded by different configurations of planets and stars, or maybe a comet sweeping by. There is always a messenger in the movement of the stars and planets that seems to portend these changes.

That's what it looks like when you're standing on Earth. When you bring in the knowledge that the stars are actually pulsating information, telling their stories, singing their songs or sending their frequencies, you can understand that what is truly happening is that a different light, a different choice, is being sent to Earth. It is still up to the individuals incarnate at that time to make the choices from the light coming in; to make the decisions of what to weave into the future.

Your eyes receive light that is bounced from your sun onto the atoms that make up your physical plane. Your brain takes this light and creates the perceived patterns within your consciousness. That is what you see as your reality, what your sun is bouncing to your eyes.

At night, only by the light reflected by your sun upon the moon, or by the energy stored by your sun that you burn to make fire, do you see.

Everything that creates light, one way or another, comes from your sun. It is the source of light by which you can view your physical reality. When there is absence of light, you cannot see physical reality. There is no colour; there is only form in the things that you can touch. All patterns of physical reality are based upon the image you receive by the light reflected from the sun.

Your brain also receives light from the stars, and this light forms a different pattern in your mind. It is not forming the pattern of the physical reality that is manifested here; the starlight is forming the patterns that you choose to weave ideas with. Just as your sunlight illuminates the different atomic structures showing you the physicality around you, so your starlight illuminates patterns showing you the choices of ideas.

As different configurations are presented, it shows you a variety of patterns available and various ideas that you can work with. When these changes in patterns happen in the heavens, you immediately have a change of pattern, in the consciousness and thought processes of the people receiving them on Earth. It is this change in consciousness, in receptivity, that creates the great changes in your civilizations and your cultures.

Those who have been trying out their hands as creators, who have had good success, by their standards, use this information. There are few so-called leaders of the world, and few so-called leaders of the business realm, who do not consult the stars. It is a common, but hidden practice in your world, and was always a common practice among those who wished to pull the strings of creation. By studying the patterns of light that are coming in, a wise soul could see which strings to pluck and which strings to keep still, thus creating the song they desired.

Think of your Earth as being a harp with light streaming from the stars as strings, and imagine having the wisdom to pluck those strings to create the tune of your choosing. The knowledge that the tune being plucked creates what humanity dances to, helps one understand how cultures and dynasties become actualized.

One does not have to study astrology to understand how this works. You simply need to feel and to listen to the ideas that are being streamed to you. You need to be in connection with creation to feel the responses to creation.

This is knowledge enough for most of the beings on Earth, but for some who wish to understand this, the study of the stars is a way of interpreting what is happening.

Yet, for many souls, the idea of being able to interpret something makes them think that they have control over it. They believe that someone who can interpret the movement of the stars can control that movement. You can only dance to it.

So, throughout history this has been deliberately kept as a great mystery. This mystery tells you that starlight brings you ideas; that starlight brings consciousness and awareness.

There has been a lot of movement in the heavens in the last decade, and a lot of awareness has been flooding Earth. A lot of ideas have been brought forward, and more and more, you may notice that people are awakening as if from a long sleep. You may notice that people are suddenly having the awareness to see the patterns before them, that five years ago, most people would not see. You may question why we can suddenly see things that we could not see before. You may wonder why certain patterns are being illuminated that have not been illuminated before. You may wonder what light is being shone now, that is uncovering so much.

The answer to that is in the configurations of the stars. We notice a scurrying in response to this by those who have been wielding these patterns as a source of control and power, as if they are trying to hide what they have been doing.

It has been easy for the last few hundred years to hide the patterns of manipulation that have been used. It has been easy in the past to go into places, cause destruction and hide the tracks, so that even those who have been calling out, trying to bring awareness to these destructive patterns on Earth, have had voices that were not heard.

Now, you have awareness in the world around you. Eyes are opening and people are saying, "Yes, that is so, and I think it has been so for a long time." I believe many will hope this awareness is an evolution, but the truth is, this awareness is illumination.

The configurations of starlight that are shining now are showing you what has been and what is. This is the same as what has happened during each great leap. The stars have configured themselves to show clearly, patterns that need to be healed, and you weavers on Earth have a choice of what to do.

During other times in Earth's history these choices have been made available. These times are illuminated in each culture's history. These points of change can be seen in the myths, stories, songs, and ceremonies of each culture. The legends of the heroes and heroines are always about choices that particular people made during these key points in Earth's history.

You are all, once again, at one of those places in time where the choices you make now will weave the reality for the next seven generations. Many of you will have to do some un-ravelling of the weavings of the last seven generations so that you can bring the lines in clearly to yourselves. This point where many of you are standing moves forward and backward at the same time.

As you are healing your history, you are re-weaving your future. You can see this in just about every aspect of life, happening all over your globe at this time. In the past, these points of configuration would often be directed to one area of the world, and it would be those points where the changes occurred. What you are experiencing on Earth now is one of those points that are affecting the whole planet; everyone and every place.

Those of you with a Christian ideology will believe that two-thousand-odd years ago your saviour came and was one of those immense points. That was one of the points on one place on the globe. His coming did not affect the North Americas until one thousand years later, and then it wasn't in such a good way. His coming did not affect Australia or Africa until a long time later. His effect was on one specific point in the world.

India had its points of the change. China had its points of change. All the places on the globe have had different points of change throughout their histories, but it has been a really, really, really long time since the whole planet was in the same place.

The last time this happened you heard the stories of the great floods and the end of all things and the beginnings of new. All of your cultures have stories from this time, all of your cultures speak of their ancestors as being the only survivors of such times, and all of your cultures will tell you your ancestors were the survivors because they were good people and all the bad people left. It's a funny thing, how, after the fact, the stories change.

The reality of those times was a little different; each point on the Earth had a different story and reaction. One area of the planet during this time believed that everybody had gotten lost and had strayed from the proper rules, and that all of those that had strayed from the proper rules were going to be killed and only one family was going to survive.

That's a very interesting story, an interesting philosophy, for even in the surviving stories it is told that

89

this one male head of that family was a drunkard, and why he was able to hear the voice of God and not anyone else is a matter of speculation. But, I would imagine that his wife, his sisters, his uncles, and brothers must have supported him in some way for anything to have happened. Clear or not, he got the job done. The people from that place were told pretty clearly to either build a boat or drown. Those who chose to build the boat are the ones who survived.

Some people might say you had to be crazy to listen to those voices and build a boat, so maybe only the crazy people survived. Some people say that this is so.

In other places in the world people just went about their business.

There are stories from some cultures where they simply made large barges and put their villages all on the barge and waited things out.

There are stories where they made long lengths of rope and had it tied to the central tree of the village. As the floodwaters kept rising, the barge kept rising up with them, and they had to keep adding more rope woven from the fibre they had stored on the barge. In some cases, as they were running out of fibre, they were thinking and worrying that they were going to snap the line, but they had to have faith that each barge had the right amount of fibre to keep weaving their ropes. A lot of really good stories like that are left out from those times!

Some people just stayed put, and some survived and some did not. No one worried too much about it; they just went about their village work.

Some say they lived underwater for a while, and other stories talk about building great big canoes and paddling through the waves, awaiting land to emerge.

Others have stories of putting people inside large hollow reeds or logs. There are stories of medicines that were given, which put these people to sleep for a whole cycle of the moon, and when they awoke they were on dry land in a new place.

Others have stories of having to ride all the way down a long slope of snow until they landed in the summer lands.

There are lots of stories of those times of how people coped, how they survived, and what they needed to do. Some of them just got soggy; they did not get flooded right out, so they survived. Everybody on the face of the Earth was impulsed to be prepared for what was happening. Nobody was left out. The stars did not discriminate; they did not pick and choose who was worthy and who was not, they simply broadcasted. They sent the information of the configurations and the Earth responded.

You, the two-legged, because you have your feet on the ground and your heads in the air, heard from both places. You hear the configurations from the stars and the response of the Earth. So you knew, and the animals all knew, and everyone listening headed for higher ground. Where there was no higher ground, some went underground to wait it out. All creatures found a way to make it through the changes. Some of the birds started migrating ten years earlier, getting ready. Some of the creatures began changing their habits generations before to get ready. But they all knew the changes were coming and everybody needed to adapt. Everybody knew!

That was the last time that your whole Earth was in the same impulse. You are there again. It doesn't mean there are going to be any great floods, although many will experience that. It does not mean there are going to be any great fires, although many will experience that. It does not mean there are going to be horrific storms, although many will experience that, too. Depending upon what each group of people believe this energy will bring, is what they will create.

There are some of you who are hoping that the energy being brought at this time will help all of humanity to make a leap in consciousness, so that you will be able to make changes in the world.

There are many who are hoping that brutality, slavery, and greed will be eliminated. There are others who believe that the angels are going to come with great swords and kill everybody they don't like, and give glory to those they do. There are others who believe that spaceships are going to come and bring the worthy up off the planet while things are unfolding, and all the unworthy are going to get killed again. There is still the belief system present that says that God is going to smite the enemy and hail the heroes.

I ask you to look at your planet and look at your stars again. The planet doesn't choose; it gives. The stars don't discern who is going to see them, they simply transmit their light. Those with eyes to see, see it, those with ears to hear, hear it and those with hands to give, give. That is how it manifests.

You are all children of the Creators and you are all given the same access. What you believe and perceive of yourself and your relationship with creation is what you weave into your realities. This is a time of great opportunity that has not been here for a long time. You can take this opportunity and make that leap in consciousness that is required to bring all of Earth to a state of grace. It is not meant that only a few masters benefit from the magic of the land or the skies; it is meant as a birthright for all souls.

There is a banquet feast spread out with long rows of tables, heavily laden with every delight, and all around these tables are one-hundred people and all can partake. We find, in your culture, that five people might step forward and seat themselves around this feast, while all the rest find themselves serving and cleaning and afterwards perhaps getting some of the crumbs. The feast is there for all who sit at it. It is there for all who say, "I am worthy to eat this feast." It is not meant to that you chop off each others heads to get to the seats. It is not meant for you to believe that you must serve and work your way up to get one of those seats. It is meant that you realize there is plenty for all. Help yourself, the Earth is bountiful.

How do we change this reality, where ninety-five percent of the people will stand back and serve the five percent? How do we change the reality of worthiness? How do we change this, unless we change the attitudes and understandings? This is not new knowledge, this is not new information, that all are worthy in the eyes of God, but it has been a long, slow process to bring people to this understanding.

We wonder what choices you weavers are going to make now. Are you going to stand back and say, "Well, they won't let me sit at the table, I haven't earned it. I wasn't born in the right family, the right place, the right country, the right reality. I don't have enough money, enough intelligence, enough fame, luck..." or whatever the excuses are. Why do you still stand back from the feast?

There is another group who stand back, and they have worn the robes of the priesthood; they have worn the robes of the poor. They have taken vows of poverty and believe that by denying the abundance, denying the beauty, denying the body and the bliss, believing that somehow they will reap great spiritual rewards. So they starve and deny themselves in this name. These ones incarnate time and time again, still trying to prove that denial of the physicality is the road to bliss.

I notice that their bellies are hungry. I notice that they will not sit at the feast, believing that they are somehow purer or better because of this, and the feast is wasted on such. I noticed many people standing back for many reasons and I wonder why.

I notice among the Christians, they are told that if they did not eat of the feast in this world they would be

93

able to partake of the feast in the next world, so they are waiting.

I notice among the Moslems, that they are taught that if they show the restraint in this world, that feast will await them in the next one.

I notice among the Buddhists, that they are taught that the feast is an illusion, and therefore is meaningless.

I notice many different cultures debating about this feast, but the supper is getting cold and maybe everybody should just sit down together and eat.

We have numerous reasons why people do not wish to partake of this great feast of ideas that the stars are currently pouring down upon you, and why many are afraid to take such a role at such a place.

Each one of you will have to look through your own histories and your own beliefs to find out why you are not seated at the table. Each one of you need to look and see where your choices are leading and if you intend to keep yourselves in the same patterns of starvation; whether it be physically, mentally, spiritually or emotionally. I

It is time for each of you to look and see what choices you are making of the realities being presented to you and to recognize that these choices are what are creating that reality. You have one billion impulses to work with, and how you pluck your strings decides what song you are playing, and that decides what your atoms are going to dance to, because they dance to the rhythms of the stars. Your consciousness decides what rhythms will be created.

I cannot emphasize enough the opportunity available to you during the time that your planet is in this position in the universe. I ask you to be aware, to look around you, to realize and recognize what is going on.

No. I'm not done here. I have more to say.
Condemned with your fiery words,
Birds, call to me from the skies
We do not believe your lies.
Lashed to the pillar
Set in the village square.
Centered there.
Every branch, dry tinder's lay in wait
To be set off by your spark, your hate.
Greasy smoke is all that's left of me

You hope.

Chapter X

The Pyramids are Shaking

I wish to bring to your awareness again, the reality that has been created in the form of the pyramid.

The ones who have scrambled to get to the top believe that they are now safe, and they believe that the laws and the realities of everyone else has nothing to do with them. Look around in every single country on your planet and notice that those who seem to be on the top of the pinnacle in the last while have been tumbling down.

Ten years ago, these folks would never have been accused of the wrongs they have been accused of, let alone be charged with them, let alone be sent to jail or thrown out of their empires! Never have you seen before, the stockholders at the base of pyramid holding the ones at the peak accountable. It is shaking! It is shaking!

Those who scrambled so hard to get to the top and believed they had made it are falling, for it is a precarious place to be. Many who have sat at the bottom feel pretty smug about this and they think, "It looks good on them." Many of them are feeling that this is God's judgment again; "He's going to flood out those Babylonians again. He's going to topple all those kings off their thrones. He's going to cast those Queens down". Many think in such a way, but those thoughts are coming from somebody who is obviously willing to stand at the bottom, or the middle of the pyramid, where most of them are, and hold things up.

You won't hear these words spoken from somebody in the circle, someone in the circle that never joined the pyramid. They notice these things happening and they have compassion for those ones. They think, "Boy, you know you believed that. You tried so hard to get to the top.

You used everything you knew. It took you twenty lifetimes to get there, and what do you find out once you get there? It's not worth it.

We could have told you that in the first place." Somebody standing in the circle is going to see it for what it is; any time you try to build something upward like that, it is going to topple. It is the law of gravity. When you build in a circle, it expands, inclusively. It doesn't topple it breathes in and out.

This is the point we are at; the pyramids are shaking. The ones on top are falling and the ones on the bottom think they can scramble up. Can you picture that? That is impossible. The ones on the bottom do not want to give up this dream, for they have been fighting really hard to be able to rise to the top. Unfortunately, as long as all the people are holding onto that belief system, it won't change and will result in a really big mess.

As the ones on the top are tumbling down, the ones in the middle and the bottom will be scurrying to get up there, all of them at once. Throughout history you have seen when this has happened.

When an empire has crumbled from the inside, from the bottom up, what you will see is spikes and peaks following, as all of the upward thrust from the ones underneath continues and there is nothing to support it. There is not a big enough base as they thrust up and explode. This is what you are seeing around you now; the thrusting and exploding of the final scurrying.

You can be part of that, or you can step aside and sit in the circle and wait. Wait until everyone has exhausted themselves and then begin to sing in the new reality. That's a choice; one the stars are bringing you.

The light coming to the Earth now contains humour and laughter and the ability to stand in a different reality and have compassion for what has been created. To wait for all who have been scurrying up to stand on their pinnacle and look around, and for them to realize that to be the king of the dust heap is not helping much. Wait until they are finished, and sit and hold your circle space open and inclusive. When they are tired of that, they will come and sit with you. Maybe you can teach them some new rhythms on your drum, because you will have been practicing this whole time.

So what are some of these ideas that the starlight is bringing? How would you know? How would you find it? How could you see it? Watch.

How does your world bring forward ideas? Most of you reading these words are living in a western culture, a culture of books and print, of movies and songs. It is in these ways that your culture brings its ideas forward.

Notice in the last few years what has caught the imagination of the people. It is stories of magic, it is stories of power, it is stories of the individuals who can rise against all odds and make magical changes. This is what has captured your attention in the last few years.

Notice the ideas that are coming forward, the truths that are being spoken and what is exciting the people.

Notice the people who are stepping forward and being shown and illuminated in the greatest light are those who are able to step forward and speak the truth, those who are standing in their own light and their own integrity.

Notice the fast-talkers and the illusion-makers, and notice that everybody else sees them, too. The veils have been dropped and things are being seen. That is how you can tell what new ideas are coming into your world.

If you lived among some of the tribes of the Central and South Americas' you would be having group dreams in your ceremonies, your medicine plants would be leading you to see what's happening and to be prepared for it.

You will also notice in the places where people are responding that magic is being used. People are coming together to do this work.

You will notice in countries where there has been great oppression, and some of the places where the people are listening; they have been able to throw off this suppression. They have been able to begin to make changes for themselves.

You will notice what armies are being shut down in some places as people are taking advantage of these times to shift their realities.

In other places you will notice a different reaction, as the fear takes hold of those who do not want to lose.

In some of the African nations, there have been a few people making an awful lot of money from a very, very rich continent. These ones do not want to lose their place of power. They have been living off of the lands and the people there for a long time and they do not want to give it up! It doesn't matter what colour their skin is; what matters is they have been sitting on top of a pyramid and they do not want to fall! So some of them are aware of the pyramids crumbling and the ensuing disruption, and are using this to incite war, one against another. All the rage of suppression of those that were forced to the bottom in one area has been pitted against the rage of the repression of others, held at the bottom of another pyramid. You can see the toppling happening, and you can see the outburst of the terror and fear of this toppling being shown in many barbaric ways.

You can see that as that pyramid begins to topple, the choice of bringing in the circle was made by some cultures, by some peoples, and an honest effort was being made to bring a different way forward. But, you can see in all of the places where this big pyramid has toppled, the waves of those trying to rush up to the top is still rippling through. The fighting between who will sit on top of this one, and who will sit on top of that one, is deadly in these places.

You can witness this happening in northern Europe, Central Africa, some places in South America, cities in the

United States and the Middle East. There are points all across the globe where, as the pyramid tumbles, the fighting for the new top place is vicious and ferocious.

What is needed is for all of you to stand in the circle, stand in the circle and hold that alternative. For those that have been desperate, life after life, to rise to the pinnacle and believe that this is their last chance to ever sit in that place, they can be shown that there is an alternative.

In those areas of turmoil there are common people joining hands and trying to hold for a different reality. These ones are the frontline fighters aren't they? They have chosen to be born into these areas of conflict which are holding fast to the old reality. These frontline fighters have made these difficult choices so that they can be there to hold a new reality and try to create something different. If they have the backup of those of you in more peaceful places, of you that are holding your circle realities here, they have more of a chance of healing the realities where they are.

Witness all of this being brought through all over your globe, everywhere. Witness the reaction of the people and witness the response of the Earth.

There are places on the Earth now where people are being asked to move, to take themselves out of there, so that those places can heal physically. When you see that your house has burned down three times, you can see it is time to move. When you see that the floodwaters have risen up each successive year and hurricanes have wiped out your towns and villages, you had better learn to build on stilts or on a barge or move. When, for four years in a row, drought has killed every living thing on your land, you know that it is not a good place to raise your children.

The population on your planet needs the freedom to move where they need to move in response to the responses of the Earth. You need to support this freedom of

101

movement so that every soul can bring themselves to their right place.

Fear restricts the movement, fear created borders that are not inclusive, but exclusive. The fear produced all of these places on your planet where you will not allow people to be. Fear has walled you in and walled others out. These walls of fear have to come down. You need to allow the flow of movement on your planet in response to the impulses you are receiving from the stars. You each need the freedom to find yourselves physically manifesting in the places of your choice, where it feels right and good for you to be.

Those who wish to hold onto the tumbling rocks of the pyramid as it falls have the choice to do that, and so they can place themselves on the points of the Earth where this is happening.

Those who choose to live, to flourish, and create the next reality, need the freedom to bring themselves to places that resonate with this idea. The old ways of the pyramid are dying and those who cling to it are dying with it.

The Earth cannot support and sustain those ideas, for they are not the ideas the stars are sending anymore.

This is a long, slow process, the movement of the Earth. It is a long, slow process, the change of the evolution of humanity, and you are at that point in time to make a choice and decision of where it is going to go.

Each of you, by the choices you make in this lifetime, can make the choice of the reality that will be lived on Earth for the next seven generations.

What you choose to live, to bring, and to create here, is creating the future for all. It is not at every point in history that this is so, but it is at this point.

Are you going to continue to grasp and hold to the promises made to you by a false god, the promises of great riches and wealth someday at the expense of all of your so-called enemies? Are you going to hold to this false promise, that if you give everything of yourself, someday you will be rewarded with everything that you have coveted?

Each of you needs to look at what you have believed about the Creators and what you have believed about life.

Is your life meant to climb the corporate ladder?

Is your life meant to pay off a mortgage so that you may say, "I have land"?

Is your life meant that you have three children, eight grandchildren and twelve great-grandchildren, and now you are done; is this your dynasty? These souls have lived and breathed before and will live and breathe again whether you are there or not.

Or, is your dynasty to weave a different reality for your great-grandchildren?

Is your dynasty to make different choices here?

Is it to re-think, re-visit and re-search the present reality?

Is this reality here by consensus, or by default?

My roots
Pushing through stone
And reaching river.
I quiver.
From the sunlight
Making me
Shiver
With delight.
More roots
Reach the fecundity
Draw from her
Stability.
Anchored there am I.
Generations of roots
Etched on my rings
That rap around us
Sings
The songs of our ancestors.
In all the languages.
Including Babylon.

Chapter XI

Individual and Collective Responsibility

The difference between individual responsibility and collective responsibility seems to cause a lot of confusion for people. As a result, most people begin to try to take on the collective responsibility and then become overwhelmed and feel helpless. The collective consciousness is like a weaving of combined realities, and when one is in that resonance it is very difficult to hold one's own resonance. It is very easy to find one accepting the dominant realities, the collective beliefs systems, and it is difficult to remind one of the realities you are choosing to believe.

I suggest that instead of thinking in terms of changing the whole collective and thinking in terms of the collective responsibility, you take it back to individual responsibility. That is all you really have ever been able to do anyway. When one soul can focus themselves to accept their own beliefs, to examine them and to make decisions as to what beliefs they are going to keep, then that one individual has a bigger impact on the collective than any of you even know is possible.

When you look at a forest, for example, you can see how the entire ecosystem works in perfect balance. The more you study the ecology of one area, the more you can see this in practice. You can witness how each individual plant works within its own group, which affects all the plants around, which in turn creates an environment for specific creatures. That one individual plant, as part of the collective, creates a perfectly balanced ecosystem. If that one plant is removed, it is not going to make such a big difference to the whole forest, but if that one plant deviates from itself, from its perfect balance, it can destroy the whole ecosystem; it can destroy the whole planet. It's a good thing that most creatures try to follow their original blueprints!

When you look at a flock of birds you can see the same thing. Each bird has its own individuality and it will sing its song, attract its mate, build its nest, lay its eggs, and teach it's young. All of this is part of its own individual life and its individual expression, and yet, it is part of the whole flock. As a flock they all move together during migration and collectively will choose specific ecosystems of certain forests or fields that align with their needs. An individual bird must follow its own individuality to create a healthy flock. If it does not, if it deviates, then the flock has lost that bit of health. Each one is individually responsible for the collective.

In your societies and in your cultures as humans, understanding this concept can assist you in knowing what your right path is. To do so, is to know what your part of the collective is.

The same way that bird knows its part in the collective is to tend to its own being, so each one of you, as part of your collective, is to tend to your own being. One bird, for instance, when tending to itself, will build a nest in the branches of a tree and it will work very, very hard to create the very best nest that it can and will use it for a period of time. The next year, another bird may use that same nest and add onto it. Whatever each creature creates, whatever each plant creates as it grows and later feeds the soil as it dies, creates something for everything else to build on. So it is the same for each one of you individually. In your lifetime, building your nest may mean starting a business, painting a picture, writing a song, or it may just mean creating a space, a life that works for you.

Imagine, if one of these birds was told where they could build their nests, and that they could only build them inside the boxes provided for them? That happens, and it is happening in your world.

So, when these birds allow themselves to be coerced, as to where they are going to build their nests, this changes the whole ecosystem and the flow of everything, as it does among your societies. You lose the choices of where you are going to build your nests and how you are going to build your nests. You lose your original plan, which each one of you had for yourselves, and your societies. Your societies lose their dynamic plan and are no longer part of the ecosystem of the land itself. They become something separate; something orchestrated, organized, but not organized by nature. The collective responsibility then becomes dictated. Your social engineers begin telling you how to build your nests, what songs to sing, how to be, and to create the collective organization that works for them.

When I look at your world I see that it is not working for you. There are very few people who are fulfilled by this type of organization, few whom I could say are happy. For the most part, people on your planet seem to be struggling and are in a lot of pain. It seems to me, the collective agreements are breaking down and are not working anymore.

The new collective responsibility is to create a different pattern to bring in something new. The individual responsibility is to find your own original blueprint, your own original plan.

Each one of you individually must go back to the very core of your own beings and decide, "What do I want to have? What reality am I going to accept and believe?" You do have choices! All of you in these cultures here, from where we are speaking, the dominant cultures, you have a choice of which histories to believe!

Any incident, anything that has happened that you believe has created your society, you will find as you follow it back, that you have many choices of which history you are going to believe and which reality you are going to believe. Most of you have chosen to believe a reality that never really happened, most of which are lies, and yet, you have chosen to take on this collective belief, chosen to make that your reality, and chosen to make your future decisions based upon that. What does that do when what you are basing your decisions upon, is not a reality that actually existed? That is called building a reality based upon denial. That's not going to last very long!

I ask each one of you to assume your individual responsibility. Look at what you believe! Look at what you are choosing. Look at the basis of those choices.

Most of you are living in towns. What do you know about where you are living? What do you know about the history of where you live? Some of you look outside your home at the trees that have been there a long time. That tree knows more than you do about the reality of where you are.

Your homes are built on rocks, built out of rocks, and these rocks know more about the realities that have been there than you do.

The majority of you are acting as if your realities started only as far back as your current memories go. Some of you think in terms of the last five years as reality, and most of you do not look ahead more than a couple of years and your reality becomes very, very limited.

What you are weaving becomes limited, and from that viewing point, it becomes far easier to allow yourself to become part of the big industrial loom. It is far easier to give up your will and allow others to do the work, but I do not see anyone enjoying the results.

So how do you change it? How do you choose something different? It begins by each individual taking the time to look at their own personal life. Take the time and energy to go back through this one lifetime. You have this one lifetime and this one body to work with. Have a look at the relationships you have right now. When did they start? What were the weavings you brought in when you were born? What stars were present at your birth? What was going on in the heavens at the time you were born? Start there! Find out what the energies that you came in on were; that's going to tell you a lot about yourself right there. Look at your time of conception; the parents you chose, the type of conception you chose. When you entrusted yourself to your mother; look at that time, look at what was going on with her. Was she resentful? Was she happy? What was going on with your father? How did he feel? Find out your own personal history.

What happened at your birth? What was it like? Where were you born, who was there and who were the first people you saw? For many of you they were strangers, people you will never see again, random people working in the night. Look at this. In what position were you born into the family?

What was the relationship to your siblings; oldest, youngest, middle, where? What happened? Who raised you, and in what geographical part of the world did you grow up? All of these are the stories of your soul. This is what you brought forward to show yourself. These are the gentle reminders of where you came in and what you brought with you. Go back and start right there. Look at your own weavings.

As you got older, what influences did you bring in, what choices did you make, and in what ways did you abdicate those choices? Did you choose domineering parents who would tell you what to do, where to do it, and what to study, or did you choose an environment that was going to give you the strength to make your own choices? All of this is going to show you about yourself, about your own original plan.

Some of you may have chosen parents to represent this, parents you had to rebel against, had to stand up and be strong to. What does that tell you about your soul, that you chose an environment that was going to make you strong in that way?

Some of you chose environments that encouraged you to question, and that was the kind of support that your soul needed. But each one of you made these choices consciously or you would not have been born. Look at it.

In the very first year of your life, from conception to one year, is the basic blueprint of everything you came in with, it is all right there. Get to know your story. What DNA did you choose? What ancestries did you choose to bring through? Look at it and study it. Why did you choose these lines? What are the stories of your grandparents and great-grandparents and great-great-grandparents that you chose to enact in this lifetime? You brought that particular DNA through to represent you. Look at it. Spend some time.

Everybody is waiting for someone to tell them who they are and what to do. You are all so used to the corporate reality controlling your lives that when a whistle blows you go into the factory or the mines, and when the whistle blows again you go home, hoping that there is enough food to eat for the week. Most of you are so programmed to this way of thinking that it is going to be difficult for you to take personal and individual responsibility. It is going to be difficult for each one of you to realize that you have to do this for yourself, because each story is going to be uniquely different. Start there. What did I come in with? What DNA? What star patterns? What are the family constellation dynamics that I arrived in on? Each one of you can follow these questions and find out about yourself. That's going to tell you the story right there.

The next stories in your life are, "Now, what did I do with it? What am I doing with it?" What most of you are going to discover is that while there are many, many, many lines that you brought in, there are very, very few that you are weaving with. Most of you are going to discover that there are a lot more threads just lying around. Some of you are going to discover that there are patterns that you can see that you do not want to carry into the future. Many of you are going to discover patterns you want to change.

So, to look at this you can realize, "Okay, I was born here with this and with this; and this is how I'm going to work with it." Take responsibility for your choices. When you are looking at the patterns, if you see one that you do not want to be woven into the future, recognize that the reason you chose to be born right there is so that you can change that pattern. Some of you, when you stand and look backwards, are going to recognize some really good patterns coming through the ancestry that you really would like to bring into the future, patterns that make you feel strong and good about yourself. Grab those threads and pull them through! They are yours. Otherwise, you would not be standing here. They are yours!

Take responsibility to look backwards and say, 'What did I bring into this reality? What did I incarnate into this reality?'

Most of you have had an attitude of having been dropped by some stork, landing on the planet, rubbing your hands together and saying, 'What do I get?' I ask you who choose to be responsible, to stand at one year of age and look backwards and ask yourself, 'What did I bring?' Some of you are going to see all the wonderful things you have brought in and you are also going to see how, as you got older, many of those threads were thwarted and snipped.

You live in a society that likes to streamline things, likes to specialize in things, a society that tells you to snip all of these lines, except one or two. You need to make a choice. Is that what you want to do? Or perhaps, these are the lines you want to snip? Starting at a one-year-old view point, look, see, what did you bring through?

Spend some time getting to know that, to understand that. Realize that all those lines are still there; all those threads and ribbons are still there. They did not go anywhere. They cannot be destroyed. Those are the lines of

111

light that you brought in with you and they are still there. As long as you are alive on this Earth, they are part of the possibility of collective weaving. It is up to each one of you individually, to bring that through, to trust that you were put there, that you chose to be there, for the specific reasons of the unique threads that you could bring in.

Some of you are going to find patterns that you do not want to bring into the future. Some of you are going to look and see that the reason you were born into a family that was carrying patterns of harm for generations past was so that you could make the decision of what to do with those patterns and those threads. They can be unwoven, they can be healed.

In this one lifetime you have the ability to look at those threads and decide that these patterns will not go further into creation, and the new reality will not be carrying these old destructive patterns. You may decide in this life that the patterns of addiction that have come through with your lines of light from the stars and with your lines of ancestry will be stopped. You may decide to dedicate this lifetime to end these unhealthy patterns.

Other people who were brought up in families of child abuse or sexual abuse may decide that this pattern will end with them. You came in on those ancestral lines contaminated with that light and you have the strength to change it. You may decide to tie those patterns up right there, using your compassion, your knowledge, your understanding, and your forgiveness. If you are able to look at your family and the blueprints you were born into, and follow these weavings back through your ancestry, you could see that it is a wide pattern coming into a narrow point, and that point is you. You have a choice. Are you going to perpetuate it, allow it to continue, or heal it within yourself?

Those of you who are choosing in this lifetime to do the work of healing these lines, when you are tying them off, do not tie them with anger or hatred. Do not chop them, but simply tie them off with compassion and understanding. For as you bring in these strands of compassion, understanding, and love, you begin to weave in the new reality.

Some of you have taken a lot of years to tie the strings off. You get discouraged and you get hopeless, and that is only because you are not seeing how far back it goes! You are not seeing what you are doing to heal it; that it is a lot of work.

Right now, if you look around the world you will see places that as the individual people who recognized this and began to take personal responsibility for whatever threads they could heal in their lives, you will see the collective responsibility happening. There are whole countries who are currently engaged in healing.

There are countries all over Africa currently engaged in great healing ceremonies, and they are trying to heal all that has happened for generations back. There are whole areas and many cultures that have entire libraries of books on how to heal. You can see in the Hebrew families that a lot of work has gone into healing what happened to their people generations ago. You can see in the North American Native communities, healing going back for generations. In Africa, you can see whole movements of old religions coming forward. All through Europe and all through South America, the old ways are coming back as a means of healing.

You can think of it as part of the light that was harmed and disrupted many generations ago that people are drawing through themselves, bringing the goodness back, the brightness back, and healing what had happened to their ancestors all the way back.

You can see, if you look, if you have eyes to see, that great healing is happening in your world that was all started by the individual willing to take responsibility for where they were born and what light they are carrying. This is good work. It is a good opportunity, and each one of you who can do this and each one of you who does this work are weaving the next reality.

Some of you will stand at this place and you will see all the brightness you were born into. Maybe into a family where there is a lot of positive things; a lot of support and lots of funding. All of this is really good. Well, some of these people begin to feel really guilty, and feel, "Oh this isn't right. I should be doing the healing work. I should be doing this or that." They want to push away the good things they have coming through because they feel they do not deserve it.

For those of you who look at this, I ask, please, do not compare yourself to someone beside you. Does the oak tree compare itself to the fungus, or do they both realize that the work they are both doing in that forest is important? Some work is to tear down and some work is to build-up; that is how an ecosystem works.

Some souls are born into the hard situations and some souls are born into places where they live upon the garbage of others; these souls are trying to heal those patterns, to make the changes to bring their family system out of that. Some souls decided to be born in the most depraved social situation to heal it. They are the ones that have to trust that their part in the ecosystem is to take that apart so that it does not continue.

Those of you who were born under stars of strength, who have had the so-called advantages; maybe your job is to look and see and say, "Okay, yes, I have all of this to weave with. Let's get busy and do it." Maybe your job isn't to take apart. Maybe your job is to build and that is why you have been given those tools and those strengths; maybe your job is to create. Each one of you can see exactly what you have to work with, and if you can trust yourselves, trust your own strength and trust the creation process, then you can turn this around.

Each one of you needs to take time to do your homework and do this—really see who you are and what you have so the individual responsibility becomes the collective. Each individual, in caring for themselves, doing their own part, is what weaves the collective.

You do not find, anywhere in any naturally occurring systems on this Earth, you do not find hierarchy. In all of these creatures, each individual goes towards what it needs and uses its strength to survive. The survival of the individual becomes very important, and they know that as strong and as healthy as they can raise their young is as strong and as healthy as the whole flock will be. They know this, because they know that the health of the whole forest is dependent upon the individual.

All species know how important the individual is, except among the humans. Here, you do not value yourselves, nor do you see how important you are. Among all creatures great and small, the individual is honoured.

I know you hear stories among the people of animals who lie down for each other; lay down their lives as food. I have lived many, many lifetimes here, and I never saw any animal give itself up passively. They fight. They fight for their lives and they use everything they have to be strong and healthy. They do not give up, and by trusting their individual survival instinct, they create the strongest collective.

There are a lot of creatures on this planet and most of them have been here a lot longer than the two-legged kind. It seems to me they might know something; might know something about collective responsibility. They might know something about trust, something about their original plan. They know what the Creators hold for them; that is to be who they are. And if who they are stamps out a big territory, they trust that. That is right for that ecosystem and that place. If who they are creates decay to tear down, then those are things that need to be torn down to change to something else for the overall ecosystem. They trust who and what they are and they follow their original plan.

If each individual who hears these words begins to take responsibility for themselves, for their actions, for their thoughts, for their beliefs, you will change the collective reality of your planet. That is the hardest thing for any soul to do, to be responsible. All the Creators have ever asked you to do, is to be responsible.

So, nowhere do you see one creature, one tree, one plant, deciding to be the boss of all the others; it doesn't work like that on this planet. It doesn't work like that anywhere, because one being, one planet, one person, cannot possibly understand the intricacies needed for the growth of the whole. No one cell in your body can have the master plan about how everything works, no one tree on the planet can know what every other tree needs to do, and no one person can know what is right for any other person.

You can see this. You do not have a dominant star; you have the star that is the closest proximity to you. A forest does not have a dominant plant; it has a system. Even among all the tribes of animals, you do not have one that is dominant; you may have one that can be the best leader or one whose job it is to hold the collective together for a period of time, as long as the group agrees. That happens, yes, but each part of that group knows it is important, each part of that group knows that the place they are holding is just as important, except the two-legged kind.

Among the system you have going now it used to be understood that a tribe, a village, was only as strong as each individual in it. If one family was weak, that was a collective problem. That family could get sick and that sickness could spread. It was everyone's problem. If someone was in need, it was everyone's problem. If someone was upset, if there was strife or dissension between two households, collectively, you knew this could begin a feud, and it could go through ten generations if you didn't put a stop to it now.

It was understood that each individual in the community was important, very important. Things were collectively looked after, and it worked. It worked in smaller areas with smaller groups of people. This system works among the animals, the ants, the butterflies, the bees, the squirrels, the ferns and the mosses; it works. But for some reason, today's people have forgotten that God knows what he is doing, have forgotten that God has a plan. You have forgotten that He gave and whispered to each one of you before you were even born, what that plan was for you. You have all forgotten that!

Follow your histories. When did it happen in each one of your ancestral cultures; when did it happen that your people stopped listening to the Creators and started listening to somebody else? When did it happen that you stopped trusting yourselves and trusting that you are all children of the Creators? When did it happen that you allowed someone else's patterns to dominate your reality?

Follow it back, each one of you; follow it back to the points where you see this happening in your own personal life, in your ancestral history, in your soul history. Follow it back and find out, where did those lines get tangled? Reach for them—pull them through. You can do that. You can pull them to yourself and you can weave with them now. They are not gone; nothing is ever lost in this universe.

You think the light that you are seeing right now from the stars is lost? It left those stars a long time ago! Is it lost or is it traveling out and making realities? Choose it. You consciously can choose it; follow it back. Where are the lines of light that you like? Bring them through you! Bring them into being, and weave with them.

Start to look at all of the lines of light you have taken for granted, "Well this is the way it is." I want you to hold

117

that line and shake it, and follow it, and see where that line goes. Where did this belief originate from? Why do you believe this? Have a look at every one of your belief systems that say, "Well, this is the way it is. It's always been that way" and all of the other statements that stop you.

Here is an example: "You have to pay the bank. That is just the way it is." "You have to pay the bank", follow that line! Right now I sit with a woman who lives in North America, and the belief system is that banks own everything. Follow it! How far does that line go, right here on this spot where we sit? How far back does it go?

Not even two-hundred years ago; not even that far back. Shake that line. Where did it start? How did it happen? Well, the line started when the bankers came in thinking they were going to help people. It may have started off in a good way. When did it twist? Follow it!

Before that, the belief system was, "The land will provide for us. How fortunate we are to come here and have this land free and given to us after coming from an ancestry in countries where there was no land, where people were hungry. Look at all the wonderful land here just free and open!" That is a whole different belief system.

On this land, further back, you would find a group of people who would pass through here, maybe they would hunt here. You know, a lot of creatures were living here; people coming and going, passing through, collecting some herbs or hunting. The expectation was, "The land is here and the land is rich. It is abundant. It provides for us. We honour it and it honours us." It was not that long ago, maybe five-hundred years ago, when this whole area was forest. Which reality is true? Which reality are you going to choose? Which one are you going to allow? Which one feels best and wholesome?

It doesn't mean go and shut down the banks, but it means to take your belief systems back further, back to the belief system that says, "This land will provide for me. It will look after me. It offers me many things." And if you are going to hold that belief really strong, then the other beliefs have to align to it.

So what happens to the banks? They become part of the land and say, "Okay, we are here to provide for you. We are here to support you." They have to change their alignment in response to you.

It is a choice of where you individually hold yourself. The one person standing there with the belief system that the banks own everything will have difficulty with that bank, won't they? They might not get what they need. They will find that they are always having to give and always having to beg.

Another person holding the belief system that says, "This land will provide for me. It will always look after me. I will be fine," they think of the bank as part of their landscape and they get what they need. It works. They are choosing to weave with a different set of rules, with different lines of light.

Now, many of the people working in the bank system who are making many of the policy decisions are often from different countries far away from here, and many of them have never even been here before. They want to hold a different collective reality. Theirs is like a big game, "We are going to dominate. We are going to get the best profits, the best this, the best that..." That is the dominant reality those folks are carrying. They are playing a game, and they will continue playing that game until enough of what they're playing with has been shifted, and then you will see that they are no longer supported.

But, perhaps a different banking institution may move up and say, "We are here to serve the people." That now fits within the collective reality. So what the collective reality supports, the systems must change to in response. For example; some companies will collapse and some companies will grow. The collective changes as each

119

individual changes in the choosing of which realities to hold.

You may still have gas stations, but if the collective reality becomes, "We are going to honour this Earth. We are going to care for it. Our needs are changing because of our relationship with ourselves, our relationship with each other, and our relationship with the planet," well then, these competing gas stations are going to have to start doing that, as well, aren't they? "We are caring about the planet; we are looking at the future, too," because otherwise, you're not going to buy your gas there. Pretty soon, they are going to have to change in response to the new idea being presented, such as, "We do not want to use fossil fuels anymore", and so these gas stations will start to offer other choices. Change takes place as quickly as the individuals change, and that can be very fast.

The ones who stand back and will not be responsible will think, "Well that's what there is, so I guess I have to take it." Well, these ones are going to be easy to manipulate. They will be dependent on those things for the rest of their lives. But those who are making a choice to change their individual consciousness will have an impact, and the collective consciousness will change.

It is easy to think that one group of people have got you in control and there is nothing you can do about it. That type of defeatist thinking has worked to keep you a conquered people. Changing it on an individual level and taking responsibility for what stars you came in on, taking responsibility for what family you were born into, taking responsibility for all that you carry in your DNA within your own spirit, taking responsibility for all that you are, and taking responsibility for all that you choose to believe, what you choose to think, actions you choose to take, that is the position of power. That is not a position of powerlessness.

From that position, you as an individual can completely change the reality that most people are living in on this planet. When you no longer hold the belief within yourself that one soul is better than another soul, that one man or woman deserves more than another; when you believe within your own soul that all are the Creators' children, that belief reflects in your being and begins to be reflected upon your planet.

When you hold yourself with respect, you begin to hold others with respect. Things that were taken for granted before are no longer tolerated, and therefore, cease to exist.

It is easy to say, "What is happening in one country far away has nothing to do with me." It is easy to think that what goes on in central Africa has nothing to do with you—nothing at all.

I want to bring something to your attention and I want to follow back some lines of light here to make you aware.

A long time ago there was a lot of turmoil in Africa and there was a lot of pain. People were coming in from different places because it is a very rich continent and they wanted things from there. They caused disruption in the ecosystem. What was happening between all the creatures, and all the tribes of people, and that land, was very badly damaged. When that ecosystem was disrupted, it allowed a lot of things to happen.

One of the things that happened is that some groups began selling other groups into slavery again. The slaves were taken across the oceans to the Caribbean and up in to the United States. They went to other places, too, but not with as much direct focus as this. Here was an absolute and intentional setup of an empire—the cotton empire. People were brought over through the Caribbean, and they were brought up into the southern states of the U.S., and then this slavery spread upwards. These people were brought over to make fortunes for others. They were brought over to grow sugar, coffee, cotton; commodities that were being sold to the rest of the world, and a market was being created for these commodities. These people were brought over in great terror and misery and were in great, great pain. I want you to look now currently. And it easy to think, "What does that have to do with us? That happened a long time ago. It happened far away".

Well, I want you to look at some of the most destructive weather patterns you have happening now. Winds are coming off of Africa. They are coming over to the Caribbean and they are wrecking havoc. They are moving up through the southern states of the U.S. and wrecking havoc. This is old pain and old misery that never had the chance to be healed, misery that was silenced, out of guilt. All of this pain and all of this misery never went anywhere; it never healed, so your planet is healing it now. Those storms are following the same patterns that this movement followed.

To believe that something that happened in the past, to think that something that happened somewhere else on the planet has nothing to do with you, is wrong thinking. It does not work. It is not what choosing your reality is about.

Choosing your reality is following the threads of action of what actually transpired, what starlight is actually coming in, what DNA you actually carry.

If you think that a volcano erupting in one place is not going to have an effect on you, then you do not know very much about the air currents, you do not know very much about how your weather systems work, and you do not know very much about how absolutely delicately-balanced it is on your planet.

The more you learn about who you are and where you are, the more you learn that every single thought and every action, past or present, no matter where it is, is affecting you. Everything that has not been accounted for and not been taken responsibility for eventually comes home to roost somewhere. The sooner you each take your own individual responsibilities and heal them, the sooner your planet can heal, and that is what she is trying to do, she is trying to heal. So if you are concerned because your weather is getting a little strange, I want you to look at the patterns. Where are they coming from? Where did they originate? Where did that storm that just killed one-hundred people or one thousand people come from? What was its course as it traveled there? What does that remind you of?

Why, in some areas, time and time again, tornadoes are swirling up and coming through where there is no known reason for those exact spots? Why those places? What happened in those places? What turmoil is held there that has never been resolved? When you look at places, where there is devastation on this planet, you will see a history of pain. There are places on your planet where people cannot live without fighting with each other, and this has been this way for a long time. You need to follow the histories and find out what has happened. Follow the historical lines the same way as you would your own individual lines and you can see the collective of each country and each place. Look at what happened and ask yourself, "Where did the present situation originate?"

If you want to follow the birth of countries, you need to ask some questions. When was it born? What was going on in the world when this country came into being? Who was living in there when the decision was made to create that country? What was going on? You will see the collective consciousness and you will see what you have to work with. Every social organization has its origins, and when it is allowed to move freely it will bring itself into a balanced ecosystem—it will do that naturally.

Even if a great storm comes through and devastates a forest, that forest will take this and it will bring itself back into balance. This planet is always changing.

Where we sit right now is an area of houses and forest and farm fields. Well, this used to be a great mountain range and this area was the foothills of the mountains. There was an ocean not so far away from here. This was very different before. There was a series of islands just west of here, in great salt oceans. That was the reality that existed here not that long ago. The Sahara Desert used to be a big ocean; now it is a desert. Many of the places that are in oceans now, used to be grand cities. The Earth opened up and swallowed them. The Earth is constantly, constantly changing.

You have a short period of time here where you get to ride upon the waves of light that created this reality. Build and create to the best of your ability, each one of you individually, and trust that where you are, who you are, and what you are, is not coincidence, but is part of a great star system. Be responsible for your part. Do not let this opportunity go to waste. Be responsible for it, stand in your power, stand in your strength, and weave; weave the realities that you want. Call upon the light to illuminate the choices. Educate yourself, learn; don't sit waiting for someone to tell you what to do. Look at the weaving of what you are and that will show you your patterns. That will show you what you are here to do. It is all right there.

Where were you born? Who are you? Time, current reality around you, will tell you the story of your soul. It is right there, moving in you. Look at your preferences; what gives you joy, what distresses you? All of this shows you who you are.

You are waiting for someone to validate your existence. You are waiting for someone to show you what to do, to make the changes for you. You sit, feeling overwhelmed, when it is all right in your hands, each one of you. Everybody has homework to do. Everybody has the ability and the time it will take to do this work, for there is nothing, nothing more important than your life's work here. Each one of you has to take your own time to find out what this is. Each one of you will be looking to find out who you are, and what you were brought here to do. As each one of you finds this and takes responsibility for your individual reality, and as you concentrate on that individual reality, you concentrate on the relationships you have.

All around you, right in your own families, your own communities, right in your own world are things that call you to do. You look up and you think the world's getting to be a better place. Suddenly, people are making conscious decisions, rather than allowing themselves to be swept along with the tides of the dominant culture.

When you become responsible for your choices of creation, there is no one to blame. There is no one to get mad at. There is no one to be the scapegoat if you just do your work. There have been many masters on Earth trying to teach this. It has been far easier to put them up on a pedestal and glorify them than it has been to do the work they have shown you to do. There have been many masters saying the same thing over and over and over; to do God's work on this planet is to be yourself, is to be all of who you are, is to choose what lines of light to bring through yourself, is to choose what lines of light you want to heal, is to choose to trust in yourself and in your own ability to know God.

There can be no armies, unless people agree to be soldiers. There can be no bombs, unless people agree to build them. There can be no war, unless people agree to fight. There cannot be any poverty, unless people agree to take away.

All that you create here, you have created collectively. All that you see around you, you have within yourself, somewhere. Every opposition you come to, you can find that opposition within yourself. Every hardship you encounter, you will find that stumbling block within your own belief system. Everything that is created on this planet, that you are aware of, you have somewhere within yourself. That is where the work has to be done.

125

You cannot do it out there! What happens out there, what you put into action, is a result of what you have done inside. Until you have decided to become conscious of what you are weaving inside yourself, you cannot be consciously aware of what you are weaving outside of yourself. When you become aware of what you are choosing to believe, what you are choosing to accept, then you can become aware of what other choices you have. Until then, you are blind.

We know where this world goes because we see the light that is streaming in. How it gets there, how it gets woven in, is up to each one of you right now in this short little time. It is up to you what you are going to weave; it's up to you how you are going to do it.

Do you want to accept the way things have been? Do you want to continue with those patterns, or do you want to build some new ones?

Those of you with ears to hear, listen. Those of you with eyes to see, look, and make your decisions based on what you see, what you hear, and what you experience personally. It is through this that the new world is born.

You are all waiting for someone to come and do it for you; whether it be a Messiah, a Saint, Armageddon, or whatever it is you think is going to come and make these changes for you. I ask you, when has God ever come and done your work for you? You've all had to do it yourselves.

Every great cataclysmic event that has ever happened on your planet has to do with where you, collectively, led your planet at that time. What you created is what you accepted as reality.

Every government system that you brought in, you have collectively agreed to let it be there. Examine it!

Every person that you have looked at on this planet as evil or wrong; I want you to look at the basis of what they brought in and what they were saying. You will find a big

126

part in yourself that believes what they present, or it would not have happened.

It is there—find it. Find those lines of light and those beliefs systems. Do you want this to continue in the world? Then hang onto them. If you want to change it, then take them apart and challenge them.

How many of you believe that if things are not organized and controlled, chaos will ensue? How many believe that forests are better off if they are groomed and cared for? How many believe that forests need be managed by people? How many believe they cannot look after themselves? Do you believe you can look after yourselves? Do you believe the Earth will not support you unless you control it? Do you believe nature will kill you unless you dominate it? Do you believe that if you go out into the wild, uncontained places, the animals are going to get you and kill you, or you are going to fall off cliffs, or drown in rivers if they are not contained? I think you will find that most of you do believe this.

Most of you are afraid of most things if they are not controlled and regulated. As long as you believe this, you are going to be living in communities that have stricter and stricter controls and regulations, As long as you believe that the wild forces of nature are out to get you, the more your culture is going to try to destroy these places. The more you believe that if things are not controlled or regulated, they will not survive, then the more fences and roads you are going to have to build. All of this is a reflection of how you are feeling about life, and the kind of faith and trust you have in the Creators. You raise your kids and run your businesses like that, based upon these belief systems of control and dominance.

How many have faith that if things are left to go the way they go, it will all work out fine? How many can have faith that given full freedom, everything will flow in the right and natural place; it will evolve to what it needs to be?

Once a desert, once an ocean, once a forest; the Earth evolves as it needs to, and change is part of that evolution. You can't stop that. You can't hold it back because it is constantly in motion.

Your societies are constantly in motion too. It's up to you to be responsible for it. What is it you want to bring in? What do you want to stop? What seeds do you want to plant for the future? That is up to you, to each one of you.

This can be done. It has been done. The difference is, I think, do you want to go along for the ride or do you want to practice being part of the creation? If you want to practice being part of the creation, find out what you have to work with, find out what you are holding and how you are living. That is going to tell you how you feel and how you think.

How many of you have enough faith to walk out your doors and just keep walking? How many of you have that faith to just go? There are some on your planet who will choose these pathways, and I think they are having fun. Well, I agree it's not for everybody, but there are those who choose this, to take a jump away from the dominant reality, and each step of the way, choose their own. You can tell who these people are; they are alive, they look alive, they're happy, they feel fulfilled, their bodies are strong and healthy. I never met anybody yet who has made the choice to follow their own lines of light who does not find themselves in the peak of health, who does not find themselves financially looked after, who does not find themselves surrounded with like-minded, loving, people.

But I find others that accept, "Well, that's the way it is," or "Got to put your time in," or "You got to do this…" or "Must be meant to be…" They are walking and they're doing what they need to do, and they are tired, and they are trained, and they get sick, and they are not too happy, and they are not having a good time. It is a choice—a choice of what you believe.

The biggest stumbling block to your personal destinies can be summed up in three words, "I can't because...".

There are one-billion-billion sentences that can be filled in after that. That is your biggest stumbling block, and that is one that can be easily taken apart. "I can't because..." Look at it, because of what? "All because that's the way it's always been?" Follow it back. How long has it been that way? Not that long. "I can't because that is the way it is now?"

Well, take responsibility; if that is the way you have woven it, then you can un-weave it. "I can't because, well, that's what they told me?" Okay, you have a choice, believe it or not, it is up to you.

For every sentence that starts with 'I-can't-because', there are one-billion answers. What you hold to be true becomes your reality it is easy. Each one of you has to follow your own lines. You have to take responsibility for what you are creating, because whether you are conscious of it or not, you are creating it.

Whether you take responsibility for it or not, you are creating it. Whether you like it or not, you are creating it.

Do you think you are the children of the Creators so that you can be slaves?

Do you think this is your birthright?

He has his Fathers nose and chin
And his Mothers sea green eyes,
Musicians hands from his Grandfather
So talented and wise.
Hair as black as the ravens' wing
The clan of his Great Grandma,
And his is a voice that was meant to sing
So smooth, and without flaw.
His is a soul who loves the night
Reminds him of where he has been,
Weaving his songs from pure starlight
And the spaces held in between.
He brings old stories of lives that have passed
Through distant times and place,
And the stories are told in rhythms of old
That show in the lines of his face.

Chapter XII

The Warp and Weft of You

Throughout the history of this planet there have been many variations and many changes that have happened. You can see this in the effects in the physical environment of the planet itself that has different concepts and different ideas. You could say different constellation influences have had their impacts on the planet.

Different areas of the planet have responded, but the parts that bring themselves up above the water become the places where these realities get to be played out. When the time comes that these realities are finished, then the environment completely changes in accordance to it.

The areas of the planet right now that are above the water are each holding a different concept, a different reality. Some of these realities are in alignment with the planet itself, and some are more in alignment with other places in the galaxy; you could say they have been superimposed here.

As long as the Earth brings itself up above the water, it is, in essence, saying that it will accept the lines from these stars coming down, and where it brings itself up from the water is where it is putting itself into alignment. The people who are receiving and living on these places are the ones who will then weave this into being. It has been this way since the very beginning of creation, and the Earth has moved itself above the surface of the oceans and back below the surface. Some places of the Earth have opened up and pulled parts all the way back inside.

The Earth has been doing this forever. And to the life span of the two-legged, the humans, those of you who are here now, it seems as if all of these changes happen very, very slowly, but if you think about the time it takes for all of this light to travel from the stars to the Earth, you can see that it is a very quick process.

Some of the light that you receive now, that you are being impacted with, is light from millions of years ago, and millions of years ago your planet looked entirely different than it does now. This light is in accordance with where your planet was, and influences the bringing up to the surface all of the movement from those times, also. In a way, all of the societal movements you have now are the echoes from millions of years ago.

As you move within your consciousness, which moves faster than anything else, you are able to receive different impulses, and the impulses that you receive have an effect on the movement of your planet itself, for this planet responds to energy, as all planets do. This one is a very sensitive planet, and it responds very easily to collective energy. It always has and it always will, for that is the nature of life here.

The parts of the planet that are up above the surface of the water right now are receiving impulses from different places in the heavens. It rotates itself around and around so that it can receive from different places in the heavens, and this is a building and creating of the realities that you are living with.

The attitudes and ideas of those who have wished to superimpose their reality here, have tried to dominate these Earth movements; they have tried to harness, change, and sculpt it into something different. You can see this in the places where cities are built; in the way the people build their homes, as if they are putting something new and different upon the landscape and the horizon. These homes are made from materials from different places that have been altered and changed in form.

Some of the cities on your planet, when you go there, do not look like they come from this place at all. They look very much like those from other planets and galaxies though, even to the tones, the colours, and the style of architecture. They are built to reflect the patterns of elsewhere, not in harmony with the planet itself. And wherever these creations are made, you'll find that the Earth and the reality built upon it seem to be at odds with each other, pushing against each other, as if the Earth is resisting the imposition of these things upon it. In these places, you will notice more and more, the Earth pushing it up and off of itself.

Where there are places and realities that are created by people in harmony with the planet, you will notice the homes, and the villages look like they are part of the landscape. The materials are made up from the Earth itself, and in these places, the Earth is holding and protecting the homes, because it is in harmony with that place.

When you are living in such places that are extensions of the Earth, you find your own mental attitudes become an extension of the Earth's attitude. Your consciousness becomes in harmony with the Earth, and the consciousness of the people around you begins to create community in accordance with the Earth itself. The feelings of these realities are very, very different.

I want you to understand that the blueprints which you all came in with match this planet. What you agree to alter and change within yourself becomes reflected in the altering and changing of the planet itself. The changes you are making yourself, as you go against your own hopes, your own dreams and your own beliefs, as you conform, usually out of fear of rejection, fear of being cut off; these changes that you make in yourself create the realities that you are living. To assist each one of you in coming to your original plan, your original blueprint, assists all of creation on this planet to be able to live out its original plan and its original blueprint.

The first recognition for each of you to look at is where you chose to be born on the planet. I know you have divided your whole planet up into squares mentally, but that is not how it really is. You need to look at your planet in terms of distance from the sun, distance from other planets, and distance from your moon. and the proximity where are you in relation to all of this solar system and the entire galaxy. If you look at the sun as the center of your little particular space in the universe, you can think of it as the heart, because it is the center and the source and all things that flow out of it into creation. Look and see where your planet is in proximity to this. There are some closer; there are a lot further away. The exact proximity of your planet to the sun shows your relationship to the Creators. You can think of it like that to start with. So, all of you born onto the planet are all holding that same proximity.

Regardless of how you like to think of yourselves, you are all, when you come onto the planet, in that proximity to creation. You are close enough that you are able to bring that energy through to create with and far enough away that the energy isn't too overwhelming for you.

Within the planet itself there are many different things that create proximity. There are mountains that bring you up higher and closer, and those who choose to live that close on those mountains, they want to be as close to the source as they can. There are those who live on the bulge of the planet, where they are getting much longer times spent in proximity to the sunlight, and these ones that live in those areas are there because that is how much time they need in the light. As far away as you are from the belt you call the equator, your proximity to the sun is that much less.

Looking at where you choose to live in proximity to the sun on this planet tells you more, again, what your original blueprint is. And even within that, there are those who live under the canopies of many trees and effectively can choose when to come out to get the sunlight and when to go back into the shade. Others choose to live in places that are in constant sunlight. Other cultures have built themselves houses like caves. They spend their time inside all day and don't get much time outside at all.

Then there are those who live further and further away from the sunlight, choosing to have equal periods of light and dark. They have long extended periods of light, followed by long extended periods of dark. Each of these choices of where you are born tells you what your soul is looking for during that time.

Those who choose to live near the big waters, choose to be near realities from the past that are still submerged. They may like the mysteries and memories of those submerged realities.

There are those who choose to live far inland away from those old mysteries, where newer realities are being played out. All of these things, you can look at.

Where did you choose to be born? What does that tell you about yourself? Where do you choose to live and make your home? Many people choose to be born in one place and to travel to another. Especially in this day and age, you have the freedom to do that more and more. Map it physically. Where were you born? Why were you born there? Physically, why were you born there? Is that how much light you need? Look at the change of choices as you change.

Each land mass, because of its proximity to the sun and the amount of light that it receives and the nature of the land itself, will tell you of the energy of that area. People will be drawn to a particular area, where they find within themselves their personal resonance to that place. The desert folk are very different from the river folk. The jungle people are different from the ice and snow people, and the plains people, again, are different from the mountain folk.

Every place that you live creates a diverse feel of energy that you purposely put yourself into. Everybody knows when they are in places that feel good to them and in other places that don't. To one person the desert is a terrible place, but to another it is home. Some people are frightened to be in the jungle, and other people are frightened to be in the plains, in the open. Each one of you know the places that feel good and right to you and the proximity to the sunlight that feels good and right to you. All of this tells you about who you are and what your original blueprint is, in the ways that your bodies are comfortable, and in the ways that your mind and emotions are comfortable, according to how you are living.

There are those who feel that they are only comfortable when they are in the artificial environment called cities. They know these environments; they trust them, they understand their sharp corners and the gridlines. It is all familiar to them, and in that they trust and feel good. Put these ones outside of the cities into the places of the Earth itself and they are frightened and they do not know how to be. These ones have lost touch with the planet and they have become enmeshed in the reality that has been imposed on this planet. There are places in other galaxies where these souls would feel more comfortable because they no longer feel comfortable on this planet.

How comfortable are you if you do not have the things of man around you? How comfortable are you to trust in the places of this planet? What places do you trust? Where do you feel safe? All of this tells you the nature of yourself, as well. Simple isn't it, when you look and see? Where did you choose to be born? Where did you choose to live?

We can see the political, social, and economic climates of each place, too. It is affected by the land mass itself. There is no earthly reason why the places that seemingly receive the most sunlight and seem to have the most of everything also have the least amount of finances. We see that all over your planet, and it makes no sense, logically, that it should be that way. The only way this can come to pass is if there has been control and change superimposed upon the planet itself, and that is the way it has happened. That is what has been created here on your planet.

After you have spent time investigating your choice of place of your birth and dwelling, I want you to look at the choice of the season you chose to be born in. This also can help you plot and blueprint what your life path is and where you plan to be.

Those who are born in the springtime, and it depends on each place of the planet what month that is, are choosing to be born at the beginning, at the first growth to push forward. You know this about yourself; you are the planners, you are the ones who bring the ideas in, you are the ones who want to ride in on that new growth, you want to come in and burst forward on this growth.

Those who choose to be born in the summer months, the time when everything is coming into fruition, you folks can see what you are like from that, too. You chose to come in when things were coming into fruition. You chose to come in and be part of that movement and part of that kind of growth. What does that say about you, about your purpose and pattern here? Does that tell you that you like to ride with the energies that are slower moving, the ripening times? Do you like to sit with ideas and help them come into being?

Those of you born in the autumn times, the harvest times; well, you are the collector folks aren't you? You like to collect things and bring it altogether. You are the harvesters of all of these ideas, and you are the ones who like to get things ready.

Those born in the quiet of the winter months, many of you are waiting. You are the ones who have to hold everything in waiting and readiness. You are the folks who like to germinate these ideas; you like to hold the energy and spend that time on the inner creations. All of this; the times, the places, show you plenty about who you are. It's all right there in your stories.

What called your soul in? What brought you here? The time of day you were born tells you more about yourself too. Were you born at the break of the day, in the mid-of-the-day, or the night time?

Nowadays, many of you have allowed others to make these decisions for you. Many of you have come in knowing you would hand over your power, and now someone else, a doctor, decides the schedule as to when you are going to be born. And for souls like you, who didn't make a decision but allowed others to, I would ask you to look at that.

Why did you choose to be born in a place where others would make the decision of your birth time for you? That's another question to ask of yourselves, for, more and more, there are souls allowing others to decide their time of birth for them. In looking at place and time, you can begin to get some ideas about who you are.

Look and see who you chose as your DNA ancestors. What biological information did you choose to bring into incarnation? For when your soul ignited the very first egg in the very first sperm, from the beginnings of your personal lifetime creation, you activated lines of DNA from all of your ancestors. You flipped those switches on and brought all of those DNA lines into being.

What ones did you to choose? What ancestors did you choose to bring through in your physical form and why? Why, with the choice of so many strands of DNA to choose from, some choose to bring in the strands of the darker ancestors or the lighter ancestors? The green eyes, brown eyes and the blue eyes; what DNA lines is your body holding? What, of your ancestors, do you most represent? Look at why you chose to bring those ones in.

What are you hoping to manifest in this lifetime? What ancestor's talents and skills, hopes, dreams and desires, did you choose to manifest?

You can see this by learning more about who your ancestors are. What did they look like? What did they do? What were their gifts, their talents, their skills? Where were they from? People have been moving around on this planet for time out of mind, but if you have the whole history of generations upon generations of ancestors in one place, you need to look and see, "Why am I pulling the threads from that place to be brought into this one? What am I weaving?"

Many of you who live in North America are bringing recent strands of DNA from many, many other places. It is interesting to look in North America and see how many lines are being brought from different places and being woven in here. What is being woven in these places?

If you look at South America you see less strands being brought in there. What is being woven there?

There are other places on other continents, for example, the British Isles which once were home to the Celts, the Picts and the Saxons, before the Romans came, wiped them out and staked claim to the lands. It is easy to see the influence of the Roman lines that were brought into those lands during those times. If you look at the British Isles now, you see many different DNA lines coming in from Africa, India, Korea, the Orient, and the Middle East, being woven into the tapestry of life there.

If you look in other areas in the world you will find that the same races that have been there for ten-thousand years are the ones that are still there, and there's not much opening or welcoming for others to come in.

So why is the land holding that, and why are the people holding that? And what about those of you who are bringing DNA strands in from different places to weave into the lands here. All of these are things for you to look at. What are the crafts of your ancestors? How did they dress? What kind of homes did they live in? Look around at the homes that you are living in now and ask yourself, in what ways are you reflecting your ancestors tastes in your own homes, your foods, and in how you dress. These are other places for you to look to understand what you are personally weaving here; what you, personally, are expressing upon this planet.

What are the family systems that you are choosing to express yourself in? What are the choices? Did you choose to be born into families that are run by the mother or the maternal? Many of you chose to be born into families with only the mother present while the father is absent. Many of you chose to be born into families that have both the mother and father, and some very few of you chose to be born into the families with just father. Many of you chose to be born into places where others would be raising you; by those who have not been biologically responsible for giving new life. All of you make choices in your birthplace and of your parents that are going to tell you a lot about who you are.

Where did you get born into those families; were you the eldest, the youngest? Were you born into families with many, many children, or you born as the only child? All of this also tells you what your blueprint is and what you came in for. Were you born into a family of sickness or health, born into a family of music, art, intellectual stimulation, political affiliations, or varying economic backgrounds?

Look at your families—look at where you chose to manifest yourself and why. And that is not even getting into the karmic relationships that you have been born in for. This is simply looking at it from afar, and that paints a very big picture for each one of you. You can get deeper into it here, as well.

What were the star systems in place when you were born? What was in the skies when you were born? Where were all the planets within your own solar system and where were the constellations that have such a big effect upon you and your destiny? All of this is very interesting for you to know about yourself.

When you graft all of these things together you get to paint a reasonably accurate picture of a person. If you wanted to pick any one person and follow all of those lines, you would have a pretty precise painting of who that soul is, what they are like, and what they are likely to do. Once you have an individual picture of yourself, you begin to see that your collective picture is made up of many individuals similar to you.

Each person coming in and holding a different place, but because of where and when you are coming in, it means the influences are really similar. So, you will see whole generations of people moving in similar directions and feeling comparable impulses, and these generations of people do not even realize why they are affected the way they are, so they do not always make the best use of the choices they have before them.

I would like you people to spend time getting to know who you really are. I would like to see a return to some of the old ways, allowing everyone to know who their ancestors are, to know who their tribes are, to understand their place with the land that they live on, and to understand who and what they are.

In most cultures of the circle societies this was encouraged; for each person to hear the stories before they came and arrived there, to hear the stories of the triumphs and failures of their ancestors, to know the stories of their mothers, their fathers, their sisters, and brothers. They also knew their cousins, aunts, and uncles, and they could see themselves as part of an entire family constellation, and within that, they could see themselves as a whole tribal constellation, and they knew who they were. They had the whole circle to reflect to them who they were and what they are made of.

They ate the foods that were growing right in their own area, so their DNA was a reflection of their whole being. All the atoms that made up their bodies were coming from the land around them, and therefore, they were entirely grounded into that place. The homes and buildings were made from the Earth that they walked on, their food was grown from the Earth that they walked on, and they were at one with all of their surroundings, and they knew who they were. Their ways led to confidence in self, faith in self, and knowledge of self.

In the circle communities the young ones were given time to know who they were. There were ceremonies for all as they passed from childhood upwards that allowed them to meet their ancestors; that allowed that they meet the land itself and ask for acceptance by that land. Nobody entered the tribe without permission from all, and the ceremonies were meant to help the people learn about themselves and learn who they were. From there comes the responsibility for these young ones to realize they were responsible to their ancestors, and they were responsible to their descendents, and they were responsible for the Earth that they lived on. They could not help but know the interconnectedness between their history and their future,; their connectedness with the land and the sky. They knew who they were and where they stood.

To be able to enslave a people you have to be able to take this away. You have to stop people from knowing who they are, you have to stop them from thinking about who their ancestors are, and you cannot let them think of future generations or they will never do what they are told. So one of the things that happened whenever the pyramid societies have come into the circle societies is they tried to make people ashamed of their ancestors.

They have often done this by killing a lot of the men and raping the women, making sure it is their seeds and their genetic lines that will be present in these new places they have conquered. They create such circumstances of shame and humiliation that the future generations never want to go back there, and thus, they effectively cut off the lines to the ancestors. They make them so afraid of the future that the people are effectively cut off from the generations to come, and thus, they have control over them now.

Well, this has worked pretty well in most places in the world. You are discouraged from discovering who your ancestors are and you are discouraged from knowing where you come from and who you are. You are discouraged from knowing much about yourself at all. I would suspect that most people in the dominant pyramid cultures here don't know who their ancestors are more than two generations back. Many have no idea where their DNA was fostered; many have no idea the different types of blood that flows through their veins.

All of this has been lost and shamed with the intentional purpose of stopping you from knowing who you are. We have seen this time and time again. Wherever tribal energies have been strong, wherever there has been tribal loyalty, wars are pitted one against the other with the idea that the two will try to exterminate those who try to hold strong to who they are.

If you look throughout your war history you will find that the peoples that were targeted for genocide were those who have held a very strong DNA identity—not a religious identity but a DNA identity, and these ones have been targeted for time out of mind. Curious, very curious if you look at that! It makes sense if you are trying to create an entire reality based upon that one blueprint.

I would like that each one of you who are hearing these words to begin to look and map out, just right around wherever you are, the country that you are in, and find out how far back the lines of the people go, how deep and how strong the connection to that land is. How long has your DNA been manifesting in that land?

If you are new here, what are the strengths that you are bringing to that land? What are the patterns that you are choosing to bring in? I ask that each one of you become responsible for the patterns that you are bringing in. Bring in the good ones that you think will add a contribution and tie off the ones that you think will take away. Decide for yourselves how you're going to weave your life.

Each one of you, look at yourselves as a being with all of these different threads gathered to yourself here; all the threads of your ancestors, the threads of your histories, the molecular and atomic threads of the land you are currently living on, all the threads of the energies of the sun that come here, the energies of the plants you eat and the earth that you walk on. Each one of these is like a different colour of thread, and all of those that you have gathered together in your hands are what you have to work with, are what you have to weave with.

I would like you to look at these blueprints and ask yourself where they came from, who has given them to you, and why they were given to you.

I would like you to begin to question all of the blueprints that come to you, because these threads that you holding in your hands are going to weave the next reality, and how you weave these threads is going to depend upon what blueprints you are following.

The reality that is woven for your children and grandchildren is going to be dependent upon the individual responsibilities that each one of you takes. As you blend all the threads you have together into a strand that is your life, what you do with that strand? How you weave in and out of everybody else's strands is what creates the next tapestry— patterns that your children and grandchildren will follow!

We are at this point on the Earth, where we know the picture that has been woven so far has come to the end, and a new picture must be woven. Each one of you is individually responsible for all of the threads that you carry, and you are culturally responsible for what you all create together with these threads.

She weaves with lavender and sage
Which she picks in the moonlight
from her garden
Plaiting them together and binding them with her own
Dark hair
She makes them into offerings.
And leaves them at the doors
Of the sick, or the sad.
Heartbreak moves her fingers the fastest.
She knows that can put someone's light out fast.

She watches them puzzle over their findings
Wrapped up in the morning newspaper
Or laid gently in a mailbox.
Some of them throw them away, true
But most, smell them, and smile.
Then look around as if expecting
Someone else.

They look right through her.
With her darkness in this land of whiteness
Where she comes to clean the houses
And heal the pain
That she sees
Everywhere.

Chapter XIII

Your Personal Indoctrination or
Brainwashing 101

After you have spent time looking at who you are and what you brought into this life, I want you to then begin looking at the training you have had, because this training shows the blueprints we are talking about. Let's look at your educational systems. What are the books you choose to read? What ideas you are exposed to? All of these are like blueprints that you can follow as you weave these threads that are yours. Most of you were put into specific educational systems that were designed by this present culture to fit the current needs of the society. The schooling systems were designed, in effect, to bring a population base to a place of understanding that would seem to be able to work for what the culture wished to represent and create.

Originally, in the circle communities everything that the entire tribe knew was passed onto the children. This was really important because the elders wanted to make sure that they had a good tribe to move back into if they decided to do the Earth walk again! It was very important that all the children learn everything they possibly could to be the very best at whatever they came to do.

The children were encouraged to pursue their own particular interests. It was understood that the circle must be diverse, that there must be plenty of opportunity for learning different things, and yet, there was a basis of knowledge that everyone possessed. The knowledge of creation, of food, of lodgings were things everyone learned, for each needed to know how to accomplish the basics so that no one would ever be hungry or cold. From this basic knowledge, some would then specialize in certain things and some in others, but everybody had a working knowledge of each other's crafts.

As time went on, people began to specialize more and more, and that was interesting and diverse within different tribal places. Sometimes whole cultures became known for particular traits and specific expertise, and all of this was part of the expression of diversity. For a community that lived near the clays, where the earth was deep and thick, these ones often would become potters, for they had access to the materials the land gave to them. Others who lived in deep jungles had access to many plants and animals, and therefore, became great hunters and gatherers. Those who lived by the sea shores became fishermen. Everyone grew out of the land where they lived and became specialized according to what that land offered. It worked really well.

People could incarnate from place to place and try out all the different cultural expressions and they learned from many things. This way worked for a really long time, but when things began to change and the system of the pyramid was set into motion, it became imperative that you trained people to be part of this system. So, no longer were people free to express and experiment and to learn the many things of the circle tribes.

As an alternative, the educational systems began to simply streamline people where they wanted them to be. Some schools were set up at this point in time for those they wished to be educated and indoctrinated into leadership positions, and only the children of the rich, the ones who had already grabbed most of the land, were entitled to attend these schools. These ones were given educations such as seemed fit for those who would be in leadership positions. From here came the leaders and the merchants of the various classes in the different places on the planet, that were under that pyramid structure. Education extended further after that when it was seen that by strengthening the people in the middle you would get a stronger pyramid, and therefore, these people were trained. As a result, schools extended and opened up to receive the children of the families who supported the middle of the pyramid. These ones were trained as accountants and clerks to uphold and run the industries of the ones who were trained as leaders. That is what opened up the educational systems to all of those ones, but it still was found that those on the bottom required more work than they were able to give.

It was then decided that they would educate the people on the bottom of the pyramid as well, so they could give more towards the top. Consequently, the education systems became public education, and here they educated the children from an early age and onward to be good factory workers. The ones who went a little further into the educational system became good clerks and administrators.

The ones who went even further, spending a longer time in the educational system, became the doctors and lawyers and the thinkers. Of course, the ones who were at the top of the system already had become the leaders and the owners of everything. And that was the system that was put into place to keep the pyramid alive and well.

The masses at the bottom of the pile were pushed outwards into the so-called third world countries, where they still do not receive such education but are left to be the slaves, as it was and always has been for the last twenty-thousand years or so in the pyramid cultures.

The educational systems you have right now are still based upon the system that has been in place for the last hundred years. It is only in place in so-called developed countries; developed, meaning; completely under the hold of the pyramid. Those of you who were indoctrinated into this haven't even questioned why it is like it is. In these countries where the factories grew in number, additional workers were needed, so they had to increase the workforce by opening up to more and more people.

This meant there was no one left to look after the children, so the education system opened up to accommodate more children. In some cases, children are brought here as young as one or two weeks of age and raised in their cubicles until they are old enough to be put back into the workforce, where they are tamed and trained workers.

Most of you have been educated within a system like this where you were not given much choice as to what you can study or what you can learn, and you were indoctrinated from a very, very young age to one expectation, to one belief system; to this one dogmatic way of being. You were encouraged to take a pathway that would best serve those on the top of the pyramid and you were forced to go into that particular cubicle that they have designated for someone of your talents and skills to fulfill.

Most of you have been so brainwashed through these systems that you do not even question what you are taught and what you are told. For your so-called leisure hours, many strategic devices were created in order for you to continue with this indoctrination.

When these systems were first put into place, with the idea of capturing and containing all of the populace so that they could be moved towards a particular ideology, even games became set to create the same end. Sports events, children's games, nursery rhymes, fairy tales and stories, what was allowed for the children to know, games they are allowed to play, games of what they were allowed to do; all were part of creating what the ones on top wanted and needed to be the basis of their support. This has continued on even further. Many children were trained to be warriors, they were trained to be soldiers, and they were trained to kill; the games and the stories were all about wars and fighting. Combat between two things or people became sports. All of this was to train warriors so that these places could conquer more and more land of the Earth. When it became that the wars were no longer fought one-on-one, the games had to change. Whereas, the entertainment and sports of the children now still involve one-on-one competition, more and more they are being trained through their games to rely upon the mechanics to become fast with their fingers and their eyes, and this type of coordination is what is encouraged now. The body is no longer important because they do not need the one-on-one bodies to fight anymore.

Now the pyramid system requires those who can fight from a distance in the abstract. The games that are put out to develop these kinds of warriors are the games you're going to see the kids playing with, because they still need masses of warriors, they still need to kill off groups of children; they still need the ability to do that to keep the pyramid in place. No longer do they need many to do the manual-type labour because they have machines doing it now, so the workers that they need have to be able to do the kind of work that involves dexterity of the fingers and the eyes. Since they do not need a lot of manual labour anymore, those are not the games that your children are playing. Look at your training and look at the kind of school system you were raised with. Were you drawn to active sports and pushed towards that? Look at what your culture is blueprinting you with. Did they look and see a good strong lad and say, "We are going to teach you how to play with the football or rugby?" Are they setting you up to be a big warrior? Or are they pushing you towards understanding the mechanics or putting you in the computer labs? Or are they pushing you to be a wordsmith, where you are not taught to think or be creative; instead, you are taught how to put into words what they want you to say? What other areas did your educational system push you into? That is your blueprinting, that is what was imprinted upon you right there.

How early or how young were you put into this system? Did you choose a family who would be unable to raise you but had to put you into the system very young? Or did you choose a family who would stay with you and keep you in their fold as long as possible? Did you choose a community where the children are encouraged to play together, or did you choose a community that isolated the children and only put them together at specific hours of the day? What is the education system that you chose to be in and how did that affect you? What were you taught and how were you taught?

For a while, in the beginning, teachers were those who had acquired, learned, and mastered understandings and were hired because of their brilliance and innovativeness. They were hired because they had knowledge and were able to teach it. Now, all teaching is a trade; people go to school for this and they are taught how to manage children and how to control children. They do not have to think about the lessons much anymore, for they are told what to teach, how to teach, and in what way, but mainly they are taught how to control the children. They even have developed pharmaceuticals to help them with the control of the children. I want you to look at what you were steered towards in your education system so that you can locate your indoctrination.

I want you to look at your hobbies, how you played, and what you played with as a child, for this is your indoctrination. Were you allowed to play what you wanted to or were you discouraged from some play and encouraged in others? How did your family and your culture indoctrinate you throughout your early years? How where you clothed? How did they look after you? What were you fed? What did your family do for entertainment? All of these questions lead you to understand the patterns and blueprints that have been given to you by your culture, so you can decide which ones you are going to accept and which ones you are not.

What kinds of stories were written in your culture when you were a child? What kinds of books did you read? What movies did you watch? What were your favourite stories as a child? Which ones did you want to read over and over again? What were the stories that your parents and teachers forced you to read? What were you encouraged to do? What movies and TV and video games did you play? How often do you sit in front of a box experiencing life through the visual contact electronics and how often do you interact with life itself? What was your predisposition? What did you like? What were you fed? What were the atoms you took into your body as a child? Were you fed wholesome foods or were you fed pre-packaged chemicals? What did you create your body out of? What kind of air did you breathe? All of this will show you what indoctrination was given and what patterns were put upon you; ones you still may be holding.

You can decide whether you want to continue with them or not. Question everything that you take as truth. Question everything that you believe. Follow the threads back. Where did I get that idea from? Why do I have that belief and where did it come from? Is it true? You can take any belief that you have, and every day you can hear people speaking as if their reality is the only one there is. So indoctrinated are they with the blueprints that have been taught that no other reality is possible in their minds. As soon as that happens to you, you are part of a pyramid and you cannot see any other way or any other way out.

I ask you to free yourselves; to look at who you are and what you came in with. To recognize that you get to decide where these weavings go and to question, question, question the blueprint you have been handed. How many souls are actually living their own dream? How many people do you know that you could say, "That person is living their life according to their own blueprint and their own will?" And how many people are doing what they have been told they have to do? I think the results of such close examinations would shock you. Looked at from the viewing point of where we stand, it is entirely understandable. This is what has been created. This is the trap that has been laid for each one of you as you get born on the Earth. This is the trap that you have allowed yourselves to get caught into, and by seeing it for what it is it is, it is the trap you can pull yourself out of.

Check every belief you have. Every time you say, "This is true," ask yourself why. "You can't survive in this world without money." Is that so? I've never known anyone to be able to boil gold coins to make a good soup. I've never seen that happen. "If you don't tow the line you will get in trouble." Seems to me the few that have questioned it and have taken their own lives in their own hands and made these kinds of decisions, a lot of those ones tend to end up being millionaires, don't they? Seems to me when I look in your culture, those ones who decided to follow their own dreams, and the heck with what everybody else says, become celebrities and stars, sports heroes, and entrepreneurs. Seems to me the ones that you look up to and say, "Well, that is an exception," are the ones who have questioned these ideas and have decided to take their own life into their own hands and make their own decisions. These are the folks who haven't said, "Okay, whatever you say." These are the folks who said, "Why? Why should I believe that?"

What would happen if you lived in a culture where everybody questioned things? What if you decided to question what you are being told and question what you are being shown and have a look for yourselves? The reality that is presented to you in your media, through your books, television, your movies, your newspapers and your magazines, is the reality the ones on top of this pyramid want you to believe. You have to believe it for this to exist. An incredible amount of money, time, and energy is put into social engineering to keep you believing this. There are entire skyscrapers filled with people whose job is to help you decide what to think, when to think it and how to think it; and huge resources are put simply towards that.

Do you not ever notice the theme of movies as they come out or what bestsellers are on the listings at different times? If you simply want to look through the media you will have a lot of fun. In the year of your birth, what were the top songs, what were the best selling novels, what were the movies that people were watching? As you were growing up, what were the kinds of films that everybody was paying attention to? What were the musical bands and what were they singing about? All of this is part of the indoctrination. There have been many, especially in the creative fields who have tried to wrestle this away from the pyramid, tried to bring in something else, some other ideas. And whenever that has happened, all throughout your lifetime history anyway, you will see excitement, people waking up, people coming alive, and people starting to question. That is how powerful it is! The many revolutions that you have seen, a lot of work went in by people who infiltrated the systems, they put their music out, they put their movies out, they published their books, and they got their words out, at least enough into the population to cause a stir.

When that stir started happening, it didn't take much if you think about it. If there were fifty different songs to listen to, all saying the same thing, and the fifty-first song comes out saying something different—that is what people were listening to. That is all it took; one book, one idea, one movie, one song, and that started things rocking. And everybody knew it at the time, "This is something different. This is making us feel alive." and people began to rock-and-roll. But it didn't take long for the pyramid system to

155

then grab hold of that movement and orchestrate it back to where they wanted it to be.

Pay attention when something is making you feel alive and woken up, as that is something calling from outside of that conformity; from outside of that pyramid. When something is lulling you back into sleep, recognize where it is coming from and recognize the patterns. When something feels dreary, as if it's going to go on like this forever, you know you are back in the pyramid. It is that simple, so watch for this.

Notice where the indoctrination comes from! Notice, even when you're watching your news and reading your newspapers that you are getting one opinion from one viewing point. You may think you are looking at all sides of it, but you are not. You are hearing a very, very small side and you will have to dig and look far and wide to get any other sides. There's not much energy pumped into seeing any other viewpoint except the pyramid, so be aware of how intricate and brilliantly this system has been set up.

You have to realize the ones at the very pointy tops of these pyramids have been well-educated and there has been brilliance fostered genetically. Culturally, these ones have been given the best food, the best medicine, the best educations—they have been given the best advantages that this planet has to offer. Do not underestimate it. It is a brilliant plan and it has worked really well! You have all fallen for it, even though you knew it was killing your planet, even though you knew it was making you unhappy, even though you knew it was taking away your freedoms, your joy, your creativity, and your expression. You have all agreed to it. So don't underestimate it—it was brilliantly laid out. But to change that, to try to bring reality into a balance that you want and what happiness you want, you have to recognize it for what it is. You have to look and see how this has influenced you. You have to look and see how you were coerced into agreeing and where the indoctrinations have taken place throughout your life. You have to look and see where you have allowed this. You have to look and see, in yourself, all of the places you are asleep, and the places where you come alive and awake, and notice this.

The pyramid is run by people who are sleepwalking all the way up to the top, where you have folks that are wide awake and very aware of how this works. During the time when we are bringing this information through, now, in the year written as 2004, there are once again, really good examples of how well this is being done, and most of the people in the world are pretty aware of what is going on. Many can voice and show proof of what is happening and they can say, "We see these things that are happening in our world. We do not think that they are right. We see where wars are being fought and people are being killed based upon lies." If you look at all the conflicts going on, on your planet at this time, they are all pretty much the same thing. They are all happening in countries that have resources that the rest of the world needs. The conflicts are not happening in countries that do not have anything; they're happening in poor countries where there are the resources that the bigger countries think they need.

Everybody knows this and everybody can see it and everybody even speaks about it, but, nonetheless, the lethargy that allows it to continue is the biggest and most predominant force. You will find a large percentage of the population, especially those who seem to be in the middle sections of the pyramid, will uphold these lies and will not see them as lies, even though it is there for them to see— will not see through the deception, even if it is laid out in front of their eyes, but would choose to listen to and agree with the indoctrination.

You'll see the ones on the base of the pyramid, those who have a lot less to lose; they know full well that this is nonsense. They see quite clearly what is going on; yet, they are herded along and comply with lies, even though they know it is not true. They do not see themselves as the bottom of the pyramid. They see themselves as the bottom of the pile, and they are also indoctrinated to believe that someday they may want to climb up that pile. They want things to filter down to them. They are not aware that they are in the position to shake the whole thing down, and a lot of effort and energy is being put into making sure they never find that out. So, sure, they can see the truth of what is going on and may grumble and complain about it, and make all the noise they want, but the ones in the middle are holding tight to the reality from the top, because they have been promised a way up, if they continue to hold tight and clamp down. You would think that the educated group in the center would be able to see this, and you would wonder why they are choosing to believe the lies.

If you can see how the system has been set up, for many generations, you can see that the terror of losing the place they have struggled so hard to climb to is bigger than the terror in any other place. When you are already on the bottom you don't realize how much power you have. When you are in the middle you have a very long way to fall and you have to give up what you have been aspiring for. That's the area that needs the shaking up.

Every now and then the ones on top will drop down, a few folks cast them into jail, or they have been assassinated to get them out of the way to make room for a few more to crawl up. But you'll never see anyone at the top of the pyramid rocking the boat; they have too far to fall. This is going to be up to the folks on the bottom to change, and those who never joined the pyramid in the first place. Be ready, be aware. Be aware of what you are creating and what you are agreeing to be part of, once you have been able to see the patterns here. That is all we are asking you to do is to look and become aware.

What you can see from this viewing point of awareness is that all of this is an illusion; all of this is the creation of belief and mindset. Things are moving in a particular direction because of the way people hold their mindset and beliefs. As you change that within yourself, it does not mean you have to quit your job at the lumber mill or walk away from the office where you work; it means that you have to bring your understandings into the reality that you exist in.

The circle realities are moving very slowly, but steadily into place as the pyramid is crumbling. There are places where the people are being prepared and are ready. There are some places on the planet where the pyramid is pulling out; there's not enough profit for them. In the places where the circle communities are strong, there have been instances where the people have simply said, "Fine, we will buy the factory for all of the workers that have been at the base." When the pyramid system left, they simply took over and ran it as a circle.

Such cooperative factories are doing quite well. They do not have child labour in those parts, or cost-saving devices, because everyone is involved and everyone has to make decisions on how it is run. It seems to be working well. In the places where the people have not been able to keep the circle community going, when the pyramid pulls out, they crash, and entire communities are lost. Entire towns and cities are lost because they have been aligned with the points of those pyramids for their very existence, and did not create circle communities to be able to support themselves. So wherever you are working, whatever you are doing, start creating those circles. There is solidarity among workers if you are helping each other. If you know what is going on in each other lives, then you're beginning to create community within your workplace.

Many of you have been trained to go from your homes early in the morning, after you wake up to the sound of an alarm that rings you out of your sleep state. You then grab yourself a stimulant that is doled out to each one of you, and you down that hot stimulant as you race to your places of work where you put in your eight hours or ten hours or twelve hours, or whatever it is you are expected to give of yourself that day.

Most of you give only your minimum, unless you are trying to advance, and most of you know there's no place for you higher in that pyramid. Then you go home to your so-called real life, where you spend maybe two or three or four hours before you go to sleep. Look at the patterns here people, where is your real-life happening? It is happening in your workplace. So what are you creating there? Most of you will say, "I'm doing what I'm told. I'm doing my job so that I can keep my job." I want you to look at how much of your life you are putting there. Why not bring your real self to it? How much do you know about the people in your work community? Do you know the person who is standing beside you or what is going on in their life? How much have you given of yourself to your community there?

What happens in workplaces where there is the solidarity between the workers? What happens in the workplace when somebody is sick? Does everybody get together and help their family out. Or if someone is in trouble, does anyone try to help? Is there is solidarity and community? What happens in workplaces where a few individuals begin creating this? I'll tell you what happens; you start creating circles, you start creating strength, you negotiate together and if that pyramid ever pulled out from there, you folks could run the place yourselves, no problem, because you already have the basis in place for it. Do not think that these pyramid folks have not seen this, and they will discourage such things unless they can be in control of it. And so, you will see many companies that have great organizations for their workers; "Here is a place you can come and do all your complaining, and you can be darned

160

sure we have listeners in there," or, "Here, you can have this great day with entertainment of this and that to make you happy and have fun, as long as everyone has fun together under our control." Notice where groups of people do try and are discouraged in not so subtle ways. " No, no, we'll put a notice up to send flowers to that sick person on behalf of the company, that's personnel's job, not yours, get back to work!"

Don't think they don't know, and don't think these pyramids will not find ways to take over what you are trying to do. If you want to bring circle community into your workplace, don't go into work with a 'pyramid attitude'. Your job is to keep casual. Keep the true circle. You do not need to be the leader there; just be a common, decent person. Just be considerate of your co-workers. Just find out about them. Be friendly. Recognize, at this point, you are probably spending most of your life with this group of people.

Those of you who work in offices, in any grouping of people, find out about the people you are spending so much of your life with. You are there for a reason. You chose to be there and not just because you are trapped by a paycheque. Look at it. Why did I choose this line? Why did I choose this company? Why did I choose these co-workers? What am I weaving here?

Those of you who are working as healers, or teachers; who did you choose as clients or students? Who are you choosing as co-workers there? What are you weaving? In whatever line of work you have decided to put yourself in, bring yourself there. Do not hide yourself away from your workplace; live in it, because that is where you are most of your days. Bring your communities, your ideas, who you are, into these places. Do it as a member of the circle, not as a self-styled leader, and you will not appear as a threat to the established order, as they only understand the threat of another pyramid!

Who do you see, in me,

By morning or night?

I try to be, what I think you want me to be,

Do I get it right?

What if I let you see,

The ones I hide, somewhere deep inside

Out of sight, denied?

Will you trigger me to betray my soul?

Will I ever, be whole

In your eyes,

Or better still, in mine?

It's a fine line

That walks between

The many facets of my being.

Chapter XIV

Daily Fragmentation

The concept of fragmentation has been presented in many different ways in your culture. I would like you to look at your everyday world, and all of the places that you have separated yourself from yourself, for to be effective as a weaver, you have to be able to bring all of the threads and lines that you have and weave with them.

Many of you begin your day awakening in the morning. For those of you who are in partnership, your relationship with your partner is but one aspect of your life. This can be a loving time, the first awakening of the morning, where strong loving connections can be made. But many of you wake up irritated or grumpy, and the person that you have chosen as your life partner suddenly becomes your abuse partner, as a secret life that exists between couples, of abuse, of subtle put-downs, of rage, of anger, and all the frustration you feel.

Every other aspect of your day is kept hidden in those pockets. For some of you, your tender loving self is hidden in those pockets and you express that self only to the partner that you wake up with. Some of you may have absolute indifference, and don't even allow yourself to make that connection when you first awaken. That is one aspect of life that most of you keep separate from who you wake up to in the morning.

On the other hand, if you wake up alone, what secret life is going on in there? Do you wish there was someone to wake up with? Are you happy to have the space to yourself? Do you regret pushing people out of your morning space? For all of you this is a very private part of you, and within this part you can find a lot more of your true self, where you're really are at and what you're really feeling in this 'who wakes up in the morning place'.

Some of you awaken and you have held in these first moments, all of the places you spent in your dreamtime; again, a secret world, a secret place, relationships that you have, and a dream place that are often not shared, not spoken of in the conscious everyday reality. For some of you, lucky enough to have a waking partner who will listen, you may be able to share where you have been going and what you have been doing in your dream space, thereby, bringing another part of yourself into that first morning reality. Some who have good practices may awake in the mornings, integrate your dream space, and begin your day in a loving manner with prayer and gratitude. Some of you who start your day out like this are integrating all of yourself into one place, but these are rare people.

For those of you with families, the next step is to fully awaken. Then there's the whole family situation; the rushing, the hurrying, getting everybody going and settled in the car, and then the racing off. Some of you race through traffic with all of these people around you, not realizing that the whole attitude is simply to get as far ahead as fast as you can. That is another reality, another fragmented place. Those of you who fight this kind of traffic each morning, what is your attitude when you are alone, encased in your vehicle, with no one to hear you?

Is this a place where all of the frustration and rage gets to come out? Is this a place where you can sing at the top of your lungs where nobody can hear you? Is this a place where you practice the speeches you have prepared to make that day? For those of you who are traveling by yourselves, what part of you comes out when you are encased in your vehicles. For those of you who collectively drive together or take a transit together with other people, what is this time like for you? What part of your self comes out then? What hat do you wear as the traveling person?

Those of you who work from your home, what are your procedures as you take yourself from your 'morning-busy-person' to the 'now-I'm-at-work-person'? What transformations do you go through? What do you do with your faces and your clothing? What is the difference between the 'who-woke-up-in-the-morning-person' and the 'who-presents-themselves-when-they-begin-to-work-person'? For many of you, you even look like completely different people, eh? You transformed from the 'one-who-woke-up-in-the-morning-scruffy-and-comfortable' to the 'one-who-is-being-presented-all-tidied-up'. That's another place where you can find different people within yourself. And the person in the workplace, the person who's doing the work they need to do, who is this person?

A person who is writing at home, or painting, have you cut the rest of the world off, shut all the doors, turned off all of the telephone devices, and locked yourself away into a different reality? Those of you who go to work in an office space, according to the office politics, who are you expected to be there; the boss, or are you a complacent worker, or are you a troublemaker? Who do you bring into those places—the same person who woke in the morning, the same person who drove?

Many of you are going to find there are a lot of different people in this day already and you have not even hit 10 o'clock yet! Then there is a break in the day; the lunch break. Who is that person? That one there is a different one from the one who was there in the morning altogether. The lunch-person who goes off with everybody to the restaurant; the lunch-person who brings their lunch pail and goes to the lunchroom and reads a book, the lunch-person who takes a break from their work and goes down to the kitchen to make tea—you are going to find a different person in each place. For many of you, your afternoon-person is putting in time waiting to get home; to finish with this day without trying, to get the day's work done, so that you can entitle yourself to be able to go home. Then there's the commute home. The 'commute-going-home' and the 'commute-coming-in' parts are different people again, with different attitudes.

Those of you who are working from home and those of you who work outdoors, can you notice who the person is at the end of the day? How have you changed? Many of you will find you are simply marking off a square; one more day, this week finished. One more day, this week finished; two more to go. Many of you will find that your afternoons are spent simply feeling pleased that you have just about put in the time for that week, for that month, and for that year, just putting in the time. Notice this 'coming-home person'. What do you feel you have achieved in that day? As you are coming home, can you look back and say, "I feel proud of myself on this day," or, "This was a good day," or, how many of you simply feel glad that it is over? This will show you how you feel about your life; this 'coming-home person', this 'finishing-that person'; this is how you view your life.

Then there is the person that comes home. Some attitudes are 'all this is supposed to be what quality time is all about, the time folks can spend together with those they love' and this the reason why you go to work all day long, is for these few hours you have in the evening. What are these few hours like? Is it rushing to get caught up, to get everybody fed, or get the laundry done? What is your reward for all that you have done in that day? I think for many of you, you will find there is a lot lacking here. How many of you folks come back into your homes and dull your minds as best you can with alcohol or drugs, televisions, and computers; how many of you do this?

For those of you who are trying to fill every moment that you can, rushing home and rushing back out again to some class, some project, some meeting, some something; look at your days and ask, "Who is the person who goes to these classes and these meetings?" Is this the same person who was there in the morning or during the lunch hour, or at work; the same person who goes to sleep at night? Who are you in your dream space? Many of you are going to discover that during the course of the day you have ten different people going on there. You have fragmented yourself in ten different ways. And who is the person who goes to church on Sunday morning? That's another person altogether than the person who shows up at the party or the person who goes to listen to a friend.

Throughout the course of any given day you are going to find that you are presenting a number of different facets of your soul, a number of different aspects of your personality. And in some of these aspects there is the wall; the party-person never meets the work-person, the morning-person-with-the-partner never meets the person-relating-to-the-children, and the Sunday-person certainly will not meet the lunch-hour person. You will find that many of you have dissipated your energy by disconnecting yourself, from yourself, in all these places. You will find different facial expressions, different ways of carrying yourself, different ways of dressing, different ways of expressing altogether, depending upon what point in the day you are at.

How can you integrate all of yourself together? Begin by noticing this as you go through your day. Are there things that you would say to your partner that you wake up with that you would never say to anyone else; ways in which you are disrespectful or rude in your morning-persona that you would never allow to speak in your afternoon and evening-persona? Who is that grumpy bear in the morning, or the tenderness if it is the tender-morning person? What then happened when you entered the workplace and became all tough? "Well that's the workplace, isn't it? That's the way it is there." Who told you this and why did you agree? Why is not safe for you to bring your true self out in all places, whether it be a grumpy bear or a gentle lamb? This is you; all of these places are you. Try to look at each one, at each reaction that you have, and ask yourself what is the stimulus that started that? Why do you behave in a certain way in your workplace in the morning; because you want to show a good impression? Who are you trying to impress—your boss? Why? Is it because you are afraid to not get paid or to not rise higher, so you give the expression that you expect is needed there? But that is not you, and so in this way you are not being true to yourself and you are giving away your power.

In each of these situations you are giving your power away to the ideologies and expectations of some social context and are not standing in your truth, your soul, and therefore, you are not effective in any of those places. What would happen if you decided to be who you are to the best of your ability in each and every moment, and each and every situation, to be honest and true, to have integrity, to look at how you are reacting and why you are reacting? Many of you do not say, "Yes, Ma'am," and, "Yes, Sir," to your morning partner. You do not treat your family members with the same kind of respect that you do your bosses; why not? Apparently those are the most important ones in your life, and yet, your respect is given on the surface to those who you feel are going to give you the most positive feedback, a paycheque.

Have a look at your day; where you put yourself and what you say. Have a look at how you react to different people. When you are talking to a policeman or talking to a person who is serving you in a coffee shop, how do you treat those people differently? What are your expectations of what those people are going to be to you? Have a look throughout the course of your day at who you relate to? Look at how you relate to those people? Question yourself, "How did I talk to this one and to that other person? Why, when I see this type of person, do my shoulders go up, and with that type of person I feel something in the pit of my belly? How am I relating to each person around me?" This will show you all the facets of your own character.

When you're walking through the city and you step over someone who is sitting on the sidewalk, warming their bottom end over a grate, do you make eye contact with them? That person is begging for money. They have a cup for money. Do you stop and give them money? Do you smile? Why does that one, sitting on the grate holding a cup for money, get one form of treatment, and somebody else ringing a bell with a Salvation Army sticker, asking and begging for money, get another? Why do you treat one, one way, and the other, another way, when they're both beggars? But most of you will have a completely different attitude from one person to the next, based upon what facet of your personality you are going to allow to be seen by each person that you encounter throughout the course of that day.

How are you going to relate? Are you being true to yourself here? Are you holding all of your lines and creating? Can you see each other as fellow souls on this Earth, each choosing to weave their realities? Can you be aware of yourself as one thread in these interactions with each person at each point of the day? Can you become so conscious of your interaction that you become aware of where your thread weaves into their day? What kind of an effect are you going to have as a thread in that day?

So, when you awaken in your day and you turn over and someone is there with you, how are you going to affect their day by how you are? If you are raising a family, and there you are in the morning interacting with other members of the household, how are you going to affect all of their days? If you are grumpy and rushing around, causing irritability, how is that going to shift their reality? If you are standing in your power, full of integrity, you can be conscious of how you're going to affect everybody's day.

When you go into the workplace, what are you bringing with you? Can you be aware of how everything you contribute that day is going to affect the company, all of the co-workers and everybody there? If you are going in with an attitude of hating the place and counting the hours to get out of there, then that is the thread you are bringing in, the expectation you are bringing in. You are no longer seeing yourself as part of a complex system; you are seeing yourself as a slave. Bringing that attitude in creates that reality. Shift it. You have the power to do that—shift it. When you are relating with your co-workers or eating lunch by yourself, or whatever you are doing at these times, recognize, "This is a moment that I have between me and my body to look after myself, to nourish and care for myself. This is the time I can relate to the other people around me and we do not have to talk about work." Use that time to nourish self in all different ways.

In the afternoon, are you looking at this time as, hurry up and let's get this thing over? The reason you came to work is so you could live these days, not just to run through them and get them over with. It is not a race, and yet, you will find, many of you, in your afternoons are racing and trying to get through the time as quickly as possible. How many of you spend your lives waiting from one moment to the next, waiting for the weekend that is supposed to be so great, waiting for a particular time, a particular date, a particular meeting, and everything you do in-between those moments is just running? Is this living life?

No, this is not living life—this is putting in time! Change that reality! Look at your afternoon as moments as times. What are you going to do with that time? How are you going to best express yourself during those periods of time? And when that part is over and you're moving on into the evening of your day and this is supposed to be your reward, for remember you are on your way home now, and the reason you are working all day and earning all this money and doing all of these things is for these evenings, for these times. That's the theory anyway, isn't it? So, why is it that so many of you bring with you into your evening times, all the stress, strain, frustration and anger? Why, is it so many of you completely numb yourselves out and spend your evenings, instead, with the television? Why is it that your reward, that you can numb your brains out? Look at it. Why are you so exhausted? Why are you so drained of energy at the end of the day?

This is not everybody. There are folks who really enjoy what they're doing. There are folks who are physically active in their work, and when they come home from the end of the day they are tired physically but feeling strong. There are those who love their work, though they are not many, and they there are those who love to come home at the end of the day. They look forward to it and they say, "This is what it's all about. This is what it's all for," but they are becoming fewer and fewer, from what we see. There are those who are enjoy their families so much that they look so forward to coming home with all kinds of surprises and fun, looking to make everybody laugh, but these are also one in one million.

So, here we are, addressing what the majority of you are doing. How you are wasting your lives by fragmenting yourselves. There is less of your soul or your spirit present in any of those places. Some of you, being unconsciously aware of this, have decided to put your essence into one aspect or one place and use all the other aspects to fortify that. These are the ones you would call workaholics; these are the ones that are putting all of their focus and energy into the current job they are holding. Many, as they start some business or organization, will work eighteen hours days, for they require it of themselves. When they go home, they bring work with them, because they believe this is the focus of their life; which is to become a partner in the law firm, or become a doctor in private practice, or head of

171

surgery, or to become CEO of the company, or the best salesperson of the day—or whatever carrot is being offered. Their morning-person gets up, eager to get going as early as possible. They may exercise in the morning simply so they have the energy to get through the day. Everything is geared towards the work because that's where they put their soul, and everything else backs this up. They will spend most of their life pursuing their work. That is where their energy goes. A partner is someone simply to keep them going so they can get to work on time. A home is the place where they can rest and do their work at home, refuel themselves, and any vacations or holidays are simply prevention of burnout. It is all geared towards the work. That is where their soul is! That is a choice.

Then there are those, their whole soul is simply relationship with their family. They will take whatever job or whatever work that will best support their family. They look at their days as going to work, as putting in time to get the paycheque to bring home to the family. Whatever work they do is in support of the family. Whatever hobbies they have are in support of the family. Whatever holidays they have are in support of the family. And yet, most of their time will be spent with other groups of people, working, and not as much time spent with the family.

There are those whose whole focus goes into their religion or into their hobby, and going to work every day is simply a way to pay for things so they can have their hobby, their sport, and their religion. The family is a necessary commodity, but life focus, where they really live, is in their hobby or sport. For these people, some of them have fragmented themselves so much that the only time they are even alive is when they get us to play their sport, their music, their art, or whatever hobby is occupying their focus. Whether it be a religion or an art, the focus and obsession is still there.

172

Look around you. How many people have you ever met who are simply living in each moment, regardless of what it is? That is the level of fragmentation you have going on in your culture. That is what people have had to do to survive.

This starts very early. How many of you, who have been parents, have noticed that when your child goes into the school place, a different person emerges? The child the teacher knows and the child that you know are often two different kids. They learn really early what is expected in one place, the face they must present, and what is expected in another place. The child that is expected to behave at Grandma's house is different than the child who is at home, and is different to the child who is in the schoolyard. Not many kids are the same in each place. Most of them learn pretty young, "Cut yourself off here—only present this here," and it is your societies and their families who teach these kids this. That you are not allowed to be playful in church; this is supposed to be God's house and the children are expected to be a different person here, as if the presentation to God must be a certain way. This has been learned very early on in your religions—your presentation to God is only one small part of yourself, your presentation to God is refined down and scrubbed clean, and that is all you get to show to God. Do you not see that God sees every moment? That when you are presenting that one face, on your Saturday or Sunday, or when you show that one face in your prayers—you think you can hide all of the other ones?

Look and see. If you were to take your soul and put it in a shape of a circle, and put a clock on that soul, and then you start dividing it up, how much time in your day are you giving to these different aspects of your self? I think you will be very disappointed, most of you, to see that the majority of the time that you give to aspects of your self,

173

you are giving to the aspects you like the least. You are expressing in the ways you like the least about yourself!

This is what we're talking about in the weaving. If you gave each one of these aspects a different colour, you with see a lot of the thread that you are bringing through into your daily life, that you are weaving into your daily reality, are colours that you don't even like. Why? What other choices do you have here? How can you bring the aspects of yourself that you do like into those time periods that you have clocked off? How can you bring different threads of yourself into all of these places? How about your organized worker-self? That could be used in the household in the evenings; the part of yourself, that can put everything into order so fast during your workday. How come that one doesn't get to come home? I wonder about the compassionate one in the morning. How come that one doesn't go into the workplace?

For many of you, you are spending more time with your co-workers than with your kids, and they are souls too. If you can reach to your children with compassion, you can reach to your co-workers with compassion. If you if you can treat your boss with respect, you can treat your kids with respect. Bring the threads to all aspects of your life. Look at all of them, and begin weaving your realities, starting by re-weaving your everyday. This is one of the places to start. Begin by looking and observing very carefully, each moment of your day.

Observe all of your habits, all the things that you do repetitively, and ask yourself why. Why is this habit there? What does it do for you? Does it make the dividing line, each one of the little habits? "Well, I get up and I do this first..." Why? "...because I always have." Why? No answer—habit. Each one of these little habits holds you in check, in place, and keeps you pulling through the same threads without question. They keep you in line, these habits! Move them around, try something different.

Have something different for breakfast in the morning, or have breakfast in the morning. Try getting up at different times. When you're setting yourself to awaken each day at exactly the same time, you're being exactly the same thing, you're hemming yourself into a box. Change things, allow a variety and flow; see what creativity comes into your life by moving the habits around. If every morning you awaken, you make yourself a coffee and you give it to yourself to wake up, you put your socks on the same way, you take the same route to get to where you're going… Move it around, try different times, try different routes, and try different foods or drinks in the morning. See what simply shifting something around does to your awareness.

When you go into your work places, what different rituals do you do? Why do you do them? What are your ritual greetings to everyone? What happens if you change that? Move it around. Actually stop with each person when you say good morning, stop and look at that person, make some comment that makes a connection between you and that person, and you have begun weaving. Bypass them, head lowered, nose buried in newspaper, coffee in hand; you have done no weaving that day. Watch what you doing, watch your habits, and watch your structures and your systems.

It would be interesting for you to make those circle clocks and write in what you're doing at each moment, and why you are doing it. Do that for a couple of days you are going to see some patterns in yourself that will surprise you. Look at the expectations that you are holding for yourself in each one of those hours; look at the frustrations you have with yourself when you cannot meet those expectations. Look at all of these things in yourself, with your days. Take the threads apart, look at them, decide where you're going to weave them, decide how you are going to weave them, and begin weaving your everyday reality with some consciousness, some planning, and some insight. Use all of yourself and purposely live your days.

This is your base for tomorrow. This is how you alter reality. You do it by being very conscious of what you are doing in each moment, by being very conscious of what you're presenting to whom, and why. You do it by being conscious of what you are not showing, what other parts you are keeping back, and asking yourself why. Question yourself. Spend a while studying who you are by how you present.

You want to change your world? Start by changing your day, your hour, and your moment. Ask yourself why you are responding like this; when someone says, "Good morning," what is your response? "Good morning," and walk on? What weaving did that leave there? Were you truly wishing each other a good day? Have you ever had anyone take you by the hand, look you in the eye and say, "I really wish you a good day today"? I bet none of you have ever experienced that. Would it take everybody off guard if you started to be authentic with your morning wishes, as if you really meant it? And when someone says good morning and you look at them, and you know they're going through a hard time, do you stop and ask, "How are you this morning? And do you ask, "Is it getting easier? Is there anything I can do to help?" Or do you just say 'good morning' and walk by, with no connection being made?

Be aware of what you are weaving. Be aware of how you are reacting. So when you wake up in the morning, and if you are waking up with a partner, how do want to treat this partner? How do want to affect their day? If you're waking up and you are alone, is this how you want to be waking up? Are you happy with this? Waking up with someone there, is this how you want to wake up, and are you happy with this? Look at the very moments of your day; the start of your day. Is this how you want to begin this day you have on Earth, and if no, how do you want to change it? Are you waking up with a hangover from alcohol from the night before, simply thinking "How am I going to get my head together?" Are you spending your morning moments trying to recover from the night before, trying to play catch-up, so that you are ready for that day? Pay attention to everything you are doing so that everything you are doing is by choice, not by default. That is standing in your power. That is being responsible for your personal reality. That is weaving consciously.

There have been many disciplines presented in your world to assist in helping people see and be conscious of the reality they are living. Some of them are quite strenuous; you basically have to hand your life over, depending upon the religious persuasion of each person. They have different attributes and different expectations once you become part of that. In some cultural traditions you must start your day off praying. You must start your day off in the habit of prayer and you end that day in the habit of prayer. This is meant to contain your day, to help you remember what you are there to do, what the point of this day is, and for some people it works.

Those of you that have experience in monasteries or in religious communities are aware of the structures. Some of you have faint memories of this way of being, where the morning begins in prayer, where the work of the day is done as a dedication to creation and then the day it ended in prayer. These structures can assist to keep your awareness in creation, but they can also block any other creativity that might want to come in. Some of them are quite strict, and although they do give you the opportunity to hold yourself centered, grounded, and aware of each thing you are doing, they do not allow for the playfulness of life to come in.

There have been a lot of teachers who have tried to bring different ways for people to try to help them create some structure of life that will allow more freedom, and then there are some who have simply tried to help people shift their realities for themselves. You all have stories in your various cultures. In the Christian culture you have stories where Jesus says to some fellows, "Well, why don't you just walk away from your fishing boats and come with me?" That is all you have left of the story. You do not know what went on before those famous words. It is much the same as what we are speaking of here. These two brothers were asked to look, "What is your life? What is the purpose of your life? What is the point of your existence? Is it to get up each morning very, very early, go out on your boat and catch as many fish as you can and bring them back? And are you trying each day to catch every bit of fish until there are none left? Is that the goal—to get all the fish from the water and put them all on the land?" Well, that was two-thousand years ago and you have almost done it, haven't you? Almost all the fish are gone, but that is another story.

So, Jesus had them look at this, "What is the point?" "Well, we are honouring our Father. He had this fishing boat, so we have to have it now." And he asked them why, "Well, because he is our father and we have to do what he did." And he asked them why, "Well, people need to eat so we have to collect all the fish." And he asked them why, and each question of why brought another excuse and reason that said, "We have to be up every morning and on this boat to catch the fish." And he asked them, "What would happen if you just walked away and didn't do it? What would happen if on this day you just decided, instead, you're going to come with me and we will learn about a different kind of fishing?"

It took a lot for those boys to walk away. It took an awful lot for them to break those customs and those habits and all of the guilt that said, "You have to take your boat out. The people are depending upon you. The family is depending upon you. The ocean is depending upon you. The fish are depending upon you." It took a lot for them to see that this really was not important at all. And they did it; they broke the habits of a lifetime. It took tremendous courage to say, "Okay, we are going to trust you on this. We're going to get up and walk away."

And they did, and they completely changed their lives, and they actually completely changed millions of people's lives. For those two became some of the best disciples, and they learned and they wrote about what they learned, and they helped other people learn. It took many months of asking the question, why, until they actually walked away.

In your stories you hear it like it happened only in one day, but it did not, it took a long time, and it will probably take a long time for you too, with all of your whys. You know, they did not stop fishing forever, and when they went back to their boats, they just were more aware of what they were doing, what, and why they did it. So, when they went out in their boat and caught fish it was completely by their choice, not because they had to please anybody, but it was their choice to do so and they did it in all consciousness. You can hear in these stories that because they were able to put that level of consciousness into their fishing, they could go out in one hour and catch the same number of fish that used to take them a couple of days because all of themselves was present there.

This is in your Bible stories, too, look it up and you will see. You can find this in stories of every culture. In the Greek mythologies, there were stories of the demigods who could bring all of themselves, all of their power and strength into one place, and were able to do feats that were unimaginable. Each one of them, in all of the stories and all of the mythologies, had to challenge their everyday patterns. All of the stories will tell a tale where, either the hero or heroine would have to leave the village or something traumatic would happen that would cause them to completely change their personal habits. That is what altered their reality which caused their soul to be brought all into one place. When this happens, when life intercedes and creates something that causes you to break all of your everyday habits and puts you all in one place; for these souls, this is the most intense power of their life.

Sometimes it is an illness that does this, that brings you completely into focus of what is important in your life and where you want to the standing, and you are transported in that moment to the realization of what is important, and whether the dust underneath the chairs gets swept up or not is no longer important. Whether you have some pieces of paper put in the right envelope by the right period of time is no longer important. What becomes important is living and the relationships of the people you love and all of the things you want to do.

Sometimes it is a war, and all around you is chaos and what becomes important is what you are fighting for; the principle that you are fighting for, whether it be land or family or the right to choose that becomes the focus. And when somebody has been put into that place where they are all-focused in one point, everything after that is flat. You will hear people who say these are the moments of their life, the true moments of their life, when everything is very clear, and once you have had that experience; to try to put you back into an office place is almost impossible

You can hear this from almost anyone who has been through those moments. It does not have to come through trauma, although it generally does. It takes coming to a place where your life and what you believe in, is actually threatened before you are able to pull all of your threads into one skein. You can do this consciously without using terror to catapult you there. You can do this by paying attention to what you are doing and asking yourself, "why?"

So the homework here for this section, once you have charted your origins, charted the DNA lines that you brought in, charted the star systems that you came in under, charted the family constellations that you came in with, then you can chart place. What country? What time periods? What was the plan, culturally? What was going on in your families? What was going on in the communities in your world? All of these are big pieces of your big puzzle, to show you where you came in. Then looking at what you accumulated along the way; what belief systems you took on, what cultural systems you took on, what religious systems you took on, thoughts, ideologies, and philosophies—all of these things that you have brought into the now.

Then, this next part is what you are doing with that. How are you weaving all of these threads? Once you have sorted through where you got them from, why you are holding them, you can now get to see what you are weaving with them. This is the work of watching your everyday movements. By the end of this exercise, and it may take you a long time to do this, you should be able to see very clearly what choices of threads you have and you should be able to, by this time, be very conscious of every single thread that you are weaving into that day. When you are at this place you can truly call yourself a master.

Then you are ready; only then, are you ready to start being aware of the big threads of this universe, and only then, are you strong and conscious enough to begin weaving with them. These are the threads of cause and effect—and the master can weave these threads on behalf of all of humanity if they so choose. Once a soul has found their place upon this Earth and is aware of what strings they are pulling and becoming consciously responsible for what they are about to weave, that soul is standing in their personal place of power. By being aware of all that you are bringing in and by being aware of the patterns that are already in place, you can then begin to weave a reality that changes the destiny of mankind.

Love ripples throughout creation,
And resonates,
Surging towards eternity's call.
Composing waves that full embrace,
All fates,
All truth, realities of all.

Earth creates metaphor of life
In her own way
With light received through sun and star.
Arranging conscious intentions
So that we may
Discover through her,
Who we are.

Chapter XV

Earth Majic

Now I want to address the nature of this planet and the nature of the reality of this planet. It has been said, and will be said again, "This planet does not need humans." There is not one place upon this planet that you could say benefits from human contact. There is not a single ecosystem naturally occurring here that benefits from the humans. The different ecosystems benefit from all of the creatures and all of the plants, except the human. As hard and as humbling as this is to hear, this planet does not need you; it never has.

What this planet has done is offered its services to creation. This is a giving planet. This is a planet of infinite expression. All of the movements of this planet are about bringing into expression. So all ideas of colour, of sensation, of idea, smell, touch, sound, sight, and taste; all of these expressions come into being on this planet. It has a diverse ecosystem that is made up of thousands and thousands of tiny ecosystems. You could compare this to the Heavens where configurations of stars and planetary systems all come together creating a whole universe.

The further in you go into the ecosystems, the tinier the systems are; like the microbiology that lives within the larger systems and the mitochondria that live within the cells of larger organisms. This planet expresses within all of her ecosystems, which make up all of the creations that are in expression here.

You have every sensation on this planet. You have every colour, every sound, every taste, and every smell. Every expression of physicality is present here and it is changing constantly; daily, momentarily. Whatever essence moves to the Earth plane comes into creation and is created into being-ness.

What happened when people, spirits, souls, first started coming here to Earth? As they came to this planet they were looking for a place of expression, and sometimes a place of refuge. The understanding was that this would be a place where certain souls could create their own reality, or certain souls would be given all that they need here, and the Earth would give it expression.

The Earth proceeded with this pattern for what you would call eons. As souls moved and touched upon the Earth, the Earth responded to those souls, which is what the Earth does. The Earth responded with form, with colour, with sound, with scent, with sensation, and the souls who chose to interact with the Earth found themselves in a dance of playful delight with the Earth. Souls found themselves touching upon Earth and taking on molecular structure and form and moving and flowing with the nuances and changes that the Earth itself had, and this was a beautiful interaction between planet and spirit. As more and more souls came to the earth plane, the interactions took different forms and the souls learned about physical expression. For that is what this planet teaches—physical expression. This planet teaches all of us how to bring ideas into manifestation, or how to become manifesters or creators.

The first souls expressing here found what you could call the garden of delight or what your current culture knows as the Garden of Eden. They found that whatever they touched, whatever they thought, could be given form by this planet, and the planet delighted in giving it form. So much was brought forward; every idea blossomed in response to the input of the spirits and the Earth would bring those ideas forward into manifestation. So if a soul touched upon the Earth with a feeling of flight, the Earth would lend the atoms to create wings, to create a sensation of wind and soaring. If a soul touched upon the feeling of taste, the Earth would respond with beautiful fruits. And if a soul touched upon the Earth with a sensation of power, you could find yourself flowing down a waterfall, cascading into the pools, or flying across treetops that reached and stretched up to the sun. For a long period of time there was a beautiful and responsive relationship between Earth and spirit.

As more spirits came to Earth with different ideas about what could be created—and this is the true story of the Garden of Eden, by the way— there came a time when souls began to think, 'How can we best utilize this resource? How can we best utilize this planet to serve our needs?' and thus began the stray from the Garden of Eden.

The forbidden fruit, the fruit of knowledge, wasn't actually knowledge; it was when spirits began to doubt that the Mother and Father of Creation knew what they were doing. Spirits began to question this and spirits began to say, "Well, why don't we take the Earth for ourselves and put it to use for what we believe?"

In their wisdom, the Mother and Father of creation, and with the Earth's permission, said, "If these souls wish to pursue this line of thought and this line of reasoning, well, why don't we let them do it? They will soon see." Now, for some of you it would seem like thousands and thousands of years of this, but in the history of this universe this is a millisecond—just a millisecond of learning. Some of you have felt like this has gone on and on and on forever, but it has not been a long time at all in relation to the rest of the universe.

Ideas began to be manifested on Earth that spoke about dominion; the ideas that the plants and animals ought to serve a purpose for the development of the souls, instead of a gift given to the souls. As these attitudes spread, there came into being a system that involved trying to harness and use energy instead of reacting and interacting with it, and this system of beliefs began to create many different manifestations.

185

Out of these different ways of relating with Earth came different cultures. Different souls began to argue about how things should be and how things should operate and what is the right way of being. They began to get immersed more and more into what they were creating here and they began to accept what they were creating as the only reality available. When arguments occurred between souls, about what they were creating, they would break off from each other, and from the breaking off, thousands of different cultures began developing. There was a lot of arguing between the different cultures and the diverse ideologies that were expressed by the various types of souls that were here, and Earth dominance became a competition between different souls who were trying to prove that their reality was the best and the most important.

The Earth and the Creators, in their wisdom decided, "Okay, fine. Maybe they would stop fighting with each other if they could each try out their ideologies and their belief systems, and we will give them time to do that. Maybe they will need to be isolated from each other.'"

So, at this point in time the continents began to divide and different languages started to emerge so that each group could try to fortify and develop their own ideologies without being influenced and interfered with by others. The belief being held was, "Well, our system would have worked fine if we didn't have the influence of those ones."

The Earth, in her wisdom said, "Well, fine. We will create different continents, we will put barriers up, and we will put you all into similar forms so you all have an equal advantage. Different languages will emerge so that your ideas and your ways can be kept isolated, and we will see how each one of you develop. We will see how this works since that is what you want to try."

Well, it took a few thousand years, Earth time, to create that system. In your stories you have some of this history still told of the time when languages were first developed, and in some cultures you can hear the stories of when all of the peoples were divided up into four directions and were sent off to prove themselves. This is also the story of the Tower of Babylon, when suddenly people couldn't understand each others language. These old stories all talk about this time period this sequence of events on the Earth.

The heaviness of thought that began to emerge through here, the repressiveness and the fragmentation of thought, slowed the spin of your planet down quite a bit and the slowing down of the spin of your planet caused a lot of changes in the weather. It created a real differentiation in places on the Earth, where some places became further away from the sun and some places got closer to the sun, and the whole configuration of your planet changed during this time because, as you know, the Earth responds.

This may have taken her awhile, but she responded to the idea that everybody wanted to be isolated so they would have no interference with whatever they were planning to do. This created isolation on the planet, isolation between different peoples, between continents, and between those in physical body and those not in physical bodies. This created isolation between the planet and the rest of the universe, and between the spirits and the Creators. But that is what people wanted and that is what they asked for. "Leave us alone. We will do it our way. We will create our reality how we want it and we do not ask anybody else for advice." Well, that has created this reaction on the Earth.

As the Earth slowed down it became less and less responsive, because the Earth, she does not like to be told what to do, you know; she likes to respond. Instead of a playful response between spirit and matter there became a dominating and a powering-over atmosphere. The Earth became slower and slower in her response and sometimes she would not respond at all. This, more than anything else, is what caused physical form to become so stagnant. As people began to move more and more into the mindset that they controlled the Earth, they believed that they therefore controlled reality.

So the Earth responded back by holding itself and not moving, and form began to hold itself and not respond to the unlovingness of that mindset. Things became set in their ways, and when the Earth was no longer responding in most places with the joyousness it naturally did, the people began to do without.

The Earth was not giving as it used to and manifested living wasn't as easy as it was before. Therefore, people began looking around them and saying things like, "Well, they've got it easier than us over there, so why don't we go over and take what they have?" They were so afraid of what was happening where they were they could not see that this was the outcome of a sequence of events; a natural consequence. Thus, life reflected the hoarding and fighting all over again, perpetuating the "dominate or be dominated" reality that has continued to this day, and continues still.

Admittedly, there were pockets of people who were learning that when you treat the Earth with respect and when you bring loving energy to a situation, it happily and joyfully responds back. But when you try to dominate or when you try to use power-over in a situation, it becomes rigid really fast. This is something folks are still learning.

There is something magical that happens when people start holding themselves in a place of love and joyfulness. But when someone is holding themselves in an unloving place or a frustrated place that is when things grind to a halt. This is no coincidence. This is how reality manifests. This is a responsive Earth.

Anywhere on this planet, if you allow the Earth to move on its own as it needs to, you will have life. It takes tremendous effort and energy to stop the Earth from creating life, tremendous effort! In most places all you need is a bit of sun and a bit of rain and you have a forest full of creatures, full of life, and for that to be destroyed—that takes tremendous power. If a volcano erupts and covers everything, it doesn't take long for life to start growing out of that. If an earthquake happens and opens up and swallows in, it doesn't take long for all of the seeds that are shaken up to start sprouting really fast to heal it. Where there are floods and after the water has receded, life grows back pretty fast.

The only places you will find the Earth not responding are the places where spirits have come in and actively poisoned or sought to destroy. The great deserts that you have on your planet are caused by human destruction. In the places where nothing grows, the badlands; trace it back and you will find the footprints of people and you will see what they have done and what they created.

The Earth responds, and everything that you have here, everything, is from the Earth. Your buildings are from the Earth, your money is from the Earth, everything you have; everything you think are your riches and your powers belong to this planet, not to you. The belief that all this could be harnessed and gathered up, brought above ground and held in the hands of a few, has created the systems of hierarchy that you have on this planet, but it all still belongs to the planet!

Once you start to understand your relationship to yourself and what you are bringing in; the next step is to understand your relationship with the planet. Why did this planet allow you to come here? Why has it allowed you to return so many times? In each life it has given you a body, it has given you food and drink, it has given you shelter, it has protected you, fed you, clothed you, and cared for you in every life you have lived. Why has this planet agreed to do it? Most of you will think that the planet has no choice, that things can be forced.

189

The important thing for you to understand is that this planet agrees, and this planet can also disagree. At this point in time it has been hoped that souls would evolve, grow, and learn. It has been hoped that by the graciousness of this planet allowing you to be here and the graciousness of this planet to give form to all of your ideas that you would be able to learn what ideas are going to work and what are not, and this planet has allowed for this.

When you understand that and you understand what it is that you believe, and why you are believing it, you can begin an entirely different interaction with this planet—a playful, fun, loving interaction. As you start to look at what you are trying to create and why you are trying to create, you begin to make conscious choices. And as you look upon the planet as a real good friend who has, for eons, offered you her services, you will begin to honour and respect your relationship with this planet.

There are laws of cause and effect here because of the way the planet is. There are laws of gravity, laws of chemistry and laws of physics. Laws are not rules, laws just are, and this is how it is set up and this is how it works.

As you understand these laws and why they work like they do, you can understand different ways to relate to these laws, and as you relate to them differently, they change! For instance with the laws of physics; "What goes up must come down". Well, that is a simple one, except in the cases where there is intent to go up and keep going up; then the intent changes that law.

The laws that say, "If it is a particular density, it must weigh itself in this way and react to gravity", except, if someone has a different intent, and that is how helicopters and airplanes were invented. If the law is, for instance, that, "What is put into something else can irrevocably change it," then that's what you have.

Now, if you decide to have a different relationship with that matter, then your intent can be different, and that is why some who study and learn about chemical reactions within themselves are able to swallow poison and not have their body react through death. That is why some are able to bless a well or a lake, or any body of water, and change the chemical compositions to neutralize the poisons.

Because the intent is different, the relationship between the person and the water has changed. You can take a cup of water and put poison in it and then you can say, "I have now poisoned this water and there's nothing anybody can do about it," or, you can have a relationship with that water and understand that water. You can learn to understand how the molecular structure of that water works, and your relationship with that water can then undo the molecular structure that is causing harm. You can neutralize it by changing just a few places where those molecules align, take them apart, so to speak, and you can find ways of doing this within yourself.

With knowledge, with intent and with understandings, this may seem like a miracle. You can take that water and you can look at the molecular composition and how it works. You can look at a glass of wine and see the molecular composition of that and notice the differences between the glass of water and the glass of wine; different arrangements of atomic structure. You can work with the water and ask the water if it will rearrange itself to match this glass of wine. The water can choose to respond to you playfully and now you have two glasses of wine! The water chose to respond when you chose to put your intent there. That is not power-over; that is playing with. There is a difference.

If you decided that you were tired of walking and you needed to be somewhere else in space and time you could talk to the Earth and you could say, "Well, you know what? You are a big planet and I need to be over there right now with all of myself." and the planet could say to you, "Why don't you drop your molecules here and go there and we

191

will help rebuild you over there?" The Earth could choose to respond to you like that. It would take absolute trust in this planet and absolute faith that if you dropped your atoms in that one spot, the Earth would help you to reassemble somewhere else. You would have to have absolute faith that the Earth was not tricking you, have absolute faith that everything would go as your intent is, and not many of you have that faith in the Earth. Most of you are secretly feeling pretty bad about the way you have treated her; somebody invites you in, feeds you and clothes you for eons, and then you turn around and treat her like this. So that guilt gets in the way of your relationship with the planet.

Those few who learn about themselves and see where their journeys have led and what they have been doing, have been able to re-establish a relationship with the planet. They pretty much come and go as they please, having the life that they desire. Of course, you never hear much about this in your reality because that would not fit in your reality. The reality that you have concocted here says you must have dominion over the fish, the fowl, the animals, the plants, and the rocks of this planet. The reality that you have concocted here says that you must force this planet to respond to you or you will die—it is the fear belief system that has created this.

Those who are willing to do their homework can see how all of this got started and can begin to have a different relationship with this planet; a much more playful and joyful one. As your relationship with the planet changes, you become aware that what you have created as your societies are only here because the planet is obviously agreeing to do it, and so if you want some changes within that system you still need to work with the planet.

You have stones and rocks that have created buildings, and other stones and rocks and trees that have created the money within those buildings, and you call this a bank. In this bank you have a person sitting there that is made up of water and stone and carbon from the planet and they are sitting in that body borrowed from the planet. You then go to them and you wait for them to tell you whether you can have money or not, and this tells you whether you can have a home or not, or food or not. You go to your places of work where raw materials are taken out of the Earth and these materials are made into other commodities, or you take ideas and create a business based on those ideas for eight or ten hours each day. Then you think you are entitled to go to that other building called a bank and you get those minerals and those trees that you call gold and dollars and somehow that entitles you to live within this reality. You think that this is truth and you think that it has power over you and you think that it has power over the Earth. The other way to look at it is more fun, isn't it?

You need to find your relationship with the planet. You need to find what this planet truly is. You need to get to know her, watch her, and pay attention to how she works, because all of your answers are here. The planet was made this way and it has stayed with its original blueprint and has not questioned it. This Earth has lovingly allowed each one of you to try out your ideas, your realities, to challenge and to grow. She has given you the freedom and the opportunity to put into manifestation whatever you could possibly dream up, and she has.

Some of these realities and manifestations cannot coexist, and so the Earth has created many levels of reality. For not only during those times past did the reality separate itself with continents and mountains and languages, but it separated itself with layers of reality, as well. So now you are living in a really complex organization that has within it a billion different realities, but they all operate under the same basic laws—the laws of response that what you put out, the universe responds to and the Earth creates. I guess that is another way of saying you still create your own reality.

That is what this planet has offered. This planet has offered to the Creators, "I will give these spirits a place to create their own realities, no matter what that reality may be, and hopefully they will learn, and hopefully they will grow and they will empower themselves." This is what this planet has gracefully done. It takes a leap of faith in oneself, a leap of faith in the Creators, and a leap of faith in this planet to begin stepping outside out of the dominant belief systems and start having your own relationship with the planet. It takes a great leap of faith to go off on one's own and trust that the Earth will respond.

This yearning, this knowledge, is embedded within each one of you, and in every culture on the planet you will find these stories. What you call your fairy tales or your mythologies contain these stories and this knowledge within them. What are the favourite fairy tales of the current culture here? Do they not speak of children who have to leave the dominant reality and find their way in the forest somehow? Is this not the story about Hansel and Gretel who went out into the wilderness where one finds sustenance? It is there, after all, but they have to overcome quite a bit in their relationship with what the wild has to offer. As a result of that they were able to bring back riches and goodness. Is there not the story of Snow White who goes out and finds a home with sustenance able to look after her and care for her until she goes back? You have so many stories of those who have to go out and seek.

You have many among the native cultures; North America, South America, Africa, Asia, and in the northern European pre-Roman times, in which this was actually ritualized. In these rituals the young men and women were sent off by themselves to learn their relationship with the planet, to learn who their helpers were and what they were going to learn from them in each lifetime. They were sent out to find and seek in their youth, so that they could bring back into their villages, into their cultures, this sense of knowing, and in every culture this was a right of passage. They were told "Go out from the village, from what you know, learn your relationship with the Earth and bring that strength and that knowledge back into your village so that this village may continue to live and grow in its relationship with the Earth".

It did not take long on this planet before people started thinking of each other as resources, not just the planet itself, and so the last thing you wanted anyone to do was to learn their relationship with the Earth. You only wanted them to learn their relationship with the social structures that were in place, and thus, rituals began to change. Rituals got put into place that instead of helping someone learn their relationship with the Earth and how the Earth works; they instead taught dependence upon whatever cultural setup was put into place.

This took form as a lot of horrendous circumstances. In some cultures children were taken away from their mothers and fathers; so frightened, that their dependency became only upon the leaders of that particular culture. In some situations children were taken away from their parents and put into whole institutions with other children, their minds absolutely trained only to learn what that culture wanted them to learn. Children were taken from playing on the Earth and put into buildings, not just for some times, but for the whole day. They are only allowed to go out and see the sunlight for fifteen minutes, and therefore, their alliances were with their cultures, not with the Earth. This has systematically been put into place.

The Earth has been covered up, the children's minds covered up, so they can only see themselves in context with their societies and whatever belief systems those societies are putting forward. Very few children these days are allowed to have a relationship with the planet, only in so-called poor, underdeveloped nations of the world are children still running barefoot on the ground, and only in these places are children still aware of their relationship to the Earth. The interesting thing is if you look at these people that are living in such a way, it is true they are not dependent upon their societies or their cultures to look after them. It is true they have to depend upon the planet to provide for them; they can only hope that they find some food somewhere, they can only hope that they can find some water somewhere, but these people can be anywhere upon your planet and they will survive.

In contrast, if you were to look at the children who have been raised with no relationship to the Earth and if you took them away from the societies that provide for them, they would be dead within a week. These other children struggle to survive, but given any opportunities, they will triumph. It takes tremendous effort to destroy those people, and tremendous effort is applied to do so.

Have you ever wondered why your current realities are so determined to take people off the land and so determined to put them into boxes? It seems to me that there is quite a lot of effort put into preventing all of you from getting to know your real relationship with this planet. A lot of effort is put into preventing you from knowing what you are capable of in your relationship with the planet.

After you have learned who you are, what you're carrying and what you are here to weave with, the next step is getting to know the loom itself, and that is your planet. She is a big loom and she allows space for absolutely everything to be woven; anything at all. But she has her structure, she has her responses, and if you weave in alignment with the structure of the Earth you will find the weaving pretty easy going. If you treat the Earth with respect, with loyalty, with gratitude, and with love, you will find a playful response in return.

There are those who have learned this. They have learned it perhaps with the plant beings. Everyone hears of these folks where plants respond to them and that's all there is to it. They can get anything to grow anywhere, and they do not need to use a bunch of chemicals and they do not need to poison everything around; for the plants simply respond. You walk into a garden where you know that soul has a good relationship with the plants because they are responding; the Earth is responding in bounty.

You can go other places where there is a forced response; plants are being grown without soil, chemicals are being used, the seeds have been tampered with, and their DNA constructed by engineers. They are growing in artificial, poisoned environments. These plants they will grow because the Earth still responds, but there will be no life-force, no energy, and there is not a loving relationship going on there, but they will still try to respond.

You can find this between people and stones, as well. There were those, in the old times, if wishing to find a particular type of stone to make arrowheads from, would be drawn right to where that kind of stone was to be found. For those who sought gold, some of them even knew exactly where to go because the Earth responded. Those that needed whatever gems or minerals the rocks had to offer would know exactly where to go and dig, very few, but those who came with loving intent, the Earth responded to. "So, here you go, you want some of the stones? Well, dig here; we have some. You want some coal? Dig here, we have some. You want to know where the oil is? Right here; we will show you." But, more and more the Earth hides. She is not willing to give anymore; not in that kind of context.

You hear stories all the time about the Earth responding to people starving, by showing them food. The Earth responds to a loving intent and a true calling. You hear stories all the time of miracles that happen when people need something, how it seems to appear or how circumstances intervene. This is the Earth responding—the Earth, giving of itself in response to the intent, the enthusiasm, the lovingness, the joyfulness, the calling of the spirit and souls. The Earth does not give a deaf ear to anyone.

You hear when the Earth is about to make a change, of the warnings she gives; there is going to be turbulence on that airplane; do not get on it. There is going to be an earthquake; do not go into your apartment building today. There is going to be a flood; get out of the area. The Earth gives warnings of every movement she is going to have and she gives warnings to every creature. Most of them, if they are free to respond, will respond. She gives warnings to all the humans, too. She gives warnings to everyone. Those who have a relationship with the planet are able to work with these laws, and will know where to be and where not to be. When you have need of something, ask the Earth with good loving intent. Ask the Earth and the Earth will respond and assist you with this.

This has been proven time and time again, and it has been the mistake, a great mistake, of most of you who are here to try to take these laws and use them for your own devices. So you look and you see somebody who has good luck with growing fruit trees, but what you do not realize is they walk through the orchards and they talk to the trees. You do not notice how they carefully look and say, "Oh, you want this branch pulled? Okay. And what do you need here... Okay?" This person has a relationship with their orchard, and because they have a relationship with the orchard, the orchard responds. Rather, somebody else comes in and they say, "Okay, what are the techniques they are using here?" and they want to take those techniques and duplicate them, and for awhile that works, but eventually the orchard dies and they think, "Well, that technique didn't work so let's try something new". That is power-over. That is coercing food. It is a very different relationship than with the person who loves their orchard and who has dedicated their whole life to loving that orchard.

All over your planet you have people like this; the growers who have their vineyards that have been tended and cared for, for generations. The olive groves that have been tended and cared for, for generations; they respond to the people. When these places get bought out by corporations who begin to run them technically, it is possible you could coerce a little more out of each tree for a little while, but eventually the tree will give up and stop producing. When you have a group of people coming together to create an economy or create a business together and everybody is excited about it, that company will produce just what is needed. Certainly you can send somebody else in there and you can start penalizing the workers and you can get it going a lot more industriously, and you will get a better output, that's for sure, but eventually that company will collapse because nobody's heart is in it. The employees will begin to drift away and without incentives and coercion nobody is going to come in to work, so during hard times it will collapse. That is very different than a joyful agreement between people when during hard times everybody will tighten their belts and help out. Do you see the difference?

You treat each other the same way you treat the Earth. You treat your bodies and your emotions the same way you treat the Earth and you can change that relationship by getting to know it.

The big secret of life that everybody is trying to figure out is this; what you have around you is what you created, and you have a choice to change that. The more you try to force and coerce, the harder it is going to get, and the more the Earth or form is going to resist you. The more

199

you engage in a loving response, the more the Earth is going to engage right back with you in a loving response.

You can find this in relationship with your own bodies, which are the Earth's molecules. As you love your body, as you love yourself, as you give yourself room for joyful expression, your body responds with health, vitality, and with life. As you try to coerce your body and force yourself to do things you really do not want to do, to say things you do not really want to say, to behave in ways you really do not want to behave; the more you try to conform and coerce your bodies, the more rigid they get. The more you flow with love and respect for self, gratitude and gratefulness to your body for maintaining your spirit, the more your body responds in a loving way, just as the Earth does. Being aware of yourself and your relationship with the Earth is the second part of the story of being a true weaver of reality.

To understand the Earth you need only to look at how she works. On the Earth everything flows and changes in cycles. The water flows through the planet, above the planet, on top of the planet, and through all the beings of the planet. It flows through the trees, the plants, the animals, the birds, the insects, the people, the rivers, the lakes, the oceans, the fish; it flows through everything and is filtered through everything. It goes down deep into the earth, back up into the sky and back down again, constantly changing form, constantly in motion and evolving, flowing in a cycle.

We can see how the Earth, which is mostly made of water, and all the creatures and plants, which are mostly made of water as well, are malleable and changeable. Water itself can be solid, can be liquid, or can be gaseous, depending on its intent and its reaction to the factors around it. It has mobility and flow, and has had this for eons; that has not changed. No matter how much poisoning you do to the water, it has its own way of changing and clearing itself by transforming to gas in the form of air and back down into liquid in the form of rain. It transforms in response to the heat of the sunlight and it transforms and filters through the solid matter of the Earth itself.

It hasn't taken humankind long to try to destroy the waters by pouring into it substances that never belonged in the clear, clean waters. It hasn't taken long for humans to try to subdue and control this cycle of water that belongs to the Earth, but as you can see, your water will decide its own cycles after all. Dams will burst and rivers will find their own way to flow. The Earth will send the waters up to the sky or pull it deep within itself according to its own patterns and the more the people try to control and subdue the cycle of water, the more you are going to see resistance to that.

The Earth has its own way of cleansing, rejuvenating, and changing. Each place on the earth has its own responses and its own cycles that it goes through. In some areas the Earth goes through cycles of temperature; through cold to warm. In some areas it goes through cycles of dry and wet. No matter how people tried to dominate and subdue it, there has not been much success in controlling or manipulating the weather.

There are peoples who have learned to interact with cycles of the weather, and there are some areas in the world where people still have that playful interaction with the weather. Many people can see this in their superstitions. You will hear people say, "Well, you know, of course it's going to rain; it is my wedding day," and for those that expect that, the Earth will respond to them. If they're planning a family picnic, of course it will be sunny and so it is. How many of you notice that if everyone calls for snow on Christmas Day you probably will get it? You have more people saying they want it to snow than you have people who are saying, "Well, of course it will be miserable," so that is what you will get. Even the weather responds, but not just according to your dictates.

There has been, in the last little while, and this has happened before, too, an intentional manipulation of weather. There have been experiments going on trying to manipulate winds, trying to manipulate moisture, and trying to manipulate the currents. There have been different gases released into the air to try to manipulate and change the weather.

There has been intentional manipulation of hurricanes, attempts to manipulate tornadoes, attempts to bring rainfall to places; there has been messing with the weather going on, once again, among people. There has been intention from some factions to try to use the weather as weaponry during wartime, or as ways to cause economic disaster in different areas, and you can see quite a few signs of that going on in your world now.

As soon as you start trying to dominate and manipulate the weather you will have a response from the Earth, and that is what you are getting. The Earth moves according to the intent that is imposed upon her. It is up to you to decide what you wish to send out as your intent.

The Earth is in constant motion and change, and if you understand this, you can learn to move and change with the Earth in response to its movements. You will find that your life will get a lot more interesting when living that way. There are choices.

You can either try to dominate the Earth or manipulate the Earth to suit your needs, or you can agree to try to flow with the Earth and be part of it. One way leads to destruction, as you can see, while the other way leads to creativity, change and growth. It is your choice. For only so long can you pour pavement upon the top of the living Earth, for only so long can you come in with your big equipment and tear away at the living landscape to try to form and shape it into what you believe you need.

Does the Earth need any more subdivisions? Is it truly serving a purpose for anyone? These are questions that you are all going to have to ask. Are you going to continue ploughing up the earth and changing it into something else because you believe that suits your needs?

Or do you wish to try something different on the Earth, and instead perhaps see if you can respond to the Earth. You can play along with it, dance with it. This would create a great change on your planet. What you are doing right now is simply causing the further destruction of it.

It seems to us that the options are not as great as you might like to think. The basic law and understanding of your planet is this; the Earth responds! You can decide what you want the Earth responding to from you!

We set our intentions so very high
And toss our questions to the sky
Mirror mirror... on star bright?
Will I have the wish I wish tonight?

He answers with a rose.
Soft silk petals,
Bud not yet exposed
To the warmth of the morning sun
Arm held high, first one
To greet the sunlight,
His gentle hand holds
The rose bud unfolds
Petal by petal
Responding to the light

Chapter XVI

Heaven and Earth

The next relationship for you to understand is your relationship with the Heavens and what you are bringing in to this Earth. What first drew you here in the beginning? What brought you forward to try your hand at manifestation? What is it you were hoping to learn and to gain? Anyone asking themselves these questions will probably get a pretty quick response. Why are you here anyway? Once you recognize what you are carrying and once you understand what the Earth truly has to offer, it is very simple to see what you are bringing here

Are you here learning or are you here putting in time? Most of you, from the looks of it, are putting in time and believe yourselves to be trapped here, and so you are. You look at the Earth as an adversary, and so it is. You look at each other as people to battle with and so you do. You create what you expect, and then you live in that.

Originally, most of you were drawn to the Earth because you wanted to find a place that would accept you and allow you to create the reality of your choosing. Many of you believed if only you were able to set things out yourself, things would work how you thought they would. Many of you believed you had a good idea and if only it was given a chance in the universe you could prove your idea. Many of you believed you had to get away from a lot of the things that were going on elsewhere in the universe. The Earth seemed like a safe place to get to; a place where you could try things out and you could see how they manifested. Unfortunately, it attracted other people with a lot of different ideas. Each one of you is going to have to look within yourself and find out, "Why did I come here in the first place?" You also need to look at what have you learned so far.

Each lifetime represents an aspect of your soul, of your being. When you look at it altogether, you can see the whole of yourself. Put altogether, you can look at how each one of your thoughts has manifested, for each lifetime represents a thought, an idea of who you are. Seen in total, you have your whole self. Most of you do not want to remember who you are. Most of you do not want to remember all of the parts of yourself, and according to the same line of thinking, the belief that what you're looking at right now is the only thing that matters. The whole is what matters and what everyone is weaving is the reality that gets created.

You can see some examples of this on Earth, where you have folks who build themselves beautiful paradises. They move to sunny, warm climates where they build themselves walled villas, and have servants, paid a very low wage, to wait on them. They have their special food flown in, swimming pools to dip into when it gets too hot, and whatever else they desire. They build themselves a beautiful paradise and there are many of these little paradises all over your planet, and they are lovely, very tasteful, and yet all around the outskirts is poverty and misery. The man who is lying on the ground in front of the walled villa with a needle stuck in his arm, dying from an overdose of heroin and the privileged one inside the villa also with a needle stuck in his arm, are sharing the same experience in different realities. Which reality is real? Which one is dominant? Are there more walled, secluded areas of beauty and privilege or are there more people born into shacks built on top of refuge piles? Which reality is being manifested on your planet here?

For a long time it was believed that these two realities could coexist; those who wished to wall themselves and keep all the beauty for themselves and those who believed they were not worthy of being sustained have been living side by side. These multitudes of realities have coexisted on your planet for a long time.

You can see where each person holds themselves, what belief system they came in on, and so the one who has the beautiful reality, nicely kept in the right neighbourhoods with the right people, can pat themselves on the back and say, "You see what a good job I did? I have created a wonderful reality. I have created beauty all around me. I have created everything just as I like it to be. I can pat myself on the back at what a wonderful job I have done." For these ones, there is truth in this, but they need to be aware that they are also responsible for what is happening outside of their gates.

They need to be aware that the maid that comes and serves them the drinks and gets paid an hourly wage has to go home and watch her kids go without. They need to be aware that as much as that maid may be grateful to have a job so she can at least feed her family, there is going to be resentment. They need to be aware that the person who is on the street outside their door is going to resent the placement that put them outside the door and them within. They have to be aware that in the creating of their beautiful little reality they are also part of creating the resentment and anger and feelings of disenfranchisement that is going on outside of their gates.

All that you create in your realms and in your worlds have consequences; they have reactions. Just as the Earth responds and reacts to you, so you respond and react to each other, and so if one person is going to take and exclude themselves, believing the justification of the beautiful reality they are creating, then another is going to resent this. When one requires more resources for their life than another there is going to be judgment and resentment for each other, and how can you coexist and create a paradise together when this kind of disparity is taking place?

Each of you need to look at yourselves and ask what are you bringing to Earth? What are you bringing into your relationship to this planet? If you can look, just at that one simple question, you can find out a lot about your right place in this universe. You can divide people up according to this question. You will find numerous people who believe they are here because they are somehow trapped, and there are a variety of belief systems about such entrapment. You will find a large number of people believing that they are here because of some great accident in the universe, some accidental mixing of chemicals that caused life, and you will find those that believe they are here because of this accident live their life accordingly; everything is an accident, so nothing is quite serious. There are those who believe they are here because of some punishment, some terrible thing they have done, and they have to pay back for it. Some believe they are imprisoned and when they are finished their sentence or learn whatever it is they have to learn, they will be free.

Some people believe they are here because this is a great school and they are students and once they have learned and passed the proper exams and the trials and tribulations, they will be free to get out into the real world. Well, you have quite a number of very interesting belief systems. There are also those who say, "I'm here because I choose to be here. That's my choice." As many different types of souls that are here, are as many different answers to that question, as you are going to discover, and each one of these are the threads that weave the fabric of the reality that you all live in.

Some souls believe they have come here to try to assist humanity in finding their right relationship with the planet and with God, and these ones treat their whole life like an adventure. They choose to learn and grow according to this belief and choose to assist according to this belief.

We are not saying that any of the beliefs are right or wrong because in actuality they are all true. Each one of you was drawn here for different reasons and you live your life according to those reasons. What we do wish to point out is that it is ultimately your choice of how you're going to respond to yourself here in the physical reality on Earth.

If you choose to believe that you are here, entrapped, until you learn something, then that is what your life experience is going to be. You will be trapped here until you learn. You will suffer and you will die, and if you do not think you are done, you will be drawn back into incarnation again. Those who believe that you are here because of some punishment will continue to punish yourselves. You will continue to try changing and adjusting your thought processes, your belief systems, your religions, your colour, your creed and your race. You will continue trying all different configurations of being, hoping that you are going to get the right one that has the magic key that opens to whatever paradise you believe is being denied you. Those who hold that belief system, well, you have a multitude of lives to go through then don't you, for there is a lot more to try out. Those who believe that it is just a big accident, well, you will know that for one lifetime won't you? You will look at everything that happens in your one lifetime as also being a big accident and as of no consequence, and that is how you will choose to live your life until the end of it; which is when you start remembering a little more about yourself.

The point is, each one of you have brought into your lifetime right now, threads and strings that lead all the way back to your original pull to the Earth in the first place. You can find within yourself what you are intending to do in this lifetime in how you treat the people around you, how you treat the Earth, and how you treat your relationship with the Divine. You will find all of these threads by simply asking yourself those important questions, and all of

209

this leads to your relationship to spirit, your relationship to light; the light that streams to Earth, the light that awakens the physical response into life.

What is your light that you are streaming to Earth? What is the intent of you streaming this light to Earth? What is your intent in stimulating this planet to respond to you, to your light? What are you bringing to Earth? This is the question for you to ask yourself. When you are bringing light to Earth, where are your alignments? Are you aligning with the Creators? Do you feel yourself as part of the Creators or do you feel yourself as something separate? Do you feel yourself as part of a community of spirit, or do you feel yourself isolated? All of this shows where your personality right now is in relationship to the rest of your spirit. Do you see yourself as one idea in expression in a multitude of ideas or do you see yourself as part of a whole picture, whether it be all of the pictures of your many lifetimes, or you as part of your family or community? Do you see yourself as part of a continuum or, do you see yourself as an accidental idea expressing in a void?

There are those who believe themselves to be something different; see themselves as very unique individuals, and there are those who believe that everything is simply the stage and setting for their story. They believe themselves to be the only important part of the story and all other people, all the objects, and all other realities are simply props in their play. Once again, all of this is truth and there is some truth in each story. For, yes, in that you choose your reality, in that you choose the people to have around you or not to have around you, in that respect you are responsible for what you respond to, and therefore, to what you allow in your own space. In this way everything could be seen as a backdrop to a great idea or play. All of these realities have truth; all of these expressions are valid.

The Earth responds to light, and because it responds, it creates. So, whatever ideas about yourself or about reality

210

that you bring here, they will come into expression, and because of this you get a chance to fully experience what you choose to believe. You get to fully experience what your ideas, attitudes, and belief systems mean, what they are. You get to see this, because the Earth allows you to. You get to taste, touch, and smell this, because the Earth allows you to experience all of it.

When you are not in physical reality and you are in spirit, it is true that there are the ideas of flowers, the ideas of trees, the ideas of waterfalls and breezes and sunlight and star-shine; there are the ideas of all of these things of every reality. There are ideas of castles, ideas of Heaven and hell, and these ideas are bright, and very, very real, when you are in spirit. But it is only when you are in the physical plane, yourself, that you can see the physical manifestation of these ideas. It is only through the eyes of the physical that you get to see these ideas manifested. Spirit can express here only through the physical forms that the Earth manifests.

The thought-form of a rose is very beautiful, the thought-form of its scent, the thought-form of its texture, of its colour, is vibrant and beautiful and very purely formed. The physical manifestation of the rose to some may seem a pale reproduction to the idea of a rose, but the physical manifestation of a rose can have a billion, billion, billion, different materializations and not one of them will be exactly alike. So, the thought-form is able to be made manifest in every possible aspect of itself, and each one is beautiful; different, but beautiful. The thought-form of a sunset, when you are in the Heavens is glorious, you can look at it and it will invoke wonderful feelings in the heart. It is very beautifully manifested on Earth every single evening. Every place on the Earth has an entirely different sunset; all of the aspects of sunset, manifested.

The idea of a song in the Heavens is a glorious choir of Angels, Heavenly hosts, the singing of the stars, as pure as song manifests on Earth. Well, how many songs do you think have been sung on Earth; billions?

Every single thought in the non-physical realm, when it is manifested in the physical, can manifest in every dimension possible, in every aspect possible, and each manifestation will be slightly different because that is the nature of the physical reality; constant change, constant motion, constant expression of every possible aspect. This is the creation of life. This is the creation of the Heavens. As every possible aspect of whatever thought-form is brought to materialization, it is like a pulsing outwards in an ever-growing and ever-expanding universe. This universe has to keep growing in response to whatever pulses, to whatever is created within it.

What we ask you to do is to be conscious of what you are creating, be conscious of the light that you are shining on this planet, be conscious of what your intention is, and as you are consciously aware of what you are manifesting, you will be manifesting all the aspects of what you like.

If you are conscious within yourself of your own destructive nature, for instance, you will become aware of where that destructive nature is coming from, why you are bringing those lines through and what is it you truly wish you could destroy. There are things that have been brought into creation, which we agree, could be destroyed.

This Earth will bring forward whatever you ask it to. You may not like some of the things that you bring forward, and thus, the ability to un-create is handy to have, but this will only work if you can be conscious of what you are creating, take responsibility for what you are creating, and decide which of these creations you wish to put your light into and which of these creations you wish to withdraw your light from. It is up to you! It is up to each one of you to make these kinds of decisions in your everyday life and to bring these decisions into a broader aspect of yourselves so that these kinds of decisions can be made on a greater level of reality.

Who are you? What do you want with this planet? What do you want with this life? What are you pursuing? What do you want to create? Time needs to be spent learning who you are, what you want; time that is found only in the physical realm, and only when you yourself are manifest here. What you bring in from the stars, what you bring in from your own soul, what you choose to bring as your light to this planet is what this planet has to respond to, and this—this is your creation.

Everyone reaches a point in their lifetime, each lifetime, when they look around themselves and ask "Is this I wanted to create?" I would expect a very small percentage could look upon this and answer "Yes, this is exactly what I want, thank you." I expect most feel pretty powerless when looking at their creations and I expect most wish they could undo a lot of what they have created. Well, you can, from this moment forward you are re-creating your realities.

Nothing stays stagnant, except ideas; ideas can be frozen into place, remain eternal, never moving, never growing and never changing. It is only when those ideas are brought into manifestation that they begin to change and grow. The manifestation of ideas is always evolving, always changing and always growing. The Heavens are full of ideas, and new ideas are always springing forth. You who have brought your idea of yourself to the Earth, you have allowed the Earth to give form to this idea of yourself, and are now streaming through these ideas and materializing them. That way you get to look at them. What ones do you want to keep and evolve? What ones do you want to take your light out of? It is up to you. This is how you will be creating the future; by what you put your light into and what you take your light out of, by what you give your attention to and what you pull your attention out of.

This understanding has long been used as an excuse for denial, but it is nothing of the sort.

It does not mean do not notice the man with the needle stuck in his arm outside of the gates. It does not mean withdraw your attention from that. What it means is to look deeper into it. What is this man struggling with? What is this addiction that causes him to put all his focus and attention upon the addiction itself, to the point that he will sacrifice his entire life and his existence to what he has his focus on? What if one decided not to put their focus on that? If you put your attention on the idea of the addiction then that is where your attention is going to be, and the more attention you give that addiction the more the addiction assumes its own reality, its own essence, and its own energy. The more focus it is given, the more it takes over and becomes the reality that that person is living. I do not say step over the person with a needle in the arm. I say look at the person and don't give the addiction your attention, give the person your attention. They are living an idea. What is the idea they are expressing, and is it an idea that you wish to give your energy to or your light to? Perhaps their idea is, 'Reality is simply an illusion, and the only interaction you have with reality is how it feels and nothing else matters except the illusion of feeling'. Those of you who believe that statement are going to be feeding that belief, the addiction, the forcing of sensation.

When you are looking at the person lying upon the ground, I do not say to ignore the reality of this person; but again, I say to look at the idea that this person is bringing forward. Is the idea that they are worthless? Is the idea that they must somehow rebel against something they do not like? Do you want to give your light to their idea of themselves, to their idea of reality, or do you want to give your light to caring for that person? Where you put your focus and your energy is the reality that you create.

To be supportive of such a person is to honour them. So, rather than stepping over and ignoring that person, thinking that by ignoring the person they are going to go away or cease to exist, try to honour that person. If that person says, "I am making a choice to stick a needle in my arm and put myself into an alternate reality by putting different chemicals in my body that I can respond to," how can you honour that soul while not feeding the ideas you do not like? You will have to respect that this is that person's choice. You will have to respect that they have their own lessons to learn, but as you walk by that person do not step over them and if they do not exist.

It would be fine to buy them a cup of coffee. It would be fine to put a blanket over them and say a cheerful good morning. It would be fine, to stop and say whatever it is you are feeling at the time. It would be fine to stop and say, "I am really sorry you are choosing this life. I am sure there is more to you than that." It would be fine to give whatever response you really have, once you have looked into yourself. Some of you may stand before this and wish to destroy it and think, "Oh, hurry up and die, so you are not outside my door." Some may wish to build buildings and put them inside, "Off the street, out of my way. Let's hope you are getting some help." Some may become intrigued by this and wish to study the situation and learn more about the hold of heroin and the reasons people seek this reality out. A hundred people will have a hundred different responses to this person.

What I am suggesting is to have your true response to the situation without giving any power to the addiction. Understand the person, their choices, what they're doing and why they are doing it, and do not empower the addiction. The very fact that enough people have managed to take themselves away from this addiction tells you how little power it truly has unless you give it to it

So many of you are empowering the things that you hate by focusing your energy towards the corruption, addiction, the military forces, the bombs, the pollution, the bigotry and hatred. So many of you are empowering these things that you claim to wish not to have here on Earth. This is what I ask you to do. Look through the whole story, the whole situation, and decide what aspects you want to give your energy to and what aspects you do not.

Do you want, when you are faced with that hypothetical man, to put a blanket over that man or do you want to give him money to buy more heroin? Do you want to feed his addiction or do you want to feed his humanity? It is up to you; each one of you. To feed his addiction you would probably take him and disempower him, lock him up in a room, force him to go through his own withdrawal, his own hell, and force him to face all the things that he does not want to face. To feed his humanity you would be honouring and respectful. You may tell him how you feel about watching him do that, but you can tell him you will respect his choices if that is what he wishes to do with his life. You may show that you would respect him even if you do not understand it or do like it, but you will respect his humanity and give him back his dignity. Honour and recognize the places within him that still can hold his head high and do not give energy to the addiction.

Your military forces are strong and powerful in some countries because everybody in that country is giving it their focus. It becomes an intent of the country's consciousness; an intent to have a military force. It becomes a conscious intention to feel powerful, and each has their own reasons for desiring this. Some wish to hold this intent because they are afraid and believe they need this force to be defended. Some, and it is out of guilt, believe, "If we have this much we should at least create a big force to protect others." Some wish to protect their own interests, so afraid are they, "We have to make sure we are not attacked, so we have need this big force." Some feel powerful and glorious, "Look how strong we are." But each person has their own reasons within each country of why they believe they must have this big military force, and that is what creates that force; the focus and the attention on it.

In countries where people become focused on other things, perhaps on health or education, or the arts, or environment, less attention and less focus is given to the military. People in these countries do not aspire to be soldiers; they aspire to be musicians or doctors or philosophers or environmentalists, where the focus is on different things. A country with a high military force has a population that is focusing on its military, just as a country with a high artistic force has a population that is focusing on their art. What each population is choosing to put their intent and focus on is what they create within their own communities. There are countries in your world that have no military, and there are some places in certain countries that don't even have a police force because that is not their focus. There are other places where almost half of the population are part of the military because that is their focus.

Look within yourself and be aware of where your intent is going. Where is your light going in your life? What do you focus on most of your time? What are you doing with your waking hours; where is your focus, what is it on? Each one of you can see quite clearly where your focus is by what you do with your time and by what you do with your responses to what is being portrayed around you. Where do you want to shine your light? Where do you want to put your focus? What do you want to create? This Earth will respond and will create wherever you happen to be putting your light. It is up to you; to each one of you individually! What you gaze upon, what you give your light to, is what you create!

So, that poor man who is sitting outside your gate, what are you going to look for in him? Are you seeing the addiction and think, "Ah, just another stupid junkie who has wasted his life..."? Or are you going to see your society and its power and ask, "Why do they let these people out? Why do they not have a place to put them away out of our sight? Why do they not have care for them?" Perhaps you are going to see it as corruption and think, "This is what it leads to." Are you going to see your particular belief systems, "Ah, probably an unwed mother—that is probably where this started—who knows?" Each one of you are going to see, portrayed by this man, what your focus is on.

Somebody else might walk by and think, "Well, someone to needs help. An opportunity—yes, I'd better stop and look after this man." Some may come and say, "Yes, I'm going to create a whole organization to look after these people," They are going to see that person as an opportunity. But how many people are going to walk by and look at this man and see his humanity? How many will to stop and look and see the many lifetimes that he has lived and all the different aspects of him? How many are going to see him in the context of his entire story? How many are going to understand that person there, not what he represents to each one of you, but who he is?

That is what is needed; for each one of you to look at each other and see your humanity, see your Godliness in each other, and to respond to that place within each other. What makes each one of you unique and alive? Not the beliefs each person has decided upon or the ideas you are manifesting, but the spark, the God spark of who you are. If you can see this in each other then you are seeing the true weaver in there. Then you are encouraging the true God spark in each person.

When you look upon one that you call enemy and you see their humanity, and you see underneath all of the threads that that soul has picked up and believe they have to carry; when you see the true spark of their being and focus on that, then that is what you are drawing into your life, and that is how you choose your fellow weavers. So, when you look at that man do you want to weave with his hopelessness, with his addiction, with his self-pity, with his self-hatred, or do you want to weave with his humanity, with your respect for him? It is your choice as all of those threads are there.

You have a choice of what parts you want to react to. It does not mean denying the other parts that are there, but it means you have a choice out of all the threads that you see with that person, which ones you choose to interact with and which ones you choose to withdraw your light from?

By withdrawing your light from the addiction, you are not saying," I am going to pretend you are perfectly fine and you do not have a needle sticking out of your arm." But, "I refuse to see you simply as an addiction and I am not buying you any heroin." What you are doing here is seeing the soul struggling, and what you may say is, "I would like to support you. I believe in this part of you. I believe in your strength. I believe you are going to get through this even if it costs you your life. I am not giving up on you." It is about not feeding the addiction, not feeding the self-hatred; not feeding any of those parts, but feeding the strength and the humanity.

This is how you can begin changing the reality around you. This is how you can begin changing how, you, yourself behave, within your family, your community, and your country; by putting your light in the places that you wish to see grow and not putting your light in the places that you would like to end. By weaving with the threads of relationship that you like and snipping those threads that you don't want to weave into the future. This is working with the laws of the universe!

I am washing in the water, of the river

Life giver

Flows through all eternity

Wise and witty

Touching all life, filling it with living

Light

Bright

With giving

Forgiving,

Wash away our sin

That we have believed within

We were capable of.

Dove

Of peace, come gliding down from the sun

Hot fire of life burns us in its transformative fun

Granting growth, giving for

Seeking shelter where it's warm

Stretch towards its light

Bright

With anticipation

Of what is to come

Tomorrow

Chapter XVII

Eden Lost

From the origins of the universe, of this particular universe; the outward flow and movement of this beginning has continued rippling throughout the universe. It has streamed through all of the planets and all of the stars with the same energy and motions. What has become manifested upon the Earth contains within its patterns all of the original ripples from the beginning of time. These ripples are waves of energy that come through the Earth that all life rides on. All life follows these same rhythms and these same ripples. When you understand this you can learn to build with these energies. You can learn to ride the waves of the universe as they come in through the Earth.

Some of the understandings that need to be brought forward can be found in the movements of the Earth itself. All the ripples of your water are caused by the movement of your Earth in correlation to the movement of your moon, the other planets, the sun, the comets, and all the intergalactic magnetic movement. That pattern of the relationship between Earth and moon, relationship between Earth and Mars, Venus, your sun, expresses in the waves of your planet. There can be disturbances on the planet itself which disrupt the waves, for instance, an earthquake or an explosion beneath the water is going to change the waves. The resulting ripple will have the intensity of whatever caused it and will change the waves until they have ridden it out. Another example would be an explosion in your oceans will cause a ripple of waves that will continue into the shore until they are finished and then that particular ripple and pattern is done.

The constant ripple that you have expressed here is from your Earth's relationship with the other beings, like your moon and with the galaxies around it. These are patterns, wave patterns. The relationship of your plants with the wave patterns from your sun is another way to see how this is expressed on your planet. There are patterns of waves or ripples found in the sands of the shorelines and deserts, as well. A desert landscape has ripples that show up in the sand that also show the patterns of the relationship between your planet and the universe. All of these images that show up on your planet, all of these waves, these pulses, all of the movement of your land, your plants, your animals; are all the physical manifestations of the patterns of the universe. They all manifest on your Earth in one way or another for you to see and understand.

Somebody who is well-versed in the ways of your Earth and understands how she moves is going to be able to predict the next flow, the next movement, where things are going to go, how things are going to manifest, because they understand how the Earth responds to energy; how physicality responds to energy. So you can watch the waves or you can watch the patterns of the animals or the patterns of the plants. When do they go into bud? When does the first leaf appear? At what time do most of the seeds begin to sprout? All of this is watching.

Some film makers using time lapse photography have filmed the opening of a forest in response to light patterns coming in; illustrating springtime. You can see the wave that goes through the forest in accordance to the movement of your planet. You can watch the waves go through as things burst into green.

One of the places you can see this very clearly is in the far north, in the Arctic lands, and if you talk to the people there they will tell you, you have to be in tune with the Earth rhythms, the rhythm that the Earth has with the other planets, in order to survive. That is how all of their ancestors survived. They are so aware of these rhythms that the Earth has that they are able to base their own lives completely upon these rhythms.

Most of you, in the societies that you have now, where you believe you are so plentiful and you are so blessed and you have so much, have become enmeshed in the rhythms of your cities. So aware are you of the rhythms of your traffic, your politics, your work and shop schedules that you are out of touch with the rhythm of the planet itself. You are not aware of how your planet relates to the rest of the galaxy any more than you are aware of how your society relates to the rest of the societies on the planet. You are as unaware of your relationship to the Earth as you are the relationship of the commodities that you call your luxuries, to the rest of society. You are as unaware of the poor in your cities and as unaware of the corruption that goes on, as you are of the realities that are created by all of the external forces.

To lose this knowledge, to lose the ability to know one's self as part of life on this planet, is to lose your state of Godliness. It is to lose your birthright. To begin to believe you are a product or consumer, to begin to believe that your destiny belongs to a corporation or a business, to begin to believe that you are owned by a country or a state, is to lose your relationship with humanity and your relationship with the Creators. What has been put in place upon this planet has tried to impose itself upon the basic patterns of life and has stolen your souls and stolen your birthright.

The way back to yourself, to your soul, is to find yourself and who you are in relationship to the world around you. Where is your planet in relationship to other planets? What does it matter, this round little ball in the midst of the universe, in the midst of a billion other planets? Is it so important to this universe? Are you so important to your community? What difference does it make if your star explodes? Will it make any difference in the whole universe? Will it matter? All of these questions that people find themselves looking at make one feel redundant and hopeless; as if it is all an accident

If the proximity of your moon to your planet has such a huge impact that it decides how your waters flow, if the proximity to the sun has such a huge impact that it decides whether life will flourish or not, if the proximity of your planet to all the other planets around decides how thick your atmosphere is, and if all of this is true, then it must be that every single placement is of the utmost importance. Then it would be understood that any disruption of any of those placements would have a ripple effect across the entire universe.

Your planet is important in the whole scheme of this universe. Without your planet everything changes. Are you so important in the scheme of things on this Earth? Without you being here everything changes. It is all with purpose.

The interrelationship between everything that exists has importance, has purpose and planning. You would have to be walking blind and deaf to not see this, to not understand this, and yet, you have entire societies that seem to ignore these realities. These societies believe you can create systems that will sustain themselves irregardless of whatever else is going on. They create systems that take so much energy to exist that it depletes all of the systems around them. Most of you in the western cultures have set up systems like this that are not in balance, that are not working in harmony with all of the other systems around, and when an imbalance is created it ripples out and affects everything in the entire universe.

So when you are creating an imbalance within your family, within your own psyche, you are creating an imbalance within your communities, your society, your countries, your planet, and that imbalance ripples out into the universe, as well. Such is the state we see your planet in right now. Such is the state we see being enacted here. It is too easy for everybody to believe that they are not important enough, that they do not really matter. It is too easy for everyone to think, "Well it's just one little planet; so what, if we mess it up?" It is too easy for these attitudes and ideas to take hold, and when it is this easy for that to happen you lose sight of who you are. You lose sight of your importance in the world and your importance in the universe. There is much that needs to happen to bring your consciousness back to Eden and to bring your consciousness back to the realization of Eden. This is a mythology, a story, meant to represent a state of being in balance and harmony with each other and with the Earth. A return to that state is a return to balance.

Now the Earth is a place to try out some of these social ideas. Some of these ideas on how to run the universe have nearly run this planet into the ground, so to speak. How do we collectively turn this ship around? First and foremost, to become aware; aware of what is missing, aware of the lack of joy that exists in the most prosperous of cultures.

In the places on your planet that are deemed the most advanced and the most prosperous, we see the most depression, the most sadness and the most hopelessness. In places on your planet that are deemed to have the most poverty, the most sickness, and the most pain, we see the greatest faith, the greatest hope, and more peace and contentment. Does that mean that all should live in poverty? Does it mean that one must suffer to find your way to the state of peace? Many religions are based on this assumption. It is common to see such a thing. Most of the diseases that you will find in the western culture are diseases of discontent.

Most of the diseases that you find in the so-called third world are diseases of poverty. So when one observes this it would appear that poverty and suffering is the way to peace, but there is much more to this story. What is observed in most of the cultures that are so-called first world, those who believe they are in the places of prosperity, is a disconnection with the planet, a disconnection with the rest of humanity, and a disconnection with the rest of the universe. It is as if you have begun to believe in the created realities that you have made, and that reality has become God, and God speaks through the profiteers, through the advertisers, and all of creation comes through the mouth of the television, and this is the creation that everybody's energy goes into and that is the creation that is materialized.

As you have all begun to believe in that reality it is spinning and spinning in a desperate state of frenzy of activity, simply trying to sustain itself. No longer do you have people in communities you have consumers. Since the consumers have to be workers as well, they feed each other back-and-forth. But so hungry are the consumers made to feel, that now you have to create a whole world of workers to create more things to consume.

As a result, you have moved into the third world countries and you have created whole areas that do nothing but produce gadgets, knick-knacks, clothing, and shoes They produce, produce, produce, for whole other sectors of society that have been set up to consume, consume, consume. This is an artificial reality that has been created, and if you really look at it, it looks pretty silly, and obviously not at all sustainable. Neither reality is thinking in terms of, "How does this affect the rest of the planet or our relationship to the rest of the galaxy?"

In the countries of the consumers, you are driven; you have to consume for the very state of your sanity. The states of your feelings, of self worth, are based upon consumption. If you do not have enough to consume, you feel less than, and a great depression comes up inside. If you do not have as much as everybody around you; you feel you are less, and this drives and drives and drives, the reality that has been created here. There must be continually more to consume. Each generation must have more for this reality to be validated.

In the realities where you are bringing your workers from, whether it is from the group of very poor within the country here or from the larger masses of the poor in the countries elsewhere, it is the same story. It is again about consumption, but this consumption is for life sustenance, for food and water. You have to go to work or you have no food, no water. You have to produce these goods that then get sold to markets over in the richer countries and these ones in the rich countries have to buy these goods or they feel they are no good and they have no status.

So locked in, is the majority of your planet to this reality, that you have made it Earths' reality. So locked in, is everyone to this reality that you have completely lost touch with who you are. You have lost touch with the rhythms of your planet. Most of you do not even know where you are in position to the rest of the universe. Many people on this planet have never seen the night sky, so blaring are the lights that you must have on to block out any incoming information from the stars.

There are those who have even grown to adulthood who have never even seen the stars, and they have no idea of their placement in this universe, for they have lost their birthright as souls. They have no concept of the rhythms of the planet, but they do know when the traffic starts in the morning and when rush-hour begins. They know by the increased sounds of traffic what time of day it must be and they know when there is a lull it must be mid-morning. The rhythms, the movements, are those created by the artificial reality that has nothing to do with the rest of the planet or the rest of the universe.

This reality is spinning so fast right now that most people are losing consciousness within it. Not only have they lost consciousness of self, they have also lost memory of self. Most cannot remember back more than a year or

227

two. Most cannot see forward much more than the instant gratification of, 'When I get enough money I will buy that.' That is the state of consciousness; a very sad and sorry state. We see most people in this reality and they are dying, they are sick and they can barely make it through a day. They use drugs to keep themselves alive, stimulated and going, and then they use drugs to put themselves to sleep. They use drugs to hold themselves in a functioning state and they use drugs to control how they feel and how they act. This is what you have created; the most unhappy group of folks I have seen since the days of intense slavery.

How can this be turned around? How can you help people understand the waves and rhythms, what they are choosing to ride and what waves and rhythms they are choosing to align with?

Every now and then a soul gets born into such a place and they are able to step back and look at those rhythms and they think, "Hmm, this is the rhythm of how this city moves. This is how the rhythm of business goes on here." They are able to look and chart all of those rhythms and then they play them. They play them really well. They play them so well that they end up with all of those rhythms and movements supporting them and their ideas. There are a lot of smart businesspeople who learn these rhythms and learn how to play them, but not enough to make any changes; just enough to exploit.

Most of the population is held in ignorance so that you are the perpetuators of this. You are the rowers of this boat and you keep rowing and rowing and rowing, while some have learned how to be the passengers. The passengers aren't interested in the rowers being able to see what they are doing. How far can this go? How much longer can this system continue?

As hard as it is to bear witness, look and see how this system is working. Have you ever wondered how the system that keeps those of you that I am addressing here in your nice warm homes with all of your push-on lights and appliances, your closets full of clothing and cupboards full of food, with all of your entertainment, all of your drugs, all of your cars and pavement, is kept in motion? What keeps it going?

Some of you have nuclear power plants that supply your electricity, which also supplies toxic waste and dangerous situations that quite possibly could blow your planet up. It is a risk, and at some point in time, if this continues on, you'll have more toxic waste than the Earth will be able to handle. Forethought was not put in for that eventuality. Some of you use coal-burning generators so that you can produce electricity that allows you to turn your light bulbs on. Coal miners die young and coal mines dry up. The same carcinogens that killed the miners go into the air and make you sick. This changes the balance and the rhythms of the air patterns and the plants and animals are all affected, but you have lights. Some people dam up the rivers and create hydro-electricity. The damming of the rivers causes great flooding and changes the course of the water, the veins of this earth. Some rely upon oil and gasoline for their energy, which are pumped out of the earth of the generally poorer countries, and this has completely disrupted the patterns of life there. These are not life sustaining realities, are they?

Where does the food come from in your cupboards? Most of it comes from the poisoning of the land, the wasting of the fields, and the exploitation of people. How many agricultural workers are dying of sickness caused from the poisons put upon the food? How much of the world's population work for pennies in the fields growing the food, a third of which is thrown away?

Even the clothing that you wear; how much of it do you really need? How much of it represents children locked in rooms as slaves to create cheap clothing for you?

How much of the reality you have built here is created through misery and through poisoning? Then when you need more of whatever you are afraid you're going to run out of, you will take over those places that are the sources of these things. Whether this is done through economic enslavement or with military is a matter of strategy. It is far cheaper to drop bombs on a place and rebuild, according to your specifications, than it is to try to negotiate fair trade.

The patterns and rhythms that these societies are run on are patterns of destruction, slavery, and death. They are the patterns of a dying star system that is blinking itself out; that is blasting itself forward into one last supernova of explosion. Can you not see this pattern here? Can you not see that the revving-up of your society is like the revving-up of the final effort of a dying star system? Where did these patterns come from? Why were they brought in and incorporated here? To whom do these patterns serve?

I have people say to me, "But, look, we are so much better off here than people are over there." They want to tell me this with certainty how much better off they are and I ask them, "Are you happy?" And it has been so long since they have been in their bellies that they do not even know. "Happy, means being able to get up and face the day, and unhappy means I cannot go to work. Happy, means I can go to work" and that is what I see people believing. When I am with people, even though where they are living is in extreme poverty where sometimes they do not know if there is going to be enough to eat, sometimes in those places we find joy.

Sometimes in those places we find peace, contentment and percentage-wise, probably just as much in either place. But when I am with people who are in tune with these rhythms, people who understand the rhythms of the Earth and who are in tune I find joy, I find contentment, and I find health. When people are aware that the days are

230

getting longer, the sun comes up earlier, and they think, "This morning I saw the sun come up. It was a beautiful golden and red sun this morning and it lit everything up, and I noticed the buds are just beginning to come out on the trees and I can't wait until tomorrow to see when the sun comes up."

These ones are with the Earth that day. They are smelling the air, feeling the wind, going about the business of looking after their physicality, but all the while being aware of the Earth; stopping because the deer are out in the morning and sitting quietly for five minutes to just listen to the deer playing back-and-forth with the rabbits and the birds. This can happen on your way to work, but the rhythm is different. These ones are putting in days of work into what they love to do, no matter what it is.

Some love to go work in a factory. They get to go and visit with everybody today and they watch and they notice, "Feels like rain coming this afternoon. Does anyone notice the feeling in the air?" They look forward to the sunset at night, "Ah, the sunset was beautiful tonight. It was all of these colours, and the first star I saw come out was here. Ah, it's going to be a clear night and the stars will be nice tonight." These few individuals are in love; they are in love with life. They look forward each day, "Ah, soon the blossoms will be out, then the leaves will come out, or the first of the fruits will be coming. Yes, the first snowfall..." They watch. They are in tune. They are in love. They are enjoying life because they are in tune with and riding the true rhythms.

When you are so aware of the movement of the Earth you cannot help but be aware of the people around you. These are the folks who notice, "You look a little down today. What's wrong?" These are the ones who comment and ask questions. They are not the ones racing forward to their deadline, or worrying about how much they have to have in the bank so they can buy that next car; those ones are too busy to notice a sunrise. The ones who have slowed themselves down to the rhythm of the planet they are part of the planet, and their atoms are vibrating along with the planet, not removed from the planet.

What is the definition of health? It is when your atomic structure is vibrating in a creative way. You have a choice of where you put your attention, where you put your light and where you put your energy. You have a choice of which rhythms to relate to, and it does not take much to start feeling. Just being aware of the sunsets help you to be aware of your planet as she turns and moves, and pretty soon you are going to start feeling.

You are going to start noticing all the life going on around you that you never noticed before. You will begin to realize that you are sharing this planet with an awful lot of other species as well. You will begin to realize your relationship as human to the planet. It is different than the relationship of hawk to the planet or ant to the planet. You will begin to realize that you are part of a really incredible ecosystem here and you will begin to feel that you are an important part of it. You will begin to know what you are and who you are, and out of this knowledge comes a caring for the future. You cannot be in connection with the rhythms of this planet and not immediately, as consequence, become concerned with the health of this planet.

As you become aware of yourself in relation to the Earth, you become a caretaker. That is what naturally happens. From this place you become aware of yourself and of your planet in relationship to the rest of the galaxy and the rest of the universe. And, you, as one being, become aware of your relationship with all of creation. You are brother and sister to all of creation in this place. What is that place where you are aware of yourself as part of all of creation, where you are aware of your place within that rhythm? That is Eden! That is Heaven! That is the state of bliss! That is the state of oneness!

What power is in there to be able to watch these waves? What power is in these rhythms to know? "First leaves are early this year; I know when to put my seeds in the ground because I am watching. These insects are already out. That is interesting. It was not like that last year. I'd better move myself into that rhythm and be ready. I noticed last night that all the birds were making quite a commotion and now this morning they are gone. I think I'd better get out of here." "I noticed that the snakes came up out of the earth last night; they are all over the place. I think I'd better be on guard today." When you are aware of what is going on in that reality you can work together with the rhythms of the planet to always be safe, to always be provided for, to always be cared for.

By being aware of these rhythms and movement you will know where food is. You will know how to provide for yourself when you know how to work with the rhythms of the Earth. When you observe and think to yourself," I noticed the animals doing this and this; hmm, I guess a storm is coming," then you are safe. You are safe because you allowed yourself to be part of these rhythms.

The disconnection that has happened with some of those folks who have put themselves in the rhythms of the cities instead of the planet, gives them no forewarning, no knowledge of what is going on, and so they feel constantly at the mercy of the planet. That is a state of fear, not a state of faith. They will never know if there is going to be an earthquake or a volcano erupting, or what will happen. They are frightened by it. Therefore, their faith goes into the army, "Ah, well, the army will come and take care it. The authorities will let us know if there is going to be a tornado; we will hear it on the radio. If a big wave is coming they will tell us and big trucks will come and take us away." Their dependency upon the structure that has become their God keeps them in a perpetual state of fear.

So more and more they try to conquer this fear by conquering the Earth. It becomes a vicious cycle. The fear of wild animals causes you to cut down all the trees and then you do not need to be afraid of that Earth coming to get you. You dam all the rivers, and then you do not have to be afraid of them flooding. Of course that causes more floods. So then you build bigger and bigger towers and more and more structures, so then you do not need to be afraid of the weather. You create more and more monitors. The more and more and more and more technology and on and on and on and then, 'we do not have to be afraid of the Earth anymore.' mentality has kind of spun out of control. The fear that is caused by the disconnection to the Earth, the terror that is caused by this disconnection to self, is what has created and continues to create such an unhealthy and artificial reality.

It is easy to change. Take a walk every morning at sunrise, a walk every evening at sunset, with your feet on the ground. In your culture you have an expression, 'stop and smell the roses'. Why? Because that is how roses transmit information, through their scent. Maybe the roses have something to say to you. They are your neighbours and maybe they want to talk to you! That is how flowers talk, through scent.

Stop and pay attention to your planet. for she is trying to talk to you. She is trying to include you in her rhythms. She is trying to bring you back home. She is not asking you to living in tepees again. She is not asking you to lie out on the ground and grow fur and tooth and nail. She is asking you to pay attention to her because only then can she include you, only then can she support you, and only then can she care for you. She cannot do that if you ignore her and if you are not part of her; consciously part of her.

How can you be part of the rest of the universe? You relate to the rest of the universe through her, as long as you are here partaking of this Earth by being in physical form. This is how you are relating to all of creation, and it is your choice which rhythms you are going to relate through.

The state of Eden is a state of consciousness as the state of Heaven on Earth is a state of consciousness. You cannot change any of these patterns that are killing you until you change your states of relationships. Until you feel the rhythms of this Earth, you cannot understand the rhythms of God. You can theorize and you can guess, you can make all of your grand religions and patterns, but you have not found it. In every one of your great religions that you have here, is somebody who went out and made their peace with the Earth. In every religion is somebody who went alone into the wilderness and heard the voice of God. All the rest of you think you can do that second-hand by reading about them, but you won't understand their words until you have found it yourself.

How many lifetimes are you going to spend on this planet until you are listening to it? How many times are you going to be born here until you listen? You can create whatever realities on this planet you want, or you can disconnect yourself and you can fight for your ideas. You can prove that you know what is better or what is best. How you know that river should be diverted over here? How you know that oil should not be in the ground it should be in your car? How you know all of these things about how things should be on this planet. You can argue that one lifetime after lifetime, and you can witness more death, more misery, more pain, and more suffering. You can populate and populate and populate if that makes you feel like you are dominating. You can exploit, and take and take and take until there is not a single fish left in the polluted waters, but what has that taught you? That you can take.

It has not taught you what physicality here has to teach you. It has not taught you about your divinity, about who you are. It has not taught you about your place in the universe, or your power. The power to take and destroy is not the same as the power to give and create. It is a lesser power, a far lesser power.

Those who understand themselves as a part of the rhythms of this Earth learn from this Earth how to work with those rhythms and how to move with them. The very act of planting a seed in the right rhythm and the right time to watch creation flourish is a beautiful gift. It is the gift of creation. The gift of being able to listen to the deer as they tell you what has been going on in the forest, to listen to the turtles as they tell you what is happening with the seasons, to listen to the dolphins and the whales when they tell you their concerns about their oceans. These abilities are gifts of creation. These are the abilities that come with recognition of self and right place.

You want to learn about your personal power? Learn who you are in relationship to the land right around you, even if all you have is one little park with blades of grass that were planted there from some seeds from some far-off continent and nurtured into growth with poisons, these are still seeds of the Earth. Start there, if that is all you have.

If you are lucky enough to have some trees around, go and get to know one. Those ones, they have their roots so deep in the earth that they know what is going on, and they have their branches so high up in the air they know what is coming in. If you are lucky enough to have at least one living thing to relate to on this planet, take your time to relate to it. Make that tree your beloved tree. Make that patch of grass your beloved patch of grass. Make this Earth your beloved and you will find you are beloved by it. As you spend time with that one tree, you will get to know the squirrels in the area, as well. You will know who is who, and they will get to know you. You will know what birds are nesting there and they will know you, and you will know the insects there too. You'll find there is a whole little world living there, and when you become part of that little world you realize that that little world is just as important as the world that is going on in a coffee shop, that normally you would spend that a half an hour in. That world is going on, as well. You realize that both are important and both are interesting.

The more time that you spend in getting to know yourself in relationship with the planet, the more you begin to know the Mother and Father of creation. They have been here the whole time. They never went anywhere, they never got lost. They have been here the whole time, just waiting, patient-like, until the children come home. They are waiting until the children come back to Eden, until they learn their right place, until they have learned their humanity, and through that, their divinity. That is what physical life is all about; learning that you are divine, learning what your power is and what your strengths are.

So there are exercises for folks to try to learn who they are. Spend time by a river, just listening to that river, just watching it flow. You have rivers that go through your body—your veins and arteries are your rivers. They flow through your body, too. Your body is based upon how the Earth works. You want to learn how to heal your clogged arteries? Just spend some time by the river; get into that rhythm and flow and watch how your energy flow changes. Watch the rhythm of the seasons and you will not be at such odds with the changing of the seasons of your own life. Watch how the Earth responds to the flow of the seasons and you will be able to respond to your own flow.

Pay attention to how everything interacts with each other and you will be more aware of how all the other parts of your body interact with each other.

Notice that when the one tree in the park that you have begun to love is cut down, how everything has to change. Suddenly the squirrels have to negotiate different trees, all the insects living in that tree have to find some other place to be, and the birds that had nested there every single year, well, they have to build a new nest now. Where is this bird going to nest if all the other trees have been taken? You become aware how each little thing is so important.

When the mower comes through and cuts all the grass, you can say, "Well that is lovely. But wait a minute—there were some little flowers beginning to grow there. I hope they didn't cut them too. Ah, too bad—they did." That changed the ecosystem there again.

When you start to become aware of this you start to become aware of your body and you think "I let my kidneys get cold the other day. I am noticing that here, and here, and here. That has affected everything else in my body, as well. I better take care of that one little place because I am noticing it everywhere else".

You become aware of yourself as parks with the rivers flowing through, your lungs, are like the trees, and all your hairs are like the grasses. You become aware that you are one with everything, that you are divine. Come back to your birthrights. It is a much more interesting place to be.

Ever notice that you run
Into the same people no matter where you are?
Sure, they have different bodies sometimes, but it is bizarre,
How often they look the same too?
Different histories, different names, but same expression.
I have a confession.
When I meet them, I call them by their other names.
Just to see if they remember who else they are. No games.
And then I just talk to them just as I would their other.
Please
Understand it's hard when they speak only Cree, or Japanese,
But I try, and I am usually right. They follow through
The flow of dialogue in the same rhythms I knew
From them before, or now.
Time does get confusing somehow
When I realize how many other circumstance
And distant times I knew that same dance
Hard to keep track of it
So many layers.
So many players
Yet so few.

Ever notice that you run..
just to keep ahead of yourself?

Chapter XVIII

Scattered Light

So here in the physical expression, as it is manifested on Earth, each soul has choice. As we have spoken of so far in our story here, all of these choices are manifest upon Earth, and where each soul puts their consciousness, where each soul puts their light, is the manifestation that happens on Earth. When there are a multitude of choices to be made in each situation, most people get into a place or a mindset that tells them whatever choice they make, there are going to be winners and losers. The mindset that says, "If I make this choice that loses. If I make that choice, this loses," has created a lot of problems on Earth. It has created a polarization of ideas, rather than an inclusiveness of ideas.

The idea that one chooses to bring into expression needs to be seen in its entirety. Every idea and every way does encompass everything else, and one has to look further in to see this. Whenever you make a choice, of going in a direction, for example; going to the left—that encompasses direction to the right in its very polarization. When you realize this you realize that every choice you make is going to encompass all, but where you put your light is how it becomes manifested.

The idea of denying one idea in favour of another has created a lot of polarization of light on this planet, and when you polarize your light in that way you will also be creating the opposite of what your intent is. As an example; say someone needs to make a choice between four different colours. When they choose which colour to put their focus on, which colour to use, the other colours are still going to be within that. But when choosing one colour and denying all the other ones, you are actually putting your light into the other ones, as well.

To put this into a physical life experience; imagine yourself being a parent to a number of children. Some of those children require a lot of your attention and energy, some do not seem to need as much attention or energy, and one of those children is born physically handicapped, needing constant attention. How do you divide yourself between all of those children, all of those choices? Where do you put your light and energy? Where are you going to give the most?

Most people will find they will deny one in favour of the other, either overtly or secretly. Some will find they will guilt themselves into trying to give equal distribution between all. But, very rarely, will you find somebody who is in a state of balance enough to be able to give what they really feel to each one. Rarely, will you find somebody who can find this balance within themselves. This can explain quite a bit of what happened at the beginning of creation where guilt got the upper hand. This is where the voices that tell you what should be get the upper hand, and then creation does not get the balance that it seeks. When you make choice A by trying to exclude choice B, you are dividing your own light. When your conscious light goes with choice A, and your denied light will go with choice B, because you feel guilty, choice B will still be empowered, but it will be empowered in a state of denial. When someone makes a moral choice that they will do one act because they judge the other act to be wrong, their strong judgment of that act will empower it to manifest.

Abstinence is a real good image of this. When one judges that abstinence is the moral way to be, the right way to be, and one judges that to engage in sexuality is abnormal and wrong, all of those emotions and feelings and options are present. So the choice to have a sexual affair with someone or to stay abstinent could be looked at as choice A or choice B. In choosing choice A as the moral or right way because of guilt or your belief systems, you force

242

yourself to make this choice out of your judgements. By denying the other choice and judging it as wrong, or bad, your thoughts will haunt you and they will keep running to choice B. Lust will grow bigger and bigger. You will see it everywhere you look and at every person you see, because it is fuelled by your denial of that choice.

Rather than restricting yourself, splitting where your focus is going to be, you can encompass all of yourself and recognize all of your feelings and emotions and have acceptance for all of this, while realizing that life is going to have a multitude of choices at all times. Then your action is not based on your judgments, your action is not based on splitting your consciousness. Whatever choice you make will include all of your self. In our example, you can say, 'Oh, I have a lot of lustful feelings. I have a strong, healthy sexuality, but I am making a choice at this point in my life not to engage sexually with somebody else, so I'm going to use that energy in any another way." You are then able to hold your focus inclusively rather than exclusively. You are not dividing your light and energy; you are making a choice that is inclusive of all your feelings. You are acknowledging everything that is going on and bringing it together to make a choice. That is a whole different way of being.

I am bringing this forward so that there is no misunderstanding when I am speaking about the fact that you have a choice of where to put your focused energy, and that is how you manifest your life. Now, I do not want people to misunderstand and think that they can deny one choice in favour of another and create whatever reality they want through denial, for it does not work. You have to include everything you want to and be able to move the whole circle in a positive direction for everyone.

When your life is in harmony and balance it is good for everyone with whom you are in touch, and it is inclusive of everybody. When your life is out of balance you may think you are following the path that is right for you, but it doesn't work out that way. Once something has been set in motion it will continue moving in the same direction that it got set in until it comes up against something bigger that will alter its course.

That is one of the basic laws of this universe—that all movement goes on out until it hits something bigger and then the energy will often deflect and divide. When your intent is going out with how you want your reality to be, that intent will ripple out until it hits something greater than it. What is greater than the intent? It is the doubt! When you send your intent out for the reality that you want to create and you hit your doubt, it divides it, and the energy then ripples off. So, again, if we have the question of, "Shall we take path A or path B, your intent may be to move out towards path A, but then you hit your doubts, you hit your denials and you hit all the places where you have not been inclusive of yourself, and it begins to fracture and the energy splits and both pathways become encompassed. The more splits that happen with the intent, the more realities get created. The one that you find yourself in is the one that has taken the most of your attention, and it may not be the one you thought you chose.

We can use another example here to help you understand this. Imagine your intent as a wave of energy coming out from the center of the universe like a comet. This comet is pushing out through the universe, but as it flows out through the universe the effects of all the planets and stars that it goes by helps to decide its course. As it ripples out through the universe, it has to find its pathway by its effect upon the other objects around it and their effect upon it. After eons of circling through the universe each one of these comets finds its right pathway through the universe through this movement. Another comet coming through that intersects with this one will completely alter its course. It will cause it to fracture, to fragment-out,

244

which may then eventually create two comets, each still continuing on their way but perhaps in different directions. The movements of the now two comets will have an effect on all the other planets and every star system that they pass thereby altering the entire universe again. That is what happens in this universe. It has already been set in motion, but when something new comes through it alters everything.

So, let us take that pattern of the universe and witness how it operates in the world of humanity. For an example, let's say we have a soul who is interested in preserving peace. This soul wishes, with their fullest intent and heart, that the world could be a peaceful place where people feed each other and care for each other, where energy is put into prevention of disease, into education, and beauty, and culture. This is their original intent, and we see this pouring forth from their heart with the beautiful pictures of how the world could be and they love this image. Along the way, they come up against those who are frightened, and therefore have chosen the path of war; who believe that the mighty must conquer, and who believe that the only way there can be stability in the world is through forcing everybody to conform to their way of living. This image is in direct conflict with the path that they wish to create. It triggers within them, immense anger, and they wish to conquer that attitude in those people. Immediately, that soul's intent fragment off and starts moving in an entirely different direction.

Then you find this person who began with the intent of beauty and peace suddenly throwing bombs, fighting against police officers, blowing up buildings, attacking people, and in short, behaving in all the ways that they were completely against. What happened to that person's intent when it came up against a conflict, when it came up against a different system, a different ideology? It allowed itself to fragment.

What that soul denied in themselves, what they did not include in themselves, got their attention; it got their light. Therefore, rather than finding themselves living in a peaceful, equalitarian community, they find themselves on the streets battling tear gas, being beaten with billy clubs, and they find themselves joining fundamentalists movements and building bombs. What happened to that soul? When that soul crosses over to this side and asks, "How did I get so off track? I know what I wanted, but I ended up there."

Every one of you can relate to this—how you start off in one place truly believing and trying to hold your focus, only to find yourselves landing somewhere else in a totally different reality than what you thought you wanted. Lifetime, after lifetime, after lifetime, you will find this pattern playing out. How did your intent, your focus, and your light, end up in what seems to be the opposite of what you really want to create?

Well, let's go back to this person who had a really good vision of what they wanted for the world. They know the blueprint they wish to create, they know what they want and to make sure that nothing gets in the way of creating this blueprint, so they look within themselves for anything that seems to be counteracting this blueprint and they try to force it away from themselves. They do not give into anger; they do not allow themselves the expressions within that they think would be contraindicative to the reality that they want to create. The more they do not want to have any of this within themselves, the more they are pushing that light out of themselves. Of course that light is going to find some other place to align. But because that light is theirs, it will call what it is aligning with back into that person's life, and then that person's focus is on what they do not want to have, and therefore, their light goes more and more to what they do not want to have and that is what gets created, over, and over, and over.

Now, how to heal that? Working with the idea of the inclusive circle, the person finds this within themselves and says, "Yeah that really irritates me. I don't understand how come people can be so silly to create these war realities. How can somebody be that vicious that they can drop a bomb on children?"

From that place of noticing the dialogue within, they begin to look and try to understand. You may choose to be born into a warrior reality like that for a whole lifetime to try to understand. You may choose imaginative ways to go into those places to try to understand. What happens? How does that come to be? You find out within your very soul what you are capable of, how much you can witness, and how much pain you can go through before you too begin to turn against the rest of humanity. You have to search deep within yourself. You have to put yourself in many different places and positions to see. How would I react in that case? What would it be like for me if I watched my whole family being burned? You find within yourself all of the compassion that you can. You look within yourself to the places where you have cut yourself off from feeling your emotions because you are too afraid to have to face memories, too afraid to face some of the realities that are going on. You find all the places within yourself where you choose to look only at one aspect, until you find the common bond with what you once called your enemy. You may realize that you are looking at yourself. No longer do you exclude that part of yourself. Instead, you encompass it and you honour it. Your choices are then made with all the aspects of yourself.

So, the warrior self, the fighter, is encompassed and you say, "Good—I've got your loyalty. I have your energy with me. We can fight for what we believe in and we can use this absolute strength of the warrior to tenaciously hold onto the reality that we want. Not to hit people over the head for it, but to hang onto it." You find a way to

247

encompass all of the aspects of yourself rather than denying them. The strength of a warrior can be strength of tenacity as well as strength of aggression. You discover how to utilize all of your energy to bring all of it to work towards the goal that you want. In that way you are not putting your energy outside of yourself and you are not giving it to the places you do not want to be giving it to!

If everyone who hears these words could practice this, life would change. Every time you find yourself in a conflict, recognize that you have come across something that is also moving with its intent, and that is as big as you, or as big as your intent is. Recognize that you have drawn this in because at some point in time, whether it is in this life or in another life, at some point in time your energy had fragmented and part of it is coming home. You can recognize it in the conflict that you are facing.

Not only do we speak of taking your light out of a situation you do not want it to be in, but we are also talking about where your light is in that situation. How did your light get into the soldier throwing tear gas at you? How did your light get in there? How did your light get into the suicide bomber? How did your light get into the diamond merchant who is exploiting that young African boy?

When you are face-to-face with these conflicts in your world, you are face-to-face with part of your light, a part of your own essence. You have to find it in yourself, accept it, and encompass it. That is how you pull your light out of the realities that you do not want to be expressed; not just by saying, "I will have nothing to do with that." That has never worked. You have to look and say, "I have everything to do with that or it would not be here in my life. I have to take my light out of that situation, out of that soldier, out of that corporation, out of that reality, that culture, or whatever it is, and put it back in me." Then whatever choice you are making has a much better chance of coming to fruition.

This is individual work! It cannot be done as a group. As soon as you start putting it into a group you start getting competitiveness, and it is too easy to brush over something when you are in group. It is in those places when you are alone with yourself, having to look within yourself, where you come to full honesty about what you are creating here. It has been so easy for people to polarize away and say, "Well, they are doing it to us." They, the famous they!

Well, I have some news here for you. They wouldn't be in your reality unless you had some light in theirs. It is not easy! It is not easy to look at every little thing you are trying to create. It is not easy to pick apart every move you are making in this reality to clear a path for yourself.

When folks have tried to do this they have often thought about giving away everything they own and finding a little cave to crawl into; but that is guilt acting there. It does not make it better for the rest of the world. It has to be done a little piece at a time. We do not expect any of you to say, "Well, you know I cannot live in this world at all. I won't be able to drive a car or heat my house. There is nothing I can buy. There is nothing I can eat that is not causing destruction somewhere." I do not expect any of you to be able to even begin to make that big of a change.

Rather, take a little step, a little bit each time to slowly turn it all around. I suggest that you start with one conflict in your life; just one. Whether it is with your government, your workplace, your marriage, your neighbour, a policy or belief; it does not matter what it is. Find one conflict and see if you can find where your light is standing on a line that you do not want it to be on. Find it in there, look your enemy in the face and find yourself in there. Reclaim that self, bring yourself out of there and back home into your own heart. It changes the face of your enemy when you do that; when you find yourself in there.

Start with one conflict, find yourself in there, and reclaim. Surely, a week later the universe will show you your next conflict! You will keep finding them one at a time. As you take your light out of those places where you do not want it to be and as more and more people take their light out of places where they do not want to be, you will find those conflicts are no longer manifesting on the Earth or in your hearts.

You all have the pattern that the Creators have been lovingly holding for all of us. Every soul knows this. It is your basic blueprint. Eden, paradise, Nirvana, bliss; it does not matter what you call it, for you all know what it feels like. It feels like the freedom to move and create, to express, to dance, full breath, colour, expansiveness, peace, and tranquility. You all know what this feels like; the idea of being able to move forward in excitement and passion, and then to allow yourself to sleep in a gentle drift. To be able to move as you feel to move, create as you feel to create; the idea that as you create there is more bliss for others around you.

All of these images you carry within yourselves as your core because you are all children of love and of creation. This is your blueprint! This is your base! So, every one of you know inside yourselves how to create this. Your work in this life and every life has been to find the places where this has fragmented off, where it has become other than what you desire, other than what you wish. Your work has been to find how you fragmented it off and to bring that light back to yourselves. As each one of you do this within yourselves, the original blueprint and the bliss of this creation begins to emerge. The reality that has been created that most of you do not like dissipates, because nobody is holding it alive anymore. It sounds really simple, but it is the hardest work that anyone has ever had to do. To be able to go into your most feared places, your most hated places, and find yourself there and bring yourself home is the hardest work any soul has ever had to do. But it is the only work that will heal this universe and bring it to that state of expanding bliss.

In your personal lives you can find this in all the places that you have conflict, especially with those whom you love. Here you have the bliss of love. You know what you want. You know how you want this dance to be, but your pride gets in the way, your greed gets in the way, your fear gets in the way, your stubbornness, and whatever judgments you give to yourself, get in the way of creating that blissful relationship that everybody yearns for. Conflict becomes a matter of life and death, rather than the bumping-up-against. We spoke earlier of the comet finding its way through the universe and about how it finds its path by how it relates to everything around it; by how it relates to that sun there, to that big planet there—it finds its path through this, it finds its perfect flow by how it bumps against everything else. It does not try to push things out of the way. It gently finds its way through by its gravitational conflicts with everything else, because it allows it. In your personal relationships you know how close to get to somebody or how much to step back by the type of conflict you have. It does not have to be seen as something negative.

In your love relationships, with those in your family, your friendships, and your community; there are some planets you want to give a wider berth to that's comfortable for you to stand at this state with that person. Then that is your right path, isn't it? There will be other people that you want a closer relationship with. This shows your travel-path through your reality, if you can trust it. When you find that you are coming up against a force causing you to split, you have to find how to keep yourself together in this. You have to find how to hold your own integrity and keep following your path. Through this you learn your own path, you learn who you are, and you learn your place in the universe.

You are finding your right place to be. In this way you're able to travel this universe forever, the bright light that you are, ever-expanding, and the influence that you have on everything and everyone that you pass and the influence everyone has on you, held in right balance. This is the bliss all of you have been longing for; to be able to express yourself as fully as you can! This is the bliss; this is the longing that everyone has inside themselves. Use this longing to pull it into reality.

Mind where your light is, where your attention is, and where your focus is. I think most of you are going to be really surprised as you explore yourselves. Those of you who really believe that you are fighting for peace, how can you be fighting for peace? How can you who say you are following God's path, be condemning of others? You cannot be condemning and loving at the same time; you will have to split yourself to do that. You cannot judge somebody and have compassion for them at the same time; you will have to split yourself to do that. You cannot be accepting of people and rejecting of them at the same time either; you will have to split yourself. Find where your light and your focus is. Wherever you think it is, where you believe it is, you are often going to find it is sitting in opposition of that, as well.

So, how do you change the reality you have on Earth? By changing what you are focusing on, by changing what you are choosing. How do you turn this planet around from the destructive direction it is heading? You do this by pulling your light out of those places. Every one of you is going to find a part of yourselves who wants to destroy it all. So angry and upset and in pain and fear are you, in witnessing what is going on, you are going to find parts of your self saying, "Well, just forget it. Let's blow the whole thing up! It is not worth it!" So full of shame and self hatred, it is far easier to say, "Let's get rid of the whole thing". Finding that within yourself, you become afraid and you start thinking "Gee, maybe this is what God is thinking too. Maybe God is thinking how much easier it would be just to get rid of these souls who are so hell-bent on destruction." That light is within each one of you, not in the Creator. It originated there with God, yes, and it rippled out, and instead, each one of you has parts of you who jumped on those waves and rode on those thoughts.

Every thought that the Creators put out are like ripples, are like waves of the ocean. Now, some people took their surfboards and jumped on those waves and they're riding them still. Others sent just a part of themselves out on those waves and they're riding them still. I am suggesting that you have a choice of which waves you are going to ride. You have a choice of which ripples from the Creators you are going to align with, and by those choices you create your realities. It is of no use to blame God and say, "Well you know what? If God created everything, then God created disease, too. Therefore, it is God's fault."

Instead, you have to look and say, "Okay, where is my energy? In what way is my energy riding those waves of disease? In what way is my energy encouraging that destruction to exist?" You have to find where your light is in that. If nothing aligns with those waves they ride right on through. When something aligns with those waves it becomes manifest. It is your choice.

Where in you is the energy of disease? Okay, what is disease? It is where imbalances are found within the body that create deterioration and destruction, rather than creation. It is a place within the physical manifestation that causes a lack of energy and a lack of creation. It is a rolling backwards, rather than moving forward. Now, what places do you find in everybody's light that does not want to give to creation, but wants to stop creation, wants to destroy it; feels frustrated and angry and upset? Do you see? Everybody has disease! Everybody has the wish to destroy and everyone is afraid of it and everyone thinks that it means that they're bad, that they're evil and wrong. Rather than being afraid of this aspect of yourself, I want you to look at it. In what positive ways can this energy work? Well, if we take it back to the ripples in creation and we see that the Creators have ripples that can ride right out of this universe; well, maybe some things do need to ride right out of this universe. Maybe some things that were tried need to just go on all the way through. It is possible that this energy might have a very positive effect. The ability to take something apart, to destroy it, can actually be a positive energy.

Your body does this all the time. It is constantly taking things apart and putting things together. You eat some food and your body takes the food apart, down to its basic components so that it can be utilized in a way that is beneficial. Those are destructive qualities and it's a good thing that they are there. Can you use this quality in a beneficial way for all? This is encompassing and embracing your destructiveness. Rather than sending it out with the intent of rage and anger, you can send it out with love. It is okay to take that apart. That stone wall was not put together very well, or that stone wall has served its purpose, and now we want to take the stones apart and build something different. That is very different than, "Let's drop a bomb on that wall." You end up in the same place really, but the energy and the intent does no harm along the way. By looking in yourself and finding where all of your intent, focus and energy is being put, each individually, just a little piece at a time, you can alter all of reality.

When you look back in history there have been some really positive changes in your world. There have also been a lot of situations on your planet, time periods, that all of you have lived through in different cultures that have been horrendously destructive and have caused great pain and turmoil in the psyches of many souls. Even things happening five hundred years ago, according to your way of thinking, still have a ripple effect on the psyches of those of you who are incarnate now at the two-thousand time period. It all has a ripple. It all has an effect.

During those time periods where it looked and felt as if all there was to experience was misery and destruction, it took some very conscious planning to change things. It took a small group of really dedicated people putting their focus so strongly on changing reality, putting their full consciousness and dedicating their whole lives, to make these changes. Most of the biggest social changes that you can see were done by just a handful of people. Their focus and their intent were so strong that it rippled out and affected everybody.

It was common in a lot of cultures in your world, not that long ago, to believe that only some of the people were human and had souls. In some cultures it was believed that only people of a certain caste and from certain families had souls or were real people and everybody else were not real people, but were beings "earning" their reality. Some cultures believed people who had the hormones to make them male were real and everyone who was female was not real or not human. Some people believed that those people who had light skin were human and those who had dark skin were not human. In some places they believed that tall people were human and short little people were not human.

All over your planet you had this. People could be banished and have their souls lost so they were no longer human. People who had damage to their brain were considered not to be human. People who looked different or sounded different were considered human or not human. All throughout your history you had this reality. Something happened to change that belief structure; something happened that helped people shift to become inclusive. It required a lot of dedication from small groups of people to absolutely change that consciousness.

Now, it still has not been eradicated, so some of the work still needs to be done. So maybe instead of pointing fingers and judging and saying, "All these people are really stupid," or, "All these people are really racist," or, "These people are really bigots,"—instead of all of the finger-pointing you could take that thought-pattern and belief system and find out where it fragmented and discover what happened. When we follow that line through we find out that right at the very beginning of creation there was fragmentation. Some souls do seem to be a lot more conscious than other souls. There do seem to be places where there is the original essence of the soul, and the light that follows that, and then there are the places where that light has fragmented or broken off, leaving less consciousness available. This did happen.

Just as we spoke about how it happened with ideas, it also happened with individual souls. There are places in your soul where you held your focus and your light moving in one direction, where most of your soul is, and there are all the places that you have come up against that have caused you to fragment off. Through seeing and understanding this, the judgment was made that somehow there were souls that have less light and were lesser. Rather than seeing how each one of you had fragmented your own light off to create this, rather than taking the responsibility for each one of your individual souls and seeing how you created this, there was further wedging and further judgment. Rather than looking and saying, "Yes, I see this soul here and I see that it is me," you began to look and say, "They are not real, so they do not matter. It is okay, we will just keep pushing that light further and further and we will marginalize it further."

That is what most of you have done with it. It began with a true understanding. There is fragmented light. There are souls that have more light than others. There are souls that have more consciousness than others, just as there are

256

souls that have more money than others. There are souls that have bigger houses and there are souls that have greater intellect. The original belief that everybody wants to have says, "All souls are created equal and every soul is equal." Everybody wants to hold that belief. You want to hold it so bad that you refuse to acknowledge the reality of what is really going on. Yet when you acknowledge what is really going on, you then blame yourself for being judgmental, for being grandiose, and yet by denying it, you are continuing to perpetuate it. You cannot look around this world and say that all are equal. They are not equal in the reality that is created here. All are different. Some have more and some have less.

When you bring the lines all the way back to the beginning of creation you can find that originally there was much light that went out and each individual soul was strong and bright, each one was different, but each was whole. Through the process of learning, of finding one's own path through the universe, there has been much fragmentation. You have lost your light all over the place. All of you have fragmented your light.

The journey that each one of you is on is the journey of reclaiming that light back and bringing all of your light into one consciousness. Then the experience that every bit of your light has had, each and every lifetime of each aspect, becomes the collective consciousness of your own individual soul. As you integrate all this light back into yourself you are richer for the journeys that each bit of you has taken.

As you have cut yourself off from your own light, you created this separation; you have disenfranchised your light. You have created lack and you have created disease. As you bring that light back in, you become more than what you started out with, because you are yourself with understanding and compassion. You are yourself with the knowledge of what that light that has gone outside you has had to go through. You are greater than the sum of your parts.

This is the journey. God was not wrong. This is what empowers each one of you. From this place of bringing your own light and your own power back within yourself you have the ability to bring the light and power back to whatever reality you are holding your focus on, because you do not have light opposing you. You do not have doubts splitting your intent, so your focus and your intent is all fully in one place. That is what it takes to create reality.

As each one of you, rather than judging yourself for where you split yourself off and rather than looking and saying, "I was bad and wrong for splitting myself and being unloving to myself," chose instead to lovingly embrace yourself and say to that part as you welcome that light back, "I'm sorry I split you off, but I'm really glad to have as part of me, everything that you have learned". You are bigger then. You are stronger.

There is a story about this in every culture. In the Hebrew culture and the Christian culture, they call it the story of the prodigal son. The part that goes off in rebellion and anger, the part that is shoved away, the part that has its own experiences, and how wonderful it is when that part comes back and is able to bring so much more into the household. If you think of your soul as a household, then all parts that you welcome come back into that household, each with their own contribution to make that is greater and bigger than what they had when they first left.

So, when conflict is resolved and you have brought your light back into yourself, you are stronger, more focused, and more mature than you were before that conflict.

This flies in the face, I know, of so many of the teachings that say God does not make mistakes. God has not made a mistake here. It is painful that this is how it had to be, but through this, the universe grows in love and in compassion, and through this, reality has a chance of manifesting on Earth in a state of bliss.

You all have the blueprint of what it feels like inside yourselves, so you all know. You just need to practice it!

The leaves fall in a tumble of colour.
Quilting the ground with texture,
Transformed from scraps of summer's heat
Is it enough?
Warmth against cold, snow, coming,
Blanketing all with forgetful embrace.
Is it enough?
To know that seasons rebound and ebb and flow forever.
How will I remember you, when the melts of March Cascade
Down the hillside,
To gather in pools on the edge
Of reason?
Is it enough?
To remember amongst the musty mould of decay
Making nourishment for future forest,
That cycles have reason
Each season
Is
Enough!

Chapter XIX

New Earth Tapestries

Once the understandings have been brought forward into the consciousness of enough people on your planet who are incarnate, there is the possibility of changing all of the base patterns that reality has been created from. This is the work that is at hand now.

As your Earth begins to go through her own healing and her own changes, so each one of you will find these changes manifesting within yourselves. For, as we have already illustrated, your bodies are a representation of the Earth itself, and therefore, as the Earth goes through her changes, so your bodies will go through their physical changes, as well. As the Earth heals herself, so must each one of you heal your own physical beings.

As the patterns of reality coming in from the universe are changing, so the patterns of your social realities must change too. For each one of you to become a part of the co-creation of what is going to be brought forward for the next thousands of years of Earth time, will require each one of you to become exceedingly conscious of the realities you create with your thoughts, your ideas, and mostly, with your expectations. If you wish to live in a balanced reality of love and peace and contentment, then that must be what you are focusing on within your own individual realities. You must look to find this reality within yourself and within everyone that you are in contact with.

These teachings are not new; they were brought forward many times but they have not been understood. Generally, when they have been brought forward, folks believed that you needed to deny all of the things that you saw in preference for a few good things, but that is not what this is about. This is about looking and seeing all of the realities being presented and making a choice of which

261

reality you are going to put your energy and focus into. And so, within every circumstance and within every person there are some things that are really positive that you like, and that are creating good realities. So when you find some negative things within that same circumstance or person, it does not mean you have to pretend that those things do not exist.

Many of you who are trying to work through and understand how you denied your own existences away, have gone a little to the far extreme of then only wanting to look at the things that do not feel good, and thus, those realities begin to be created in all of your lives. The balance here is to be able to realize all of the realities being presented to you and consciously make a choice of where you're going to put your focus and your energy and. therefore, what you are going to bring into being. You do not do that by pretending that the other realities do not exist. You do that by encouraging the realities you want, by focusing on those ones.

Once this is understood by enough people you can start creating together. Be aware that as much as you have doubts in your ability to hold your focus on what you want, so those doubts will come to manifest in what we will call the naysayers. So, as you look and say, "You know, we really could turn this community around and make it in such a way that that drummer in the park could become a focal point for many folks who have to work in these terrible office conditions." That way the whole environment gets moved around. Maybe every afternoon in the park there can be a place that these workers can come down to, and maybe that drummer will teach them how to make rhythms. The policeman's job will be to just simply make sure there is a good space available for the people, to have this break from the tedious nature of the reality they are choosing to be in. Now, that is bringing together the possibilities; that is bringing together all of the realities and making them help each other. The naysayers will be the ones who will try to stop such a thing for whatever reasons they believe they should be stopped and each one will have their own ideas of why this needs to be stopped. But if the collective makes an agreement that they want reality to start taking a different form, then that is the way it will go. If the collective decides that they are going to allow themselves to be intimidated by the one or two folks who hold a loud enough voice to become the naysayers, then they are doomed to hold the reality they were given to hold, rather than what they choose.

Of everything that this Earth has to offer and teach you the biggest thing she has to teach you, is that whatever you are holding in your ideas is what your life will manifest. Whatever that it is! You cannot pretend that you are not holding things there and think that they will not manifest. And you also cannot only focus on the things that you do not like and think that that is not going to make them manifest. You have to realize that you are all, each one of you in a position of immense power here in that whatever you are holding to be true is what you will create.

If you're holding it to be true that the naysayers have all the power, then you will be giving your power to them and the drummer will not be able to help the office worker find their heart again. If you believe that your world is forever going to be in the clutches of those who hold power over others, then you will forever be holding yourself in slavery. Rather, see that this was a choice; a choice collectively made based upon belief systems that were collectively held. All the realities that you see before you, when narrowed down to a single strand of DNA, you will find the pattern of the belief system. There you find what everybody collectively held to and here is what it created.

Every seed that floats through the air on the winds, every one of those seeds, has within it a whole story from whatever plant it came from. When a tree sends its seeds out on the winds and they fly for miles and miles, that seed holds within it the whole story, the entire pattern of that tree. It knows everything about that tree. It knows all about how it lives, what it needs to grow, what size it likes to be and what its fruit and leaves will be like. Everything is all in that one seed. It goes forth from that tree and finds a place to put itself and if the conditions of the environment are there for it, it will create that tree. It will create what that original tree believed about itself and it will grow in that place wherever it has landed.

All of you do this every day with your thoughts, your ideas, and your belief systems. They go out from you like seeds from a tree. They get carried on the wind, they plant themselves, and if there is an environment for them to grow in, they will grow. And pretty soon, if you look up you might see your worst fear because that is what you sent out. You might see your best hope because that is what you sent out. There are all the seeds you sent out and if there is any place for them to land and be given life, they will, and they will walk back into your life. Every doubt you have about yourself, or about what you can do, will walk back into your life and say, "Hello, I do not believe you."

For those who are trying to change these patterns, these realities, you all have your doubts and you cannot deny them because when you deny them you are putting them out on the wind. You have to take those doubts and realize that, "The seeds are not ready to go from me yet. They have more maturing to do and they are not pollinated properly." You need to hold those ones until they are ready. So if they are doubts, you keep them with you. You do not send them out. You keep them with you until they can evolve to be the seed that you want them to be. So, if the doubt is there that says, "Yeah, well, it has always been this way. This control has always been on us. The Earth has always been like this. That is just the way it is," that is a belief system. Do you want to send that one out into the world? That no matter what you do, you are going to be entrapped again. Instead, you keep that seed within you and work with that belief and say, "Okay, here's the seed and I see that it says "no matter what I do it is not going to change; it has always been that way". You look at it and you learn a little bit more and you may actually discover that have been lots of cultures in the world from many different time periods where things were not like that, and this is really just one little planet in a whole vast universe where I bet there are lots of different ways things could be." Pretty soon, you know that adamant statement, 'always has been — always will be' starts to get broken down.

It's just like you would break down the DNA, and then you start to change the patterns. Pretty soon it becomes the statement that says, "It's been like this for little while, and lots of people think that it's okay to be like this. Maybe they are learning something from it or maybe that is what they need to experience." You will come to all these different conclusions. You know, that one seed of that one little statement, it starts to grow now. It gets other genes to get turned on inside it instead. A gene may get turned on instead that says, "Well, you know I remember now, in this lifetime that I lived in a culture where we all made collective decisions and that is the way that whole society was run." That little gene light comes on and it changes that structure, doesn't it?

Then you start to remember parts of your soul in other places in the galaxy where things are really, really different, causing a whole bunch of genes to ignite like little switches turning on in the chromosomes within this thought pattern, this belief system. So, by the time you're ready to let that seed go out into the world, instead of the seed that says, "Always has been—always will be," you now have a seed that says, "There are billions of possibilities. What can we create?" And that is the seed you send out. You never hear anybody come along after that

265

and say to you, "Well, you can't change anything—that's the way people are." Instead, you're going to be meeting really interesting archaeologists who say, "You know, we are on this dig and we just found out that there is this whole culture…" Instead, you are going to be hearing from people who have amazing ideas and dreams. A whole different reality is going to start coming back to you because that is the seed that you put out, because you did not send out your doubt before you had a chance to help it evolve. That is what we mean by looking for the bliss and looking for the goodness in it. Any statement, any belief system, that any of you can find within yourself that you are afraid of, that brings your energy levels down, take that and evolve it within yourself. Do not let it get out on to those winds, because those seeds, they plant and they create.

Think about how you are with each other. We can go back to the stories about the drummer, or any of the stories we have told here throughout these pages, and look and see that there is a choice of how you're going to look at that person. Are you going to see a dirty bum sitting in the park making erratic noise? You could see that if you want to see it. Or, you can see a really, creative, young person wanting to give of themselves. Or, you can see a mystical teacher. You can see whatever you want to see and what that one holds before them; because, believe me, within that young person's whole being are billions of genetic choices, aren't there? Just as within each one of you are billions of genetic choices. So you get to see whatever you want in that one.

It's a funny thing, you know, about people; when you expect something from somebody they genuinely will try to live up to that, whether it is a bad expectation that is going to do harm or whether it is a good expectation. So when you look at that drummer there, what are you holding to be true about that one? They are more likely to try to move into being that, aren't they? So if you are looking and thinking things like, "This is never going to change," and,

"That is a bad person," then that is what you are putting onto that person, and they are likely to try to conform to that, consciously or unconsciously. That is what happens.

Now, what if you look at the person and you say, "Yeah, you know what? There are some things there that I really do not want to be around, but I am sure there are things there that other people might want to be around, so for right now, I am going to move myself back because I really do not want to listen to the drumming. I have a headache…" or whatever is going on. That is okay because you are not putting a negative expectation upon that person for them to fulfill, but you are also respecting your own self enough to know that whatever configurations are going on with that person's energy right now, it is not a good energy for you to be around. That is loving and respectful to self, as well as others.

The seeds that go out that want to make a good strong tree are going to avoid places that are not good for them to grow. That willow tree sent its little seeds out to blow around on the wind and it does not really want to grow on a sandy dune, but rather, it hopes the wind will propels the seeds to land on a nice riverbank. That is the right place for that seed, and if you give it its own way, it will find its right place to be.

So, when you have sent out the right seeds from yourself, the ideas that you want to put out into the world, the attitudes that you want to put out into the world, the reality you want to create, you have to trust that it is going to go to the right place. That is not an act of blind faith; rather, it is allowing the law of attraction and repulsion to come in. So if you have an idea and you want to bring it out into the world and you come in contact with a person who seems to be repelling that idea, then maybe that is something for you to trust and say, "Good; thank you. You are blowing my ideas on the wind somewhere else, to the right place for it to grow," and to trust this. As you're

267

moving around in the world there are places that are going to repel your ideas and there are places that are going to encourage your ideas. There are people you are going to be able to talk about things with that are dear to your heart, and there are people with whom you can't. It is like wind that is blowing your seeds so they go to the right place.

So do not get discouraged about this, but trust it—trust it. And so, with that boy who is trying to find a park that he can drum in and that policeman who is coming and pushing him out of there; he does not have to get mad. He can say, "Fine, I will move to another park," until he finds the one with the people who are going to appreciate his drumming and invite him to come back. He'll find a park with people who are going to benefit from his drumming, changing that whole reality. If all of you can trust that as your Earth is going through the changes that she needs to go through, there are places that are going to repel you, there are places where your ideas are not going to be able to take root, and there are places where they are. Find the places where they are. Find the places that have acceptance for the bliss you want to create, the reality you want to create, and you plant those seeds. That is how you change reality. Whole forests completely change because of the actions of just a few creatures. Sometimes the actions of a simple little crawling creature can come in and completely change an entire species; completely change an entire forest and an entire eco-system. So if these little creatures have the ability to do that, if they have that kind of power, do you all honestly think you don't? If one little creature can get into a human body and change the ecosystem so much that that body begins to cave in upon itself and die, what kind of power can another creature have, as small as they are, in changing an ecosystem into something healthy?

If there is so much power in this world, as you look around you and as you all believe, that has created what you all call evil, how much power is it going to take to turn it around into what you would call good? How many of you assign power of destruction far, far more energy than you assign the power of creation? If you search within yourselves you will find that most of you believe far more in death than you do in life. You believe far more in destruction and misery than you do in creation and joy. Most of you believe that the world is a bad place to be and that there must be unhappiness, there must be misery and there must be pain. Far more of you believe in that than those who believe in goodness and love. Those are the seeds that are going out that are planting the gardens of your realities. If each soul, individually, can start to take full responsibility for the ideas, thoughts, attitudes and beliefs that they perpetuate in this reality, your entire reality can change overnight. That is how fast it can go!

It has happened where ideas have spread like wildfire from one person to another person to another person, until enough people are standing together who absolutely and utterly demand change. And you can see this as long as you do not get lulled back to inaction. As long as you are willing to stand in your strength and your power and hold responsibility, then you can change yourselves, your families, your communities, your countries, and your world, in whatever direction you choose.

It is all in each one of your hands. It is so simple. How do you collectively get this moving? I hear people all the time saying, "Well you know, that is all very well and good for me. I can do this all I want, but nobody's going to listen, no one in my community is going to change and it is not going to make any difference." I hear people say that all the time and I say, "Oh is that the seed you are putting out?" Hold that thought to you and let it evolve. That hasn't always been the way; sometimes something else happens. Sometimes things can be different. Maybe you cannot wake anybody else up, that is true, but maybe all it's going to take is waking yourself up.

269

We are the rising of the tide as it swells the seventh wave

To ride us in to shore.

We are the whispers of the winds

As it prepares to move the heavens

We are the rolling of the rocks

And the quaking of the ground,

As it swells beneath us

We are the pulsing of the fire as it makes

Itself sacred to all.

Listen!

We are everywhere,

Drawing the same collective breath,

Letting it out slowly......

Fanning the flames.

Look!

We flow with the same water through our veins,

Blessing it with our loving awareness

As it passes through our internal rivers.

Feel!

The Earth as she makes us up

From deep within her dream.

We are here.

We are everywhere.

We are!

Chapter XX

Weavers of Light

I have explained to you how each one of you individually is interconnected with so many others on this planet. I have shown you how many of the seeds that have been sent out from your soul have taken root and are growing in different places.

There is a DNA connection, and this is the closest way I can describe it with the understandings that you have been presented with on the Earth so far, as to how life works. There is a DNA connection between species, between all trees of a similar seed line, between all grasses, all plants, birds, animals, and human souls. So, for instance if one pine tree is having a problem with an attack from some organism, this particular tree will be able to communicate with all of the other trees of the same species within a very large radius. This tree will let them know something is going on here, "There is an organism coming in and we need to be prepared for it," may be the message, and it can send this information through to the other pinion trees.

It has to do with the laws of resonance, where one particular alignment of pattern will resonate directly with a similar pattern, and information is passed this way from tree to tree. It happens with the insects, as well, and many of your scientists have been having fun studying these things lately, wondering how it happens. The insects all know when to hatch together and they all know when to collectively move together. All through history you have stories about those hoppers who can come into a collective mass from all over and pinpoint one place to go to. How do they do this? How do they know? How do they all know where to get together and go to one poor farmer's field and eat the whole thing at once? It is the resonance between their patterns; they are all from the same seed. They are grasshoppers, locusts, and they all originate from the same pattern. They are a collective, like individual cells of one being, and so they know, all it takes is one impulse or one idea to spread through.

How do you think all of your flyers, your birds, who come together, "Now, today it is time to leave the north and go to the south." They know how to come together from all over, where they need to go, and what they need to do. They communicate this to each other. How does one know and fifty miles away another one knows the right time? "Let's go tonight. We will meet you here." They communicate through the laws of resonance, so when one gets an impulse it is communicated to all other of like species. Similar frequencies create similar DNA and the laws of resonance work through that, so they know.

This works in all species on your planet and it works for you too. So, when you get an idea, and it might be a really, really good idea, you formulate your idea, get it all figured out and you decide you're going to take it to the patent office, only to find out that thirty people have already come in the last week applying for a patent for this same product. First, you realize you have been a bit slow getting your product ready and second thing you realize is, "I wonder what those people are like? Are they like me?"

Chances are you'll find they have a similar energy and similar vibration. An idea has come through and this particular vibration of soul has picked this idea up collectively. Sometimes an idea comes through and one person works hard on that idea, but they are impulsing this out, so anyone of similar frequency is going to get that idea, too. They are going to pick it up. All of you have experienced this. Here you are figuring something out and you find out, "Ah, that's just what my friend over here was thinking about, as well," or, "Similar circumstances have manifested in so-and-so's life." You can see that there are similar patterns of understandings and growth and that there are groups of you, that when one person learns something, everybody around starts to learn it too. Even if you don't speak to each other for five years, you may find out, "Ah, yes, that person of a similar vibration has picked up what I am doing and they are going with it, and we are relating, so it comes back to me and I learn."

All of you have experienced this and I do not think you have put this together with what the hoppers, the ducks, the squirrels, or the pine trees are doing, but it is all the same thing. One holds a particular energy and that energy ripples out and all of like-vibration pick up those ripples. It alters and changes within each individual who picks up these ripples, as well, and causes you to vibrate differently than you were. It changes your patterns and your belief systems.

When you understand this, that one pine tree that some scientist released caterpillars on, has now changed the whole forest because of what it has sent out, then you realize that if that one tree can do that, what more can you do as an individual? So if you want to send out "It's not going to work. We're not waking anybody up. Nobody's listening..."? Okay, that's fine, you send that out, and then you get to sit back and watch your garden growing. Those are your seeds.

Or, do you want to say, "You know what? I believe I am as powerful as a pine tree, or as a duck, or as a cricket. I am just as powerful as all of those beings in God's creation, and therefore, what I decide to send out, to believe, to hope for, to create, can be just as powerful, and hopefully, I will have the wisdom to send it out to like-vibration where it will be manifested tenfold." For as it goes out from you to those places of similar vibration, of similar understanding, so they vibrate and they send it out, and on and on it goes until you have a collective shift in peoples' consciousness on the whole planet. This has been done many times before.

If you look through history, as bleak as it may seem to some of you, you can witness that there have been great changes in the consciousness of people, which have created great changes in the social structures around you. Even though some of you may think that it is taking too long, or it seems too slow, or the patterns are too ingrained; you have to hold enough consciousness within yourself to realize it does not matter how long it takes. Time, as we have already mentioned, is not what it seems. It does not matter how hard it seems at first to get things rolling. What matters is that you are sending out the seeds, the ideas and thoughts from yourself that you wish to create with. It matters that what you are putting out from yourself is exactly what you want to be putting out from yourself; that you are each individually, fully aware of exactly what you are doing and why.

This Earth is giving each one of you an opportunity to learn about being a creator. You are not here just to salvage your life a little longer; your life was forfeit from the beginning. This Earth is only lending you her atoms for as long as she is choosing to, it never was your life in the first place and it still isn't. But, you are being given an opportunity here by the graciousness of this planet to learn to create and to be a creator, and each one of you, by witnessing what you are creating around you, are going to see all of the seeds that you have been putting out. It is hard work to look at these seeds. It is harsh to see what ones are out there and which ones are getting manifested, and it is harsh to realize that you may not have been the originator of all of the patterns that have materialized.

Take, for example, that poor pine tree; it did not ask for all of those caterpillars to be put upon it, did it? But that is what happened. So that pine tree has to follow its own right course, and its own right course is to send out the

274

message to all of the other trees that this is what is going on, "This is what is happening to me here in this spot and I am letting you know what I am experiencing so that all of you are prepared." That field of grain did not ask for all of those grasshoppers to land on it. It did not want that, but when those grains were under attack they would have liked to have sent out the message to others of similar vibration to let them know, "We have a problem here. These creatures are laying their eggs under the ground here, so next year there is going to be an even worse problem."

Unfortunately, some of those grains cannot do this because someone has tampered with their DNA; therefore, they are unable to send their message out. They have been silenced. That is too bad. However, the surrounding grasses can send their message out and all of like-vibration are going to be able to listen, and then those grasses can raise their tannin levels and make themselves bitter to the taste and these creatures will not land there.

Unfortunately, some of the places where the plants have had their voices silenced by people, who think they know better about DNA than God does; well, they have no warning, as their eyes, ears, and mouths have been silenced. As a result, these modified plants will probably be eaten by those hoppers. So, when you want to send your message out into the world, there are places where people cannot hear; they have become unaware, they have tampered with their own systems, because, you know, their doctors know better than the Creators, and sometimes these people think that by taking all these different chemicals into their body it is going to help them to be of similar vibration to everything around them. Unfortunately, when that happens and the call comes out, they cannot respond. They cannot hear any more than that tampered wheat can hear, so they do not know. You are all going to be up against that, as well. That is the reality you see out there in the world.

As you start thinking that you can tamper with your own bodies, your own so carefully balanced chemistries, as you change and altar yourselves, your states of mind, and states of being to suit whatever your culture wants you to be, so you have started creating that within the plants and within the animals, too. It is not working very well.

It is easy for God to come in to command the atomic reality to completely and utterly change. It is easy for God to come in and say, "Let's just shift all of these patterns into the obedience of My Will." It is easy for God to step here and lay his pattern across the land, of which all will have to conform to, like holding a giant magnet for all of the atomic reality to turn itself north or south according to that plan. That is really easy to do. It is a lot harder to leave all of you here on this Earth until you have learned that you are also the magnets that can turn things around. If God wanted your atoms to all fall back to the Earth, your spirits would all go back into the Creators.

Many of you have asked for this, many of you have asked to have your power taken from you because you do not want the responsibility anymore. You want God to come and take you all back within Himself so that you no longer have to think for yourselves. So afraid are you of making a mistake, that you hand your power over to whatever greater authority seems to be available to you, and many of you believe that God wants you to hand your power over to him, so that you can become, once again, one part of the whole collective.

God did not send you out from himself simply so you could say, "I want to go back in." All of you who are alive and birthed upon this Earth were sent out from your mothers' bodies, not so you could go back in; you were sent out from your mothers' physical bodies so that you could learn to govern your own lives. You were all sent out from God so that you could learn that you are part of God, part of the collective, responsible for what you create, responsible for the reality that gets manifested in your image, responsible for your lives, and for the lives that you touch around you. It is a hard thing to learn. It is a hard thing to step up and take this responsibility and claim this power and do something with it.

Most of you would like to believe that you are helpless children of the Creators but not allowed to create; children of the Creators, but victims of circumstance; children of the Creators, but without any power whatsoever. Most of you believe this about yourselves, and with this belief system you set about struggling to try to make a life. Whether this life is on a dung heap in the Sahara or at the top of a high building in Detroit, it does not matter; with those belief systems and those ideas, what can you possibly create?

Every now and then there is somebody who realizes, "If we are all children of the Creators, maybe we are creators," and these ones set about looking at what they can change in the world. Their whole lifetime can be dedicated to fun and playfulness, trying to have a little influence here and a little influence there; raise a few eyebrows over here and generate a few comments over there.

So, when we witness these souls who know who they are, who have an inkling of the power they might have, they do not go anywhere without causing some type of movement, do they? Everybody looks with envy at those ones and they think, "Well, if I could be like that..." instead of realizing that that is a soul who is beginning to have an inkling of who they are. That is all, just beginning to have an inkling of who they are. Ha, what is going to happen when all of you realize who you are; that you are children of the Creators?

You are all creators in training, and you are here on a planet who said, "Okay, come on folks; I will give you an opportunity here to plant whatever seeds you want and see what you grow." That is what you are all doing here on this

Earth. This Earth has held a lot of these ideas for you folks; she has held a lot of your beliefs. She held a lot of things within her until she got sick.

So, now your Earth, she says, "I'm not holding this anymore. I am putting them back out and each one of you will have to take your seeds back, your ideas back, and you have to re-evaluate and reassess them." Each one of you will find that this is manifesting in your lives now as you take these seeds back. You are going to have to decide; are you going to evolve them? Are you going to heal these seeds, these ideas, these attitudes? Are you going to decide the structure of the DNA of the seeds that you are going to put out into the world again? Just like when you toss those seeds in places where they cannot grow they wither and die, so that is what the Earth is doing now. She is giving them all back to you and you have to decide which ones you are going to give back to her.

You have to re-evaluate what you are going to believe, what you are going to live by, the standards you are going to live under, and be really, really sure that what you put out in this world is really what you want to be putting out, because it will grow; it will grow right back to you fast. That is the state that your world is in as she heals herself.

These are going to be trying times for some, hard times for some, but for others they are going to be very fast and really powerful. There are those of you who will probably flounder and those of you who will soar. The Creators will not choose which will be which. The Earth will choose, and the Earth will choose by what each one of you have put into her. The Earth will choose by what attitudes, belief systems, actions, thoughts, words, and deeds you have planted within her; the Earth will show it back to you. That is going to be hard for some, easy for others, but all of you are facing this at this point in time in your history. The collective reality has created destruction and the collective reality must change, for this Earth is not capable of destruction; this is a planet of creation.

This is a time of great hope and of great doom, depending upon what you wish to create. Some of you have been holding, for eons, a belief of a way that souls can flourish and live on Earth, where all of the multitudes of realms can all come together and co-create together. Some few of you have held this vision of unity, of collection, of consciousness, of diversity, and joy. Some of you have seen the diversity of souls as different instruments in an orchestra with the Creators as conductor, and some of you have seen this as all the different colours of a spectrum that make up a beautiful painting, all the seeds that make up a garden, each unique part bringing its own beauty and vibration.

Some of you have been holding this vision of reality and hoping and hoping that you will find a place that will be receptive to this, a place where this dream can grow. There have been little pockets in some places in the world where people have come together and respected each others' differences and honoured each others' gifts. They have been few and far between.

The dominant collective belief system has said, "One species; one way must conquer and overcome all others." A belief system that says, "There can be only one way, only one reality, and it must dominate," has been creating a destruction of ideas and a destruction of differences. A belief that thinks that as long as there are differences there will be conflict is based upon the belief that there can be only one way with no differences. Look around you. This Earth, she loves to evolve differences; she loves to bring forward variations. This Earth is all about expressing the differences.

Those of you who have been trying to hold the reality of the symphony of souls of the multi coloured garden, of the variety of humankind, are going to have to continue holding this in the face of all opposition. You are going to have to hold your faith in this by loving each others' differences, by honouring each others' differences, by allowing yourself to move towards and be attracted to that which feels like resonance, and allow yourself to be pushed away by that which does not.

Have you ever noticed that seeds, when they tumble to the ground, will stay for a little bit and roll around and get responses from all the plants around and sometimes they will allow themselves to be picked up by the wind and float on again? Maybe as they rolled around they thought, "I feel this plant and this plant and they do not feel like they are going to want me to be here," and they allow themselves to move on until they land somewhere that says, "Yes, I can grow here." There are plants whose job it is, is to repel other plants. There are creatures that repel other creatures out of their territories, force them to move on, thus forcing diversity.

There are people like that, too. Do you feel like you can be around this person? Will your ideas be accepted? Will you be nurtured here? Does it feels good, so will you stay for awhile? There are other people that you come in contact with who will argue with your ideas and will fight you on them. In one way you can use that to strengthen yourself and say, "I'm really getting a good hard shell around this nut. I am getting really clear about what my ideas are here, and I am making a good strong shell around them from all the buffeting happening around this person." But that is not where you ought to be planting. This tells you right there, that is not a good place to plant. It is a good place to harden the nut, but it is not meant to grow there, so allow yourself to move on.

If you trust the area, the people, all of the energies wherever you are, you will know if it is the right place to be. It is going to let you know if this is the right place to share your ideas. Is this a good place for you to get your drum out and play, or is the lobby of this bank a place where they do not really want you in there drumming? Maybe it is not a good idea for you to do that because you could get arrested. But, over here, you are welcome to get your drum out and start drumming. There is the place that welcomes you. "Is this a place where I can share these ideas and the understandings that you have received?" You feel it. You know. "Can I put these seeds here? Is there receptivity for them?"

Now, sometimes you will find, you know, there is acceptance for a little bit and then you'll see the winds will start pushing you out and it will feel a little cold in there, and you say, "Okay, I've said enough, time to stop." You can all feel it, just trust it. "Okay, that's enough, time to move on." Sometimes all you can do is give a hint of a seed in some places, so you are going to have to trust that that is going to cause some vibration. But if there is any resonance in any of the souls that you are talking to, what you are saying is only going to vibrate a little bit in there and you will know when it is enough. Sometimes just that little bit of vibration is enough to get that soul rocking and then those of like-vibration to that particular soul will be affected, as well.

As you sit here contemplating these ideas we are putting forward here, some of these ideas are going to vibrate in places within you. Some of you are going to shut this book and walk away, and some of you are going to like some things and not others. But, these ideas are going to you now and they will vibrate within you and all like-souls around you will be vibrated also. You might find yourself talking about some of these things and that will start vibrations within someone else. Sometimes all it takes is one song, one story, or one painting to change a whole world. Sometimes it simply takes the face of one person who holds their vibration, who holds their truth, who has an effect on all others around them, to change a whole world.

During these next few years as your Earth goes through all of her healing pangs and all that she needs to go through to throw off the sickness that has been implanted within her, you are all going to find yourselves going through this, too. You are going to find things move really fast. If you are putting out a positive, strengthening influence, that is what you will create around you in your communities and in your societies. If it is doubts, fears, old angers and injustices, they will be coming back really fast, really fast. If it is thistles you want to plant in your garden; that is your choice. Thistles are a really good plant but they are warriors and they can hurt, and if that is what you want to fill your garden with, you are not going to be able to walk through that garden. You might find the thistles are good to be on some of the edges though, for everything has its right place.

Some of your barbed words that you want to put out in the world have a right place to be, but do you want them in the garden that you want to live in? Where do you need them to be? I do not say to you, "Don't get angry." I do not say to you "Don't talk about things you do not like." What I say to you is to be absolutely responsible for that. So if the energy you are putting out has the intention to tear down, be conscious and aware of that. That when you are going into a place and saying, "I condemn you for these reasons and this, and this, and this... I do not like what you are doing," some might say that one is putting negativity out.

Yes, you can look at it like that, although you could say that one is going in and is pulling apart a structure that they do not like, so they can build something else. Sometimes that is the energy that is needed. Sometimes that is the most loving energy, if you are fully conscious of what you are doing. If you are doing it out of a sense that you have been disempowered or if you're doing it simply because you are upset, you are going to create discordance, which will very rapidly turn around to create an authority figure to come in and push you down. But, if you go into a situation being consciously aware and making a conscious choice to pull some of these threads, hopefully to unravel what you see here as inappropriate, well, when you go in with that intention that is exactly what you will do. You will unravel it and there will be no repercussions because you don't have any.

So, for instance, let's say that the young drummer wants to go into the lobby of the bank. Perhaps the people are far too uptight in there and really need to get themselves moving because the atmosphere in there is so stagnant. Maybe what is coming through the air conditioner is making everybody sick, causing employees to take the week off. So this drummer says "They need to dance, they need to get moving, they need to get their windows open and get some air flowing through there." Maybe there will be a healer working there who says, 'He's right! We have to do something about this environmental health problem. Our employees are getting sick."

Maybe all the people who are coming from meetings, or standing in the line-ups at the bank applaud, and say, "Very good, this is a fun bank and we like it." What kind of power did that young man have in that situation? But if he went in because he does not like establishment, with the intention of causing trouble; the security guard will cut him off fast; very fast.

I do not say "do not hold yourselves back because you are upset about something." I say 'take that seed, be fully conscious of it and know exactly what you want to do and why you are doing it, and then put it out there. Because one can say, "I am going in with a positive input and I'm going to start drumming in the lobby there," very positively, but inside them they haven't taken the time to reason out why they are doing it. They have not been maturing the consciousness of the decision that they are making, so they do not know why they are doing it.

Maybe they are doing it because they want to prove a point. They want to prove that positive is more powerful than negative, many of them, and the reason they want to prove this point is because they do not really believe that so they want to prove that it is true. Does that not say it is the exact opposite?

So, of course the security guard will cart them off too, and be very disparaging of them, as well. People won't even take them seriously because they are not taking themselves serious enough to take the time to think about what they're doing and why. It is all about being fully conscious of what you are putting out into the world and why. It is all about being fully aware of what energy you are working with, within yourself, so that you are fully aware that that is what you will be matched with. The Earth, she does not discriminate, she matches. What energy is put out is what energy comes back. Thus, you have created reality, all of you; your personal reality is your collective reality.

You are all afraid now; afraid of where your Earth is going, where your societies are going, and what life is going to be like for your great-grandchildren. Of course you are all afraid. You have to look and see what you have created and then you have to stand back in your power and realize you can create something different. How many of you can take the challenge in your individual lives to start creating what you want? Start being really conscious of what you want and start planting the seeds of exactly what you want. How do you want your reality to look, how do you want it to feel, what colours, what sounds, kinds of people, what kinds of plants will you invite? How many of you are ready? I hope, a lot, because you need to be.

Your Earth is changing. She, in her own consciousness is making changes in her patterns. You have a choice; a choice of working together with your planet and with the Creator, or not.

It is really easy to see what direction your planet is going in, so those who wish to go in a different direction are going in a different direction. You still get to have your reality, you still get to create your reality; only the Earth will no longer be giving it form. It is her choice. You will find that the seeds that you wish to plant that are no longer in harmony with the Earth will find no place to land.

So those of you who wish to move yourself into a positive reality that is a reality of creation, a diversity of colour and sound, then you can be prepared for a fun time ahead. Those of you who wish to try to control and conquer and dominate and suppress creation into one form, will still have the opportunity to do this, but not on Earth. She no longer wishes to give form to these ways. So it is your choice of what you want to make, what reality you want to live in and what you want around you. You have all the tools and you have all the understandings.

We have said nothing new here. It is all around you; everywhere you look are these answers, everywhere you look are these stories and these patterns. In all the stories these patterns are found. You simply have to stop and look to see it. Any questions you have of the universe can be answered by standing on this planet and looking around you, at any time of day or any season. Anything you put out, this planet will have a response. Any guidance that you need is right there and the understandings you need are right there. It is up to each one of you now. Go ahead and create.

Just be really, really sure that the seeds you are putting out are exactly what you want to be manifesting, because they will manifest. Be really, really aware. Some of you think you are putting out something very positive, only positive, but tied right to it is the flip-side of that positive idea; your worst fears. Hold your ideas until they are ready to be put out. Make sure you have them how you want them to be and make sure you are fully conscious of what you're doing.

When you go out and knock upon someone's door and say "I have come here to talk to you about God and about being good", you have to look at the flip-side of that. Why do you feel you need to broadcast this? Are you in such doubt? Why do you feel the need to convert others to your way of thinking? Is it because you feel you need to have enough collective consciousness to make it real? Why do you feel the need to preach to others about what they should or should not do? Is it because you're not sure within yourself?

On the flip side of all of that kind of movement is the fear, is the rejection, lack of faith within your own self, and that is what you will manifest and that is what will be created. The doors will slam in your face and people will argue and ridicule you. If you held that within yourself you would find your own doubts, your own fears, and you would find all the ways within yourself that you are lacking and you would heal it.

Then you would not have the need to go and tell anyone all these great revelations. You simply smile. That is all you need to do, because you know. Others will notice that smile and they will come to you and ask, "How did you get so peaceful? How come you look so young and bright and happy? Why is your life different than mine?" You may then find yourself sharing some of your ideas in that very receptive fertile ground that is ready.

There have been masters time and time again on your Earth that do this. They lived it their whole lives, and they never said to anybody "go forth and conquer with this one idea." They simply lived their lives and hopefully touched gently all those lives they came in contact with. These masters changed a lot of souls' vibrations forever. It is time for each one of you to become masters!

It is time for each one of you to transform all of your ideas and beliefs until they are whole.

It is time for you to go out and plant God's garden!